Messages *from* Home

Phyllis Levenstein AND Susan Levenstein

Messages
from Home

The Parent–Child Home Program for
Overcoming Educational Disadvantage

Revised and Updated Edition

TEMPLE UNIVERSITY PRESS Philadelphia

Phyllis Levenstein, Ed.D. (1916–2005), founded The Parent-Child Home Program in 1965. She was its Executive Director until 1997, after which she continued to work as the Program's Senior Investigator and as a clinical psychologist in private practice. Edward Zigler, the father of Head Start, describes her as "an icon" of the field of early childhood intervention, and Hillary Clinton has called her one of the United States' "finest child advocates, innovators, and clinicians."

Susan Levenstein, M.D., is a primary care internist practicing in Rome, Italy, and a clinical researcher. She has published widely on the interactions between psychological and physiological factors in disease and has collaborated with her mother on studies of The Parent-Child Home Program.

Temple University Press
1601 North Broad Street
Philadelphia PA 19122
www.temple.edu/tempress

∞ The paper used in this publication meets the requirements of the
American National Standard for Information Sciences—Permanence of Paper for
Printed Library Materials, ANSI Z39.48-1992

Library of Congress Cataloging-in-Publication Data
Levenstein, Phyllis, 1916–
Messages from home : the parent-child home program for overcoming educational
disadvantage / Phyllis Levenstein and Susan Levenstein. — Rev. and updated ed.
p. cm.
Includes bibliographical references and index.

ISBN 13: 978-1-59213-676-6   ISBN 10: 1-59213-676-1   (cloth : alk. paper)
ISBN 13: 978-1-59213-677-3   ISBN 10: 1-59213-677-X   (pbk. : alk. paper)

1. Child development—United States.   2. Learning ability.   3. Education, Preschool—
Parent participation—United States.   4. Mother and child—United States.
5. Academic achievement—United States.   I. Levenstein, Susan.   II. Title.

LB1134.L48 2008
372.119'2—dc22   2007049496

2 4 6 8 9 7 5 3 1

To Sidney, Danny, and Alvin

Contents

Foreword

KATHRYN E. BARNARD, RN, PH.D.

*"Mothers who approach a young child's learning through play
with spontaneous joy will have a child who continues to find joy
in learning."*

—LEVENSTEIN, 1986

I am honored to be asked to write a foreword for this second edition of the book about The Parent–Child Home Program. Phyllis Levenstein was a truly remarkable individual. She had foresight to develop an effective intervention that has proven to be relevant to academic achievement of children, especially school readiness and high school completion. More than forty years ago, when she developed the pilot work, there was no empirical evidence, as we now have, about the impact of a low-verbal environment on a young child's development. However, as a strong advocate of developmental theory, she was guided about the importance of communication and language skills at toddlerhood. She also had a correct assumption about the importance of involving the child's parent by enriching the interaction and communication between the parent and child. Thus, as Urie Bronfenbrenner proclaimed (Bronfenbrenner, 1974), the Levenstein strategy was distinctive in that the intervention had the target of the mother–child dyad, not the child alone, but the interactive system. Because the target of intervention was the parent and child, the intervention established a process of mutual adaptation and learning that continues far beyond the program duration.

The manner in which Dr. Levenstein started the pilot project and then quickly developed a randomized trial of three communities (Levenstein, 1970) and later studies that randomized individuals demonstrated the scientific rigor of her work. The commitment to research design principles such as randomized trials, appropriate outcome measures, intervention-integrity monitoring, trials with independent investigators, and follow-up studies all demonstrate the commitment she had to improving the odds for children born to invalidating environments. She tested many questions about the intervention. What was the best age range? For which populations was it effective? How could it be integrated into the educational system? Finally, how could systems be persuaded to adopt the intervention model? Questions remain to be tested, and one of the most important in today's world of evidence-based practice is more randomized trials.

Most researchers adhere to the canons of science. However, very few researchers have the same commitment to the translation of the findings for practice. She was a tireless advocate for The Parent–Child Home Program. She communicated with everyone who would listen and even persuaded those who were not initially interested. As in the research effort, she followed through with efforts to expose the positive results of this intervention strategy to persons of political and social influence. I know of few other individuals who can be credited with such a persistent effort to bring the message about intervention both to the community and to the halls of power. She, fortunately, lived to see The Parent–Child Home Program become widely recognized and accepted.

Other investigators have created and tested other early intervention models. In general, their approaches have differed in time, duration, and scope from The Parent–Child Home Program's model. The projects with more comprehensively focused interventions have failed to demonstrate positive cognitive, language, and school achievement outcomes equal to what The Parent–Child Home Program has repeatedly shown.

I think The Parent–Child Home Program results have been so outstanding and consistent for several reasons:

1. Intervention was focused on the dyadic communication. This focus set in place a structure wherein the parent and the child could have fun by imitating the model of interaction demonstrated by the home visitor.
2. Demands on the parent were reasonable and thus they could be successful. The rate of program completion is the highest reported in early intervention trials.
3. Frequency of the home visits, twice a week over two years, established a habit of playful communication between the parent and child that did not fade away after so many repetitions (forty-six sessions each year).
4. Emphasis on verbal communication came developmentally at the prime time for the child's transition from paralinguistic to linguistic modes of communication and thought.

5. Cost of the program implementation was reasonable.
6. Replication of the program established standards for training, monitoring the process, and constant evaluation.
7. Desired outcomes were valued by both the parents and the greater public.

Levenstein and her daughter have emphasized and discussed several features in this book that I feel are important for home-visiting intervention models in general. One has to do with the ethics of intervention. There is great stress on the fact that the home visitor is a guest in the family home. As the guest, the home visitor should continue only when wanted. She or he has a specific purpose for being there and should not intrude in other issues. Family confidentially must be honored. The home visitor must be respectful of the parents and their culture.

The nine great messages summarized in Chapter 10 of the book are what I would call lessons learned. Several of the messages I want to emphasize are the hope, the parent–child network, strivers and hesitaters, and closing the gap messages.

Hope

The Parent–Child Home Program has given us hope that early learning is truly essential to later achievement. The results demonstrated that in environments where parents are not likely to provide the motivation for learning, a structure of promoting the communication and joy within the parent–child dyad can create the motivation for lifelong learning of both the parent and the child.

Parent–Child Network

Lasting effects of early intervention efforts must build the parent–child bond to be a positive and reinforcing agent for the development of a secure relationship and as a source of constant refueling of energy for learning and exploration.

Strivers and Hesitaters

Identifying individual differences in motivation and function within low-income parents enables the interveners to plan the approach more effectively. *Strivers* are ready to go, given a few toys and directions, whereas *hesitaters* need more time and encouragement to recognize their importance to their child's well-being and motivation for learning.

Closing the Gap

With such success shown by application of The Parent–Child Home Program, why has it taken so long for communities to adopt this strategy? Changes do take time and resources. In 2007, sites in twelve of fifty states had adopted The Parent–Child Home Program. Change theory predicts when at least 20 percent of a population (statehoods) has adopted the innovation, the spread should be automatic. However, when we look at poverty communities, the penetration is probably less than 5 percent. How can we increase the adoption in these communities of interest? The best tool is to create awareness. There needs to be mass media attention to The Parent–Child Home Program in venues such as books, newspapers, education journals, films, and videos that will bring awareness of the hope for school-readiness innovation to the community and its leaders. There should be sustained efforts to reach the political and social will of communities.

Following awareness, there needs to be deliberate outreach to poverty groups and communities to persuade people to investigate how this successful model can be brought to their community by talking with successful implementers they respect. After the awareness of The Parent–Child Home Program model has been made and the community has been convinced this is the model for them, the National Program office has the structure for assisting communities in adopting the model to their community and structuring the faithful replication. The process is similar to car sales: Public media convince you of the car you want. Then the car dealer knows how to persuade you to take a test drive and makes it possible for you to purchase the auto; this is marketing.

Dr. Levenstein created and tested a wonderful solution that can close the achievement gap for children. With her legacy, we must take responsibility to create the awareness and adoption of this solution. This second edition of her book aids our work.

Seattle, Washington

Coauthor's Preface

Susan Levenstein

"Every man is a piece of the continent, a part of the main."
—John Donne

Few people have a life's work and still fewer get to see it take wing. My mother was one of these. In her forties, she had the intuition that she could combine her humanistic ideals with her various skills—as a clinical psychologist, a family therapist, a play therapist, a former teacher, and a former social worker with experience making the rounds—to produce a method for helping disadvantaged families help their own children to escape from poverty.

Having founded The Parent–Child Home Program, a pioneering home visiting intervention, she never looked back. During the 1980s, she held the Program together with spit and twine, writing the original edition of this book at a moment when the future of the Program looked particularly uncertain. In completing her unfinished second edition, whose purpose is laid out in her prologue, it has been a pleasure to be able to edit out her many references to shrinking numbers of replications and dried-up funding now that The Parent–Child Home Program is booming.

My mother was just out of college when she got her first job as a teacher of children's literature in the Detroit public schools, forty-six when she conceived the kernel of The Parent–Child Home Program, sixty-six when she embarked on writing a book as part of her campaign to keep the Program from disappearing, eighty when she found a superb new executive director (Sarah Walzer) to ensure her program would live on after her, and nearly eighty-nine when she died knowing that it was thriving and self-supporting.

In my opinion, one of the most important *"Messages"* of this second edition of her book is that with a solid theoretical base, elbow grease, and perseverance, it is possible to carry a good idea a good long way.

They say genius is 1 percent inspiration and 99 percent perspiration. The creation of The Parent–Child Home Program certainly required inspiration—to quote from one of my mother's e–mails, "There were no models in 1965 for a home-visit intervention except for the vastly different Visiting Nurses." But it is her perspiration that made the Program the only one of the Consortium for Longitudinal Studies models to have survived and, probably, along with Head Start, the longest running intervention program of any kind for disadvantaged families.

Going through her papers, I have found letters to governors, journalists, scientists, writers, anybody who had made a statement carrying a hint that their author could become a convert to The Parent–Child Home Program. If a journalist wrote an article about why disadvantaged children fail in school or about the malleability of IQ, he or she received a letter; my mother kept a copy attached to the original article. She wrote to New York Governor Cuomo after he talked about the need to help young children, to Arkansas governor's wife, Hillary Clinton, when she was first looking into pre-preschool programs, to the author of a scientific review of early intervention programs that failed to mention The Parent–Child Home Program. I had seen some of the letters people wrote to her about our 1998 paper on high school graduation (Levenstein, Levenstein, Shiminski, & Stolzberg, 1998), but it wasn't until I went through her computer files that I realized she had mailed off literally scores of hard-copy reprints to people important either in the early intervention field or in the history of The Parent–Child Home Program, every one with a personal (often chatty) cover letter asking for comments and suggestions.

My mother was a woman of principle for whom the moral and ethical imperative came before all else. Her Parent–Child Home Program was not chiefly a model, a piece of scientific research, a tool for obtaining a doctorate, or a road to admiration and fame—it rarely even helped her earn a living. It was a social program aimed at ameliorating, if not at helping to eliminate, many of the ills of society. That's why she paid such attention to dissemination and why she donated so many hours and weeks and years of her life to the Program she had created. She aimed high for her program, not for herself.

She was a committed humanist who had us reciting "No man is an island . . ." in chorus over dinner; an inveterate listener who, on her way to an airplane, would draw out the whole life story of the wheelchair attendant between the check-in desk and the gate; and a hopeless optimist. All her life she maintained an unshakable faith in the capacity of individuals for personal growth and accomplishment, and of human society for progress. These qualities stood her in good stead for her profession as a psychotherapist and for rising above the losses, diminutions, and indignities of old age.

In The Parent–Child Home Program, these personal qualities translated into an enormous respect offered to client families and an approach that emphasizes families' strengths rather than their weaknesses. More than many programs that share the aim of promoting literacy, my mother's empowers the child's parents by placing the primary creative role squarely in their hands (rather than in the hands of educators whether in the home or in a preschool center); explicitly trains Home Visitors to avoid intruding on the parent–child relationship; and concretely emphasizes its trust in the parents' capacities by giving them open-ended, though focussed, guidance rather than precise syllabi, homework, and other explicitly didactic tasks.

Comments from a Medical Point of View

As a physician, I was interested to see my mother's faith in her method echoed a few years back by an editorialist for the *Journal of the American Medical Association*, who proposed that parenting interventions focused on positive verbal interaction could help to decrease the mortality gradient between rich and poor (Williams, 1998).

Involvement in the art and science of medicine brings inside acquaintance with the struggle to balance intuition, experience, and experimental evidence. From my clinical practice, I understand the value of the kind of evidence-based guidelines the early intervention field is seeking but also the limitations of such guidelines and of the research basis they rest on. All that glitters with scientific method is not gold.

My own area of medical research concerns the influences of psychological factors on organic disease, making me even more acutely aware of the spanners that can be tossed into the works of scientific inquiry by methodological problems. The difficulties The Parent–Child Home Program has encountered with accomplishing airtight subject-randomized experimental research resonates with me because psychosomatic medicine is another field whose research is haunted by the ghost of systematic bias. It is very difficult to demonstrate irrefutably an effect of psychological factors on disease, because the distress and subjective stress caused by illness can lead even the most sophisticated researchers into the trap of a Type I error, thinking they have found a causal nexus from psychology to disease when in reality the connection is the other way around. In clinical psychosomatic research, the problem is further compounded by the self-selection of more distressed patients to participate in studies.

Writing the Second Edition of
Messages from Home

When she decided in 2002 to revise *Messages from Home* for a second edition, my mother threw herself into the project body and soul. She was in good health and planned to complete a century of life—"my100self" was her usual Internet password—but at eighty-five, she was sharply aware that her productive capacity might end from one day to the next. So she would dine on sandwiches, Fresca, and M&M's in her apartment to keep the interruptions of her hours in front of the computer as brief as possible. Especially in the last six months of her life, she did and thought about little else.

It's my impression that few people maintain an unshaken intellectual curiosity and fervor for their life's work at an advanced age. Many in their fifties are surprised to find themselves beginning to become casual or indifferent to what used to impassion them; pushing ninety, Phyllis Levenstein had not yet reached that point.

She started with the hard parts of the book, first drafting a prologue to have a clear synopsis of her vision to show around to interested parties, next completely rewriting the theory chapter, and then moving on to the research material. Though she had been complaining that her typing, her eyesight, and even her thinking were slowed down by age, through persistent application of *sitzfleisch,* she accomplished all that plus taking a first look at most of the other chapters and writing a brand new one on pitfalls in research methodology. When she did suddenly die at my apartment in Rome in May 2005, shortly after arriving radiant from the fortieth anniversary celebration of the Program she had founded, the book revision was well on the road toward completion, making it relatively easy for me to carry the project through.

I had been hearing about The Parent–Child Home Program since before it was born, when my parents were hammering out the basic concept around the kitchen table. Many years afterward, when I was involved in research of my own, it was a privilege to be able to collaborate in my mother's studies with statistical suggestions and with a little editing (as she in turn contributed some excellent turns of phrase for my medical articles). When it came to the second edition of *Messages,* she involved me in the writing and editing in part, I'm sure, to be certain that the book would be in reasonably knowledgeable hands if she died before it was finished.

My aim in this work has been to carry out my mother's mission as much as possible, to be loyal to her vision, to write only what I thought she would have written. I'd estimate that about 25 percent of the text of the finished manuscript survives from the first edition, and 40 percent more was written or revised by my mother. In addition to the changes described under the specific chapters, I have permitted myself some editing throughout for style and clarity, and have slightly altered several of her chapter titles.

• "Prologue to the Second Edition." This piece is published as my mother signed off on it in early 2005, and so it contains a few minor anachronisms.

• "Introduction." I have updated this brief introduction to The Parent–Child Home Program, which had opened the first edition of the book.

• Chapter 1, "Two Mothers, Two Children: Program Participants." The chapter that introduces the concrete practice of The Parent–Child Home Program is the only one that has been left virtually unaltered from the previous edition, in homage to the early years of the Program. The reader should keep in mind that the two families' stories are authentic case histories dating from the 1970s and written up in the 1980s, so that some of the language and family circumstances are not what they would be today.

• Chapter 2, "Poverty in the Twenty-First Century: Parental Love Fights Back." For my mother, the revision of the material on the Program's social context and purpose would have been a piece of cake. She followed the sociological and political evolution of the United States very closely and was clear on what she thought was important, especially in terms of what related to her program. Unfortunately, she died before getting around to this chapter, so the task was left to me, a much less expert author. Obviously, considerable reworking was required to bring the material abreast of the changes in public assistance programs and in the face of American poverty since *Messages from Home* was first written in the 1980s. However, the overall picture presented by my mother has regrettably changed little, and her approach to remediation remained intact, so the gist of the first edition's chapter was solid. Its organization and surprisingly much of its content have survived in my revision.

• Chapter 3, " 'Show, Not Tell': The Parent–Child Home Program Method." The chapter portraying the Program's approach in detail has obviously needed retouching, but this proved relatively limited, reflecting the stability of the Parent–Child Home Program model. With the help of National Center staff, I have updated the history, the description of the method, and the examples of home sessions.

- Chapter 4, "Underpinnings: The Theory behind The Parent–Child Home Program." I contributed little to this account of program theory, which had already been thoroughly revised and updated by my mother.

- Chapter 5, "How Effective Is The Parent–Child Home Program?" My mother revised the opening sections and intended the rest of the effectiveness chapter to be made up of an extensively annotated bibliography she had created for this edition. She and I debated the value of inserting into this chapter a narrative summary of Parent–Child Home Program research. The final decision to include such a summary was made after her death, so the job of writing it fell entirely on me. I hope my summary does not, at too many points, betray her thought or that of others. The annotated bibliography has been separated out as Chapter 11.

- Chapter 6, "Methodological Issues in Intervention Research: Lessons from The Parent–Child Home Program Experience." This expansion of material that had been presented briefly in the first edition was first written by my mother for possible journal publication, with the intention of also including it in *Messages from Home* as a chapter. When she died, she had not gotten around to making the planned chapter version. I have tried to tone down the somewhat technical language of the piece she left, but given the nature of the subject, it was challenging to match the more colloquial tone of the rest of the book.

- Chapter 7, "From Laboratory to Real World: Successful Replication of a Successful Intervention." My mother had planned to clarify and expand her ideas about replication, ideas that have allowed the extraordinarily faithful dissemination of The Parent–Child Home Program through time and space; with her gone, nobody can do this. But she had arranged with Sarah Walzer, the current executive director, to help with more straightforward aspects of updating, and Program staff members have been generous with their input to ensure that what is written reflects current Program practice.

- Chapter 8, "Preventing a Dream from Becoming a Nightmare: The Ethics of Home Visiting Programs." The ethics of home visiting was a subject my mother felt passionately about—as she did about many subjects—and had written about extensively. It seemed reasonable to expand the section on ethics from the original edition of the book into a chapter by incorporating other writings of hers (Levenstein, 1979a; Levenstein, 1981).

• Chapter 9, "Ludic Literacy: Prelude to Instrumental Literacy." One of the major findings of Parent–Child Home Program research was that trying to stuff information down the throats of tiny tots gets you nowhere. The unpublished 1992 piece on Ludic Literacy, which I found among my mother's computer files and included in the book after minor editing and updating, extends her theorum on the crucial role of enjoyment for learning in toddlers to a corollary about the crucial role of enjoyment for learning in adults. (Isn't that part of what computers are all about? The world wouldn't be full of edifying PowerPoint presentations if they weren't so much fun to make.)

• Chapter 10, "Messages from Home: Meditations and Conclusions." This chapter, which summarizes the heart of what my mother meant by The Parent–Child Home Program, has suffered from the absence of its chief author. Her reflections on the broader importance of the Program would surely have been considerably changed on the basis of twenty more years of thinking. Although, unfortunately, she did not complete her intended rewriting, her prologue gives some hint of the directions it might have taken. I have limited myself to adding the material about actualization of cognitive theory, which she conceived and formulated in the last months of her life (Message Eight), and to carrying forward the revising and updating that she had begun. I considered trying to cobble together other new messages—on play, for example—but in the end I felt I couldn't do so without a psychic to "channel" my mother's mind.

• Chapter 11, "The Parent–Child Home Program in Writing: Publications by and about the Program, 1968–2007." To my mother's comprehensive annotated bibliography, I have added some documents that were published after her death or that were not (as far as I can tell) known to her, eliminated multiple reports of the same data, and cut out conference presentations and grant reports unless they included important material not subsequently published in other form. I have checked the content of nearly every entry—two or three originals were unavailable—and have taken the liberty of revising some of my mother's listings accordingly. I also added various reviews and meta-analyses that included The Parent–Child Home Program, irrespective of their conclusions.

• Appendix, "Outcome Measures Created by The Parent–Child Home Program." I have collected into an appendix three measures used in Program research, while eliminating all three of the first edition appendices. The original edition's listing of Program replications, which is in constant flux, can be more appropriately accessed at www.parent-child.org, along with information about the National Center staff, board, partners, and sponsors, hot-off-the-presses news, and more. The appendix with examples of books and toys appeared unnecessary, and the one listing technical materials seemed irrelevant as these are supplied as part of replicators' training (this is not a how-to book).

Acknowledgments

Messages from Home is really my mother's book, not mine. The revision project was her baby, not to say her obsession, from the start and until the end. We were discussing possible publishers hours before she died. To complete the manuscript for publication, I have had to lean heavily on others, in the hopes of preventing my mistakes from being too many and too major. I am indebted to LaRue Allen, Becky Knickelbein, Jim Shiminski, Michelle Higgins, and Patricia Hrusa Williams for graciously sharing their research findings, and to Dianne Oliver for giving me a feel for the Program in action. To Carolynn Wiplich and to the creators of Google, for making my research much easier. To Linda Mewshaw and the Kirby Foundation for material and moral support. To John Spitzer, Geta Carlson, Michael Zweig, and Lenore Goldman for useful suggestions. To Lois-ellin Datta, Gloria Rodriguez, and the late Irving Sigel for their encouragement and advice. To Jerome Bruner, Edward Zigler, Katharine Ogden Michaels, and Larry Rosenthal, and particularly to Richard Walker and Harold Bourne, for their support and their useful comments on various drafts. To my editor Mick Gusinde-Duffy for his patience, professionalism, and calming influence, and to Temple's anonymous reviewers for their sharp critical eye and for suggestions that have been invaluable in improving the text. To Kathryn Barnard for her kindness, help, and enthusiasm, and not least for agreeing to write the book's foreword. Special thanks to Sarah Walzer, the Executive Director of The Parent–Child Home Program, for all kinds of assistance, in particular the vast jobs of ensuring that terminology and descriptions of Program procedures are up to date throughout the book and of contributing greatly (along with Michele Morrison, Training and Program Support Director, and Cesar Zuniga, Research and Training Associate) to the revision of Chapter 7. To Daniel Levenstein for invaluable insights, suggestions, legwork, and editorial comments. And, most especially, to my husband Alvin Curran who has tirelessly nurtured me through this project on love and lentils.

Prologue to the Second Edition

Messages from Home was first published in 1988 as an introduction to the background, theory, and effectiveness with low-income children of the two-year intervention then called the Mother-Child Home Program. It was addressed to educators, social service personnel, policymakers, and present or potential Program staff members. Nearly twenty years have elapsed since that book was written, and much has changed in those years with regard to the Program and its social context, although many of the latter's negative aspects unfortunately have not improved.

The chapter introducing real-life examples of Program families (Chapter 1) has remained essentially unchanged in this new edition, and the description of Program method in Chapter 3 has required remarkably little updating, but the rest of the book has extensively revised or expanded content. The new edition will outline recent developments in the background of societal problems and issues, will expand the basic theory of the Program through recent studies relevant to family verbal interaction, and will recount the Program's recent expansion and current status worldwide. It will contain the latest research further bolstering the evidence for the Program's impact on school success and explicitly discuss several issues (such as research methodology, ethical considerations, and the actualization of cognitive theory) that were implicit or mentioned only briefly in the first edition.

The most obvious change in the Program itself since the first edition of this book is a slight but socially important alteration of its name. It is now called The Parent–Child Home Program, reflecting the growing and welcome emphasis in this country on the roles of both parents in rearing their children. The change was intended to acknowledge the growing numbers of fathers participating in the Program and to convey to all fathers their indispensable place in their children's lives and therefore in the Program's method and aims. Less visible has been the expansion and stabilization of the Program's central office, related in part to improved and more reliable funding.

However, the nondidactic method of the two-year Parent–Child Home Program as practiced in 2005[1] is still essentially the same one that evolved forty years ago between the start of the Program in 1965 and its full development by 1968. That method is based on the multidisciplinary theory that a young child's cognitive and emotional growth develops from concept-inducing verbal interaction with a cherished parent figure. That interaction consists in a conversation that is demonstrated by a Home Visitor (formerly called a Toy Demonstrator) around gifts of books and toys in home sessions that involve, together, both the parent and the pre-preschool child. I consider it a good sign that there is little new material in this second edition concerning the Program's simple *show, not tell* procedure. Occasionally, minor variations have been added, with the National Center's approval, by the Coordinators (local directors) of certain replication sites. For example, some have added parents' discussion groups or parties for the families at the end of a Program year; others have increased the number of home sessions and play materials. And the specific toys and books used have, of course, varied over time and according to local preferences. Still, the basic method has proved to be surprisingly durable in the many years since it took final form: easy to learn, fun to put into practice for both Program participants and Program staff, and found again and again to be effective in preventing at-risk toddlers' later educational disadvantage. Most parents join and stay with The Parent–Child Home Program to its end; parental cooperation is an obvious necessity for a parent-involving program.

The Parent–Child Home Program's creation in 1965 could be considered a prescient response to a challenge published thirty-three years later:

> Parenting practices almost certainly have more impact on children's cognitive development than preschool practices. Indeed, changing the way parents deal with their children may be the most important thing we can do to improve children's cognitive skills. But getting parents to change their habits is even harder than getting teachers to change. Like teachers, parents are usually suspicious of unsolicited

1. This prologue was written by Phyllis Levenstein in early 2005, two years before the rest of the book was finalized.

suggestions. This is doubly true when the suggestions require fundamental changes in a parent's behavior. (Phillips, Brooks-Gunn, Duncan, Klebanov, & Crane, 1998, p. 46)

For countrywide—indeed worldwide—replications of The Parent–Child Home Program, the established rigorous requirements of staff training and ongoing quality control through interaction with the National Center have continued to ensure that local implementations are true replicas of the Program. As a result of the scrupulous maintenance of training and certification standards, the Program has not become watered down over time even in its most far-flung replications.

Dissemination of the Program through replication has expanded greatly since the 1988 edition of *Messages from Home*, from nineteen local sites in that year to more than 150 in 2005, especially since several state governments (Massachusetts, Pennsylvania, and South Carolina) have begun systematic support for such Parent–Child Home Program replicators as school districts, social service agencies, community health centers, and other auspices. There have been two changes in the National Center's method of disseminating the Program to sites away from the original site of its development. One is altering the training of the professional staff in most replications from the original one-on-one approach to group training; this change was initially necessitated by the adoption of the Program by many sites in a state at one time. The other change is for training to occur in two stages: the first three-day training institute equips the new site's Coordinator with full information and tools to begin the Program immediately at the Coordinator's site; in the second stage, the Coordinator undergoes a one-day training review after a few months of actually conducting the Program.

Important longitudinal research data indicating this intervention's long-term educational effects have emerged in the years since the book's first publication and have been published in juried professional journals. These new findings have demonstrated that the Program increases at-risk children's readiness for school (Levenstein, Levenstein, & Oliver, 2002) and increases their probability of graduating from high school many years later (Levenstein, Levenstein, Shiminski, & Stolzberg, 1998), achieving graduation rates that match those of middle-income students. The high rate of parents' acceptance of the Program in local replications (usually over 90 percent) and of parents' cooperation throughout the two program years, already indicated by pre-1988 research, has been confirmed in all subsequent studies.

To understand the social importance of these data, we must recall that many hopes and much fiscal support have been invested during the last four decades in non-Parent–Child Home Program center-based and home-based interventions aimed at the cognitive enrichment of at-risk children. Although some have documented positive effects on both parents and children, their lack of substantial impact on the future education of their preschool participants has seemed to be disappointing unless expensive components are added, for example, extension of preschool features into third grade. The Parent–Child Home Program's demonstrated success suggests that hope can be revived. There is good research evidence that the Program is an effective, popular, and relatively low-cost way (costing about $2,500 yearly per child) of preparing low-income children to succeed in school and thus take advantage of public education and the self-sufficiency to which this can lead.

American education, in general, has been blamed by many for what has been judged its failure to erase poverty-linked educational disadvantage. This disadvantage usually becomes apparent as early as children's entry into preschool or kindergarten and is even more evident by high school when the dropout rates of disadvantaged students continue to be high. The low literacy rate of many subgroups of children has been a special object of attacks on schools.

These problems have persisted or even increased during the many profound changes that have occurred in the world since 1988. Advanced technology at first seemed to promise dramatic improvement in educational methods. Yet the speed of technological developments has tended to render more visible the educational problems of students from low-income families rather than to come to their aid. For example, the access of most middle-class families today to computers and to the Internet is not shared by families in poverty. Schools may acquire computers for students' learning, but skepticism seems warranted as to the degree to which such learning will occur in disadvantaged students when the progress of these students is not supported by computers in the home. One potential educational equalizer, television, was available to virtually all American families, including Parent–Child Home Program participants, by 1988, yet most of the available programming was—and is still—of doubtful educational value to young at-risk viewers.

Public education, on the other hand, gives almost all children in this country a real chance at the pursuit of happiness, however imperfect some schools may seem to be. Education is the gateway to success in a chosen career and to the gratification that this can bring. For virtually every occupation past the unskilled level, education is essential for admitting people to the careers they want. Plumbers, physical therapists, Webmasters, electricians, teachers, mechanics, lawyers all require education in varying amounts and degrees of complexity. The number of jobs at the totally unskilled level, requiring little or no formal education, has dropped over the last half century, decade by decade, so that now relatively few employment opportunities are available for people who do not have at least a high school diploma.

Yet during those same decades, a very large number of students, especially those from low-income families, have been unable to take full advantage of public schooling to escape from a life of poverty. The high school dropout rate is startling, and the academic lacks of children still in elementary or high school are alarming. Countless young people who may have been ill prepared for school to begin with fill the ranks of the jobless after having left school before earning a high school diploma. The first edition of this book addressed the unhappy results:

> From their ranks come recruits for street crime, for welfare dependency, and for other social problems. Ironically, as those ranks are swelled in ever-increasing numbers by high school dropouts without job skills, the work base of our society is becoming so transformed by technology toward a services/skills orientation, that a high school diploma is the minimum requirement for almost any satisfying and well-paying job. (Levenstein, 1988, p. 3)

This thought is even more true today when a college degree is coming to be a minimum requirement for many occupations previously filled by high school graduates or even by high school dropouts. In desperate attempts to eliminate one resulting social problem, the widespread dependence of families (especially those headed by women) on monetary support from welfare agencies, draconian laws have been passed at national and state levels during the last decade that, in effect, forbid welfare dependency. Most lawmakers seem to have ignored, much less attempted to remedy, the frequent root cause of such dependency: the lack of sufficient education to qualify for self-supporting paid jobs compatible with the unpaid job of mothers raising their children.

The Parent–Child Home Program was created in 1965 when the need was already clear for an effective early intervention to prevent the educational problems of disadvantaged children. The main issues in evaluating program success at the time of the first edition of *Messages from Home* were: Does The Parent–Child Home Program produce significant postprogram cognitive boosts in its child participants? Does it show in later years the predicted positive school effects for its child participants?

The answers to these questions at the time *Messages* was first written were positive, as far as they went, and are still pertinent. But since the publication date of the first edition, more and longer term follow-up data have accrued for the substantial long-term benefits of the Program. These achievements seem vital to the escape of these children from the family poverty that could be predicted to so handicap their academic progress as to close off their chances at future satisfying work careers.

The 1998 and 2002 reports of The Parent–Child Home Program's positive effects on at-risk children's school readiness and on their high school graduation rate, published in peer-reviewed professional journals, have aroused much interest in education and public policy circles, and the Program's dissemination has expanded by leaps and bounds since the first edition of *Messages from Home* was published. This new edition will enable readers to judge for themselves whether The Parent–Child Home Program has fulfilled its promise to be a way for economically disadvantaged children to avoid educational disadvantage when they start school and throughout the years they spend in the educational system, so they can continue their way up from poverty.

Acknowledgments

This prologue gives me the opportunity to express heart-felt thanks to my coauthors of the 1998 and 2002 articles mentioned above: Susan Levenstein, Dianne Oliver, James Shiminski, and Judith Stolzberg; to the many who furthered the expansion of The Parent–Child Home Program's dissemination, although limited space allows me to name only a few: Barbara Baskin, Michelle Morrison, and especially the executive director of The Parent–Child Home Program, Sarah Walzer; to the program officers of the many private foundations and federal agencies that have supported the development and dissemination of the Program, particularly the late Barbara Finberg, who oversaw the Program's progress through six years of support by the Carnegie Corporation of New York; to The Parent–Child Home Program's Board of Trustees and its current chair, Charles Butts;[2] and, above all, to the dozens of Program replication site Coordinators whose commitment to Parent–Child Home Program standards has made it possible for thousands of families to receive the benefits of an unadulterated Parent–Child Home Program.

2. As of June 2006, the PCHP chair is Brenda Di Leo.

Chronology

1965: Phyllis Levenstein's pilot study, in Freeport, New York, of a method
to increase verbal interaction between disadvantaged mothers and their
toddlers

1965: Verbal Interaction Project founded as a program of the Nassau
County Family Service Association

1967: Inauguration of a model one-year Mother–Child Home Program in
Freeport

1968: First Program research publication in a peer-reviewed venue (Levenstein and Sunley)

1969: Phyllis Levenstein becomes a Doctor of Education at Teachers College, Columbia University, with the dissertation, *Cognitive Growth in
Low Income Preschool Children Through Stimulation of Verbally Oriented Play Activity in Mother–Child Dyads*

1969: The Mother–Child Home Program expands to its present two-year
format

1970: First sites outside the model program (New Jersey, Massachusetts,
New York City)

1971: Affiliation with the State University of New York at Stony Brook

1972: Endorsed by the U.S. Office of Education as one of fifteen compensatory education programs considered to be national models

1976: Publication of cognitive and achievement data through age eight
(Madden et al.)

1976: First site outside the United States opens in Bermuda

1978: Endorsed as one of five best childhood programs by the U.S. National Institute of Mental Health

1978: Endorsed as "a program that works" by the Joint Dissemination Review Panel of the U.S. Department of Education

1981: The Verbal Interaction Project, Inc., established as a not-for-profit, 501(c)(3), organization

1981: End of affiliation with the Nassau County Family Service Association

1982: Consortium for Longitudinal Studies reports effects through age ten on cognitive gains and grade retention (Lazar and Darlington)

1982: The Verbal Interaction Project, Inc., closes its model program and moves to Wantagh, New York, to concentrate on broad dissemination of the Mother–Child Home Program

1983: Effects on socioemotional competence published through age eight (Levenstein et al.)

1984: Home Again study of cognitive testing and mother–child interactions (Madden et al.)

1986: Publication of the most comprehensive analyses of parent–child network (Levenstein)

1988: First edition of the book *Messages from Home*

1997: Phyllis Levenstein retires as executive director, replaced by Sarah Walzer

1998: Pittsfield high school graduation study demonstrates that the program prevents dropping out (Levenstein et al.)

1998: The Mother–Child Home Program becomes The Parent–Child Home Program

1998: The Verbal Interaction Project, Inc., becomes the National Center of The Parent–Child Home Program, Inc.

1999: Massachusetts funds multi-million dollar statewide expansion of the Program

1999: Founding of the Home Visit Forum

1999: Launching of The Parent–Child Home Program Web site, www .parent-child.org

1999: South Carolina funds statewide expansion of the Program as part of First Steps to School Readiness (now reauthorized through 2013)

2000: Number of sites exceeds 100

2001: Endorsed as a "wise investment" by the Comptroller of the City of New York

2001: *Christian Science Monitor* article on the Program

2001: Pennsylvania allocates $12 million over three years to expand the Program statewide

2002: Publication of South Carolina first grade school readiness study: 92 percent of Program graduates pass first grade skills assessment (Levenstein et al.)

2002: *Education Week* article on the Program

2003: Endorsed by the California Children and Families Commission as one of six programs most closely aligned with its goals

2004: *American Educator* article highlights the Program's effectiveness

2005: Endorsed by the New York State Education Department as "a science-based Safe and Drug-Free Schools and Communities Act program"

2005: Endorsed by the National Governors Association Center for Best Practices as one of six recommended programs

2005: The Board of Directors adds its first member who had been a child in the Program

2005: Fortieth anniversary of the Program

2005: Phyllis Levenstein dies on May 28

2006: Endorsed by the Council of Chief State School Officers as one of three recommended programs

2006: Endorsed by the Children's Trust Fund of Washington/Washington Council for Prevention of Child Abuse and Neglect as one of three evidence-based home visiting programs

2007: Publication of New York University study showing that the Program bridges the "preparation gap" (Allen et al.)

2007: Inauguration of alumni program for adult Parent–Child Home Program graduates

Introduction

Humanity's most ancient dialogue—the verbal exchange between parent and young child—is at the core of The Parent–Child Home Program.

The Parent–Child Home Program is a low-cost pre-preschool intervention, developed between 1965 and 1982 using $3 million of federal and private funding, to help low-income parents prevent their toddlers' future school problems. It first reached into the homes of families in a poverty pocket on Long Island, New York, and it has been implemented widely elsewhere since. By now, four decades of experimental research have examined the results of The Parent–Child Home Program and tested its hypothesis that children's best preparation for school is their early participation in cheerful, casual exchanges of concept-building conversation with their parents at home.

Talking to infants comes naturally to all parents and all parent substitutes. For most of them, talking to baby becomes conversation. The dialogue is often focused around the toys and books that middle-income parents can afford. The Program theorized that this verbal interaction gradually fosters a parent–child network that is both intellectually and emotionally supportive for the child, whatever the family's ethnolinguistic style.

Social and emotional bonding between parent and child is the matrix for this supportive network. Important as the parent–child bond is for the child's emotional development, it can evolve with scarcely a word being said. But exchange of language taking place within the context of that emotional relationship creates cognitive skills that enable children to meet increasingly complex intellectual challenges. The child's growing intellectual abilities send positive messages to the parents about their own constructive roles in the child's competence, which in turn encourage parents to continue the good work by sending more of their own pleasant cognitive *strands* to the child. Child and parent together thus weave a network that has both emotional and cognitive links. The Parent–Child Home Program conjectured that this network lasts into the children's school years and reinforces their skills in accomplishing school tasks—that its support can, in fact, be crucial to children's school success.

The Program's view was that family factors linked to poverty often hamper the full development of the cognitive aspects of the parent–child network. For children who thus become at risk for educational disadvantage, an effective intervention should therefore begin at home when the children are about two years old, at the start of a key period for building cognitive skills through language. Such an intervention should center on books and toys of high quality that are gifts to the family and used as the focus of the child's reading, conversation, and play with his or her parents. The intervention must be imbued with trust and respect for the child's parents and should build on their personal and cultural strengths. Through their participation, many parents might be expected to make gains not only in parenting skills but also in self-esteem.

Pointing the Way toward a Way Out?

Through research both at the original model program and at other sites (*replications*), The Parent–Child Home Program has explored whether the way out of poverty for many disadvantaged children might start at home, long before a child enters a classroom preschool program. The research has aimed to find out whether the shared joy of young children and their parents—playing, laughing, and talking together in their own homes—could lead to the serious business of school success.

Is it really possible that a modest, low-key pre-preschool program to aid playful parent–child interaction, in the family's home, can appeal to most families, regardless of their cultural or ethnic background, and can mitigate the educational disadvantage of low-income children? Can economically disadvantaged children thus enter first grade with a more reasonable prospect of graduating from high school? And can the strengths of The Parent–Child Home Program be maintained during widespread dissemination?

This book will describe in detail the nonobtrusive, nonpedantic, inexpensive, and deceptively simple Parent–Child Home Program, as well as the systematic research that has attempted to answer these questions about

Program effectiveness. From a theoretical point of view, it was important to study whether children's school competence was indeed related to early verbal interaction between parent and child: Does the parent–child network really exist? But the most socially pressing research question was and remains whether the pre-preschool Parent–Child Home Program, predicated on that network's existence, would achieve its goal of preventing the educational disadvantage of low-income children while fostering parenting skills and self-esteem. Might the Program, in fact, be able to help point the way out of poverty for children at risk for school failure—and for their parents?

1.

Two Mothers, Two Children

Program Participants

The Invitation: July

Ms. Willard and Carol

The July morning was hot. Ms. Willard was awake, had to be. Two-year-old Carol had dragged the sheet until she had almost tumbled her mother out of bed. Demanded breakfast. Paid no attention to the heat in the small room, which was crowded by a loaded dresser, a chair without a back, and several overflowing boxes. Ms. Willard's welfare checks didn't provide much furniture. When the sun came around to that side of the housing project, it would beat into the curtainless window. Yet better to lie still now than get up.

But Carol wanted breakfast. She was crying and pulling. The three older ones could get their own cereal off the shelf, their own milk out of the refrigerator—and leave it on the table to sour. At twenty-five months, Carol

This chapter, which graphically introduces the workings of The Parent–Child Home Program using two genuine case studies, has been carried over virtually unchanged from the book's first edition in homage to the early years of the Program. It was written by the first author twenty-five years ago from staff observations that go even further back, to the mid-1970s, when the families described in this chapter participated. Some of the language and descriptive emphases may, consequently, seem dated. Participants' names and identifying information, as with all Program clients in this book, are disguised, and their inner thoughts and feelings were extrapolated from their Program records. Staff members are identified by their real names, and quotations from the records are exactly as originally written.

couldn't do those things for herself. She could run to her mother and scream and even talk. Ask questions. Sometimes Ms. Willard thought she was a nuisance, wanted too much. The older ones seemed to have gotten used to doing things for themselves, not bothering her with their inquisitiveness.

Then Ms. Willard heard the sound of mail being pushed into the empty oblong spaces in the entry hall, into what had been a set of mailboxes. One space had "Willard" penciled across the top. She heard the mailman say "good morning" to someone in the hall, not too far from her own apartment door. "Must be around ten," she thought. Carol had a right to want her breakfast.

Ms. Willard, a statuesque, calm-featured, brown-skinned woman, walked heavily to the bathroom, threw cool water on her face, and felt better. By the time Carol was sitting in the tiny kitchen, with cold cereal in a bowl hastily rinsed from the pile in the sink, Ms. Willard was ready to see if anything had been pushed into her own mailbox. She slipped through the door, leaving Carol at the table and the coffee for her own breakfast—still enough from yesterday—heating on the stove. Quickly came back with an advertisement and a long white envelope addressed to "Ms. Helen Willard." She crumpled the ad, put the envelope faceup on the table, searched out a sweet roll from a bag, and started to eat it with her coffee. "Hush, Carol," she said gently as the little girl jabbered away about a cartoon she had been watching on TV.

Presently she opened the envelope. It appeared to be only a typed letter with an unfamiliar name at the top: "Parent–Child Home Program."

"Dear Ms. Willard," it began. Before she could read further, Carol began clamoring to get down. At the same time, the six-year-old twins—girls—burst into the door, shouting and hitting each other. The letter and envelope slipped into the puddle of milk that surrounded Carol's cereal bowl. They were thrown out that evening when a space was cleared on the table for someone's supper.

A Few Days Later

When Ms. Willard answered a knock at her door a few days later (the bell had long since given out), she saw an unknown woman standing there, brown-skinned like herself. A briefcase was in her hand. Welfare worker? Saleswoman? Ms. Willard braced herself.

The woman smiled. "Ms. Willard? I'm Myrtle Crawford. I wrote to you about our free Parent–Child Home Program a little while ago. Ms. Bailey told me you might be interested in being in it."

"Yeah." Ms. Willard's face relaxed fractionally. She liked Ms. Bailey, a social worker at the twins' school who had helped her get an extra welfare allowance for Carol's crib.

"In the Program, we visit you and your two year old together twice a week, starting in October and going on till the end of the school year. Every week we bring a toy or a book for—what's your little one's name?"

"Name? Her name? Oh—Carol—her name's Carol."

"Well, if you join the Program, Carol will get a new book or toy every week. A Home Visitor will bring it and will show you both how to use it, especially you, so you can use it with Carol on your own. The books and toys will be yours to keep. We think if parents use them with their children every day, it will help get them ready for school when they start later on."

Ms. Willard thought of her son, Vincent. At age eight, he had just entered a special class for slow learners.

"Yeah. Well, what will it cost?"

"Not a thing. If she's between sixteen and thirty months old, we are able to offer you The Parent–Child Home Program without your spending a penny. Can you tell me her birthday?"

Incredulous, skeptical, Ms. Willard looked at the stranger. But what harm could it do? Maybe it might help Carol keep on being as smart as she was now, not end up in a special class like Vincent. "I guess it's OK. She was two years old last month—June. But what would I have to do?"

"Just be there, together with Carol, every time the Home Visitor comes, twice a week—and watch what she does—and try to do the same things with Carol, a little every day. Most parents think it's fun—and the kids sure do. Even the older ones sometimes play with the toys and books."

Ms. Willard made up her mind, faster than she usually did. "All right; I'll do it!"

"Great! You can always just stop if you change your mind any time after the Program begins. Now I need to ask you a few questions so we can help you better—but you just answer the ones you want to. May I sit down?"

Still hesitant, Ms. Willard showed Myrtle Crawford to the sofa in the living room and sat down herself on the chair crowded against it. As it turned out, she tried to answer all the questions: the names and school grades of Carol's older brother and two sisters; her own age (thirty-one years) and last school grade (eleventh); a little about her health; whether Carol's father lived at home at all (he didn't, and in fact Ms. Willard didn't know exactly where he was living); about the grandparents on both sides (she couldn't tell anything about Carol's grandparents on her father's side). There were no questions about things Ms. Willard preferred to keep to herself, such as why she had come up from South Carolina four years ago, whether she had been legally married to Carol's father, and where he was now.

Myrtle (she said to call her that although she called Ms. Willard Ms. Willard) told her when she would be back with Ms. Willard's Home Visitor, to introduce them. The Home Visitor and Ms. Willard would set up a toy chest, first thing. Then the Program would begin.

When Myrtle asked if she had any questions, Ms. Willard couldn't put anything into words, but she had plenty. Mainly, would Myrtle and the Program really do what they said? Would there really be toys and books for Carol? Would they really leave it to her how much she did in the visits, as Myrtle had implied? Or would they nag or talk down to her like teachers in school? What was the catch?

Ms. Carter and Jo-Jo

It was a hot July morning. Ms. Carter let cool water run over her hands as she washed dishes at the kitchen sink. She was a small, trim-figured, brown-skinned woman with a mobile face. She looked as if she could be Jo-Jo's sister rather than his mother. Jo-Jo had had his breakfast and was experimentally opening a low cupboard in the kitchen. "Jo-Jo, stop!" she ordered, automatically stern. "Go watch TV!" She plunked him in front of the television set, which was already on, and loud. A children's cartoon animated the Saturday morning. Her six-year-old daughter, Dee-Dee, had for once deserted TV. Ms. Carter had given Dee-Dee ready permission to go out. That left her with two-year-old Jo-Jo, but she didn't object too much. He minded pretty well. He learned fast from briskly slapped hands and reprimands. He was smart. He was beginning to talk a lot—too much—even had started asking questions as the older one had done. But he was already beginning to learn, as the six year old had, to mind his own business. She wanted him to grow up polite, like Dee-Dee, maybe do well in school, get a good job. Someday she hoped to get a good job herself and get off of welfare. But sometimes Ms. Carter felt so discouraged that she couldn't get herself to figure out how to do it.

She glanced out of the neatly curtained window of the bare little kitchen to see the mail carrier coming up the walk. That was one advantage of living in a ground floor apartment of the housing project. That way she could get to her doorless mailbox in the entry ahead of anyone else who might take a notion to investigate its contents. She scooped Jo-Jo up and quickly went out to the mailbox. Two advertising flyers (she noticed a couple of the orange ones on the floor where they had fallen—or been thrown—from other mailboxes) and an envelope.

She went back to her own door, fast, to shut it behind her before she put Jo-Jo down to look at her mail. The orange ad was about a prewinter sale of school clothes, sizes to ten. This she laid open on the table, bare now except for a pencil. The other flyer was a general admonition to "shop your mini-mall!" This she crumpled and threw into a paper bag standing ready near the sink.

The third item was a long white envelope addressed to "Ms. Nancy Carter." She studied this for a moment and then opened the envelope. It appeared to be a typed letter with a name new to her at the top: "Parent–Child Home Program."

"Dear Ms. Carter," it began. Before she could read further, Dee-Dee came running into the apartment from outdoors, loudly complaining about a neighbor's child.

"Sit down!" she ordered Dee-Dee, glaring the six year old into instant obedience. In the mutinous silence that followed, broken only by Jo-Jo's noisily sucking his thumb and the television's loud voices, she read on:

> We are happy to tell you that a new program for two year olds and their parents is starting in your neighborhood. It will be free and will be conducted in your own home. Ms. Bailey, Dorothy's school social worker, thought you might like to join. We will visit you in a few days to find out if you do. Or, if you wish, you are welcome to call me at 611-5017. Then we can make an appointment at your convenience.
> Sincerely yours,
> Myrtle Crawford, Program Coordinator

Ms. Carter looked reflectively at Jo-Jo, ignoring Dee-Dee's squirming and her rebellious face. Then she said sternly, "You. Watch Jo-Jo. I'll settle you later. And don't either of you move while I go across the hall to Ms. Smith's."

The two subdued children heard her knocking at the Smith door and a moment later asking, "Can I use your phone? It's a local call."

A Few Days Later

The woman knocked on her door precisely at two o'clock, at exactly the time and on the day Ms. Carter had arranged by telephone with The Parent–Child Home Program.

"Hello! Ms. Carter? I'm Myrtle Crawford, the Coordinator of The Parent–Child Home Program. We talked together on the phone about your joining our program. I'd like to tell you more about it so you can decide."

Ms. Carter's face was solemn as she gestured Myrtle Crawford into the living room to sit down. She sat herself on the edge of a worn chair. Jo-Jo wandered in and she lifted him on to her lap without looking at him or at the curious face of the older sister hanging back in the bedroom doorway.

The Program Coordinator launched into her Program description as she had with Ms. Willard.

"You mean I get to keep the toys and books? And none of it costs any-thing? How come?" asked Ms. Carter.

"I know it sounds sort of unusual, but we're lucky enough to be funded by the government and some private foundations especially to give this Pro-gram to you and other mothers in the neighborhood, along with their two-year-olds. That's why Ms. Bailey was glad to give us your name, to give you a chance at the Program, if your little one is the right age. When is Jo-Jo's birthday?"

"His name is really Harry; we just call him Jo-Jo. He was born June ninth, two years old last month. Would that make him OK, Ms. Crawford?"

"Just right. By the way, most people call me Myrtle. Would you like to participate in The Parent–Child Home Program?"

"Sure would. When do we begin, Myrtle?"

It wasn't so hard to say the first name as she had feared, nor to answer Myrtle's questions. She told Myrtle that Jo-Jo had only one sister, Dorothy, who at age six was going into first grade and was nicknamed "Dee-Dee." She herself was twenty-four years old and had graduated from high school. Like Ms. Willard, her own health was good, she was a full-time housewife, and she and the children were supported by welfare. Ms. Carter could tell a bit about Jo-Jo's father, who lived away from them: He was her age, had been born in Georgia (she had been born in New York City), was a high school graduate, and was a park attendant. She said that both of her parents had had "some college" and that her mother was a nurse but that her father's occupation was unknown. The father's parents were high school graduates, she thought. His mother was a domestic worker, but his father's occupation was unknown. Ms. Carter noted with relief that the questions were few and innocuous. She could see for herself that the answers would probably help them to understand Jo-Jo better.

Ms. Carter drew a deep breath after the door closed behind Myrtle Crawford.

"OK, Dee-Dee, you can come in now. Jo-Jo and I are going to school at home. Right, Jo-Jo? I don't want you bothering the teacher when she comes, hear?"

Children's Evaluations before the Program: September

Ms. Willard and Ms. Carter enrolled in The Parent–Child Home Program in July, although the program was not to start until October, to allow time for careful preprogram evaluations of their children. The Program's major aim for these toddlers was to give them a good chance for future school success through encouraging their concept-building verbal interaction around play with their mothers, based on the ideas of a series of cognitive theorists. Because their school entrance was far in the future, Carol Willard and Jo-Jo Carter were given cognitive tests whose scores usually predict school performance (intelligence quotient, or IQ, tests). In effect, these tests were measurements of their future ability to learn school subjects when they eventually would be exposed to them in elementary school. They played test games at the Program's office, sitting on their mothers' laps, with blocks, with small pegs that fit in to round holes, with a tiny painted cat that could be hidden under a little cup.

Carol and Jo-Jo seemed to enjoy the test-games. Their preprogram scores on the Cattell Infant Intelligence Scale were similar, both on a low-average level. Carol's Cattell score was 93, and Jo-Jo's was 91. These scores predicted moderate school difficulties in later years. Most classroom activities in their suburban town were geared to the abilities of children whose cognitive skills met or exceeded national cognitive norms of 100. Moreover, they risked the gradual downward slope in their IQs which often occurs in low-income children. If the theories behind the Program were to be borne out, their cognitive test scores not only should improve by the end of their two years in The Parent–Child Home Program, but also should be high enough to make it likely that Carol and Jo-Jo would do as well in school as students from less disadvantaged backgrounds.

A related Program aim was to enhance the parents' verbal competence (and perhaps self-respect) by making them the principal agents of their children's good progress.

First Year of Parent–Child Home Program: October to June

Ms. Willard and Carol: Year One

First Half of Year One

When Myrtle Crawford first brought Ms. Willard's Home Visitor, Ann, to meet her early in October, Ms. Willard couldn't make up her mind whether she liked Ann. She seemed a little young and didn't use much better grammar than Ms. Willard did herself. Ms. Willard found it awkward, but sort of fun, to help Ann build a toy chest from a big flat package that Myrtle and Ann had brought along. The toy chest stayed right there in the living room when it was finished.

Ann got Carol interested from the start during the home sessions, which they arranged for a time when the older children were in school.

While Ms. Willard watched silently from the backless chair she had carried into the living room from her bedroom, the woman showed Carol in the first home session the colored blocks in a little cart she had brought. She told Carol the colors and then said, "Show mommy the blue block."

And Carol did!

Ms. Willard's face came alive when Carol showed her the blue block—then a red one, a yellow one. Then she retreated into voicelessly watching the Home Visitor play with Carol. In almost no time, Ann said to Carol, "I have to go now, Carol. Please help me put the blocks back into the cart."

Ms. Willard waited for Ann to put the cart and all the blocks back into her own big white shopping bag that read "Parent–Child Home Program" on it. But she didn't. She helped Carol put them into the empty toy chest that she had put together with Ms. Willard. They were keeping their promise! Good thing. The mother could tell that Carol really loved that toy. She would cry a lot if she ever had to give it up.

The following week Ann brought a book for Carol. This time she sat right down near one end of the sofa and patted the place beside her, in the middle of the sofa, for Carol to sit. Then she said, "Mommy, you come too—you sit on the other side of Carol—we'll read to her together."

Ms. Willard hesitated. She hadn't counted on that. She didn't read out loud so well. But she came and sat down on the other side of Carol, who snuggled against her. A sort of jealous feeling she had begun to have about the Home Visitor relaxed. She herself listened as Ann read a book called *Pat the Bunny*, pausing at each page to tell Carol to do something such as, "Now show Mommy how *you* pat the bunny!"

Afterward Ann, a former mother-participant in The Parent–Child Home Program herself, wrote some comments on that early home session for Myrtle Crawford to read:

> Mother, child, and I sat on the sofa together. Carol sat in the middle. Mother and I held the book, Carol turned pages. Carol smiled very friendly during the session. She also patted the bunny, played peek-a-boo, smelled flowers, pointed to parts of her face while Ms. Willard named each part for her. Ms. Willard also re-read the book to Carol. After the session was over, mother commented that the session was very interesting, and that she will be looking to see me next session.

On a standardized Program-rating sheet, Ann judged that Ms. Willard had been "verbally interactive" during 16 percent to 30 percent of the session.

Second Half of Year One

Year One of the two-year Program was eight months long, from October through May, with time off for school holidays.

Early in January Myrtle Crawford visited Ms. Willard to find out how she liked the Program thus far. Ms. Willard had no complaints and even said that she and Carol liked her Home Visitor. Myrtle wrote about the visit:

> Ms. Willard said she is quite satisfied with Ann, her Home Visitor, the time and the days of the sessions. She said that Carol asks her mother to read to her every day and then goes through the book by herself.
>
> Ms. Willard tends to be nonverbal in the sessions. When she does contribute, she often seems to be nervous. I re-emphasized the importance of her participation.

A few weeks later Ann described another home session:

> Carol, Ms. Willard, and I sat on the living room floor with the VISM. (VISM is the acronym for Verbal Interaction Stimulus Material, the book or toy, which in this case was a large toy barn and its many inhabitants: animals, people, and farm implements.) Ms. Willard encouraged Carol to name some of the animals, also to try to get the child to tell what the cow says and some of the things other animals do. Carol named most of the animals. She was counting along with her mother how many people and how many animals were on the farm. Carol played mostly with the tractor and trailer. Pretending to bring food for the animals. Mrs. Willard also got the child to name colors of the animals.

Ann judged Ms. Willard to have been verbally interactive during 30 percent to 45 percent of the session.

By the end of Year One, Ms. Willard had kept her appointments for forty-four of forty-six possible home sessions. Thus, she had participated in 96 percent of the sessions.

Myrtle Crawford came around to Ms. Willard's apartment to ask her some questions after the last home session of Year One.[1] She wanted to get Ms. Willard's reactions to The Parent–Child Home Program now that she and Carol were halfway through the two-year Program. She also wanted to find

---

1. In recent years, parents' end-of-year comments are generally collected by an anonymous questionnaire rather than in a face-to-face interview.

out what other intellectually stimulating experiences Carol had had. Finally, she needed to know whether Ms. Willard intended to complete the Program by enrolling in Year Two of The Parent–Child Home Program in the fall.

Ms. Willard was now used to the Program people's asking her questions and noting her answers carefully on printed pages. After each session, her Home Visitor had noted down her answers to a few questions about the week's events. Now Myrtle sometimes just circled a number and sometimes wrote down exactly what Ms. Willard said. It made her feel good that Myrtle Crawford took everything she said seriously enough to write it down, one way or another. In fact, that was how Ms. Willard had begun to feel in the home sessions: taken seriously by the Home Visitor and by Carol. Most of all by Carol.

Myrtle checked off Ms. Willard's answers to multiple questions: that Carol spent most of her time playing with her mother or by herself or with neighborhood children or with her brother and sisters. Sometimes she watched TV, and sometimes she just followed her mother around. Sometimes she went shopping or to the beach with her mother, and sometimes other children would take her to a playground or to visit people nearby. She never went on family outings nor to a library nor to church. Ms. Willard (and no one else) read to Carol several times a week (aside from home sessions), played with her for about a half hour a day, and let her watch TV cartoons, her favorite programs. No other adults did these things with Carol. Carol was in no other preschool program aside from The Parent–Child Home Program, and Ms. Willard had no regular activities outside of the home. She thought the Program was "very good," adding that she enjoyed the books and games. She was satisfied with the amount of her participation in the home sessions. In spite of the actually rather low amount of her verbal interchange with Carol, she was able to put into words, with fair accuracy, the Program's goals: to get her and Carol talking with each other so that Carol would be more ready to learn in school later on. She felt that she had also benefited from the Program, commenting spontaneously, "We got closer—now I realize how to help her learn." Ms. Willard hoped that Carol would become a nurse when she grew up and that she would go in school as "high as she can." She had no suggestions for the Program and thought it was all fine exactly as it was.

To Myrtle's question about whether she would participate in The Parent–Child Home Program for Year Two in October, Ms. Willard said "yes," but hesitantly. It was June now. Who could tell what would happen by October? Even August seemed far away. Planning from week to week within the Program was okay. A month was almost too much. Who could tell about October? Myrtle said she'd be back at the end of the summer. Ms. Willard could make her final decision then.

Ms. Carter and Jo-Jo: Year One

First Half of Year One

Ms. Carter made sure that her Program home sessions were arranged for the times when Dee-Dee, her six year old, was in school. She gave Jane, the Home Visitor, a warm welcome when she was brought by Myrtle for an introduction in October. Along with the introduction came an unassembled toy chest that Ms. Carter and Jane put together, the two of them, the very first time they met. With neither of them skilled with a screwdriver, Ms. Carter felt they knew each other pretty well by the time the toy chest stood finished. It seemed to stand for their promise of gifts of toys and books since she had already been assured that she would keep the toy chest to be filled by Program toys and books.

The small living room was neat, and Jo-Jo was in a little blue suit recently handed down from the child of a friend when Jane knocked at the door the following week.

Ms. Carter sat on the floor with Jo-Jo and watched carefully, making a couple of enthusiastic exclamations when Jane pointed out the shapes and colors of the blocks from a little cart to Jo-Jo. When Jo-Jo could show his mother the things about the blocks named by the Home Visitor, Ms. Carter smiled in delight and imitated Jane's praise of Jo-Jo for following the directions correctly. She was only a little surprised when the toy ended up in Jo-Jo's new toy chest. They were keeping their promise!

She had picked up other cues from the Home Visitor. By the second home session, she began to initiate praise as she read most of Jo-Jo's new book and talked with him as they sat together on the sofa.

Jane wrote in her home session record some comments on another early session that focused around *Pat the Bunny*:

> Today was a very verbal visit with Jo-Jo. He was right at the door, holding his book, when I arrived. Ms. Carter told me that Jo-Jo enjoyed showing his sister his book. We all sat down and began to look through the book. Jo-Jo's interest centered on the mirror, the peek-a-boo cloth (which needed to be re-glued) and the flowers. Jo-Jo insisted that these didn't smell anymore.
>
> After five minutes of looking at the pictures, Jo-Jo asked if he could bring out some of his own books. Ms. Carter said he could and I did not discourage him. They started with his dictionary. While looking through it and identifying the pictures, Jo-Jo became engrossed in finding pictures of the water and objects under the water. He found a picture of a sunken boat, Donald Duck, scuba diving, fish swimming. He really was quite excited and

talked to his mother throughout the session about what he wanted and what he was looking for as they went through the books together.

Jane (a college graduate volunteer with no prior experience as a mother in the Program) judged that Mrs. Carter's verbal interaction activity with Jo-Jo during this home session had occurred during 90 percent to 100 percent of the session.

Second Half of Year One

When Myrtle Crawford came back in January, she asked Ms. Carter how she felt about The Parent–Child Home Program, now that she and Jo-Jo were almost halfway through Year One. Ms. Carter was enthusiastic. Myrtle wrote:

> The family was resting, as mother had been running back and forth to the hospital, due to her mother's illness. Talked with Ms. Carter briefly while the children slept.
> Program and Home Visitor are working out fine.
> Mother enthusiastic, very involved with her children and indicated that she tries to expose them to as many learning and social experiences as possible. She continues to pursue higher educational aspirations for herself.
> Re: the Program, Ms. Carter wondered if the change in her daughter's school hours would affect Home Sessions. She thought we would have to ask to have Dee-Dee excluded from Home Sessions, now that she would be at home when they took place. I assured her Dee-Dee's inclusion was all right with us if it's all right with her, but she could work it out with Jane.
> Ms. Carter had no criticisms and thought well of Jane.

Some weeks later Jane wrote about a home session focused around the toy barn and its contents:

> Such enthusiasm! Jo-Jo loved the farm—every item. Ms. Carter loved it too. She and Jo-Jo set up the farm immediately. The cow and horse bent their heads up and down while they drank from the trough. The dog moved his head back and forth. They all went up to the loft and jumped down. Just about every activity was labeled by Ms. Carter.
> Ms. Carter also encouraged Jo-Jo in imaginary play. They made up a story about the farmer's family going to town with the cart to buy supplies and food for the animals. We all had fun.

Jane rated Mrs. Carter as having been verbally interactive with Jo-Jo during 91 percent to 100 percent of this session.

Jo-Jo Carter's last home session of Year One with his mother and their Home Visitor occurred on June 2. It was Home Session 45. Of a possible forty-six sessions planned for Year One, only one had been cancelled by Ms. Carter. Ms. Carter had thus honored 98 percent of her home session appointments in Year One of The Parent–Child Home Program.

Jane reflected in her home session record notes on Session 45 with Ms. Carter and Jo-Jo:

> Jo-Jo knew where Charlie was in all the pictures. In fact, he "read" the story to Ms. Carter during the session. Ms. Carter did her usual good job with the book. She is really a highly motivated mother, and she knows how to accomplish her goals. In fact, I am sure she worked closely with both her children before she became involved in the Program. Both of them are well prepared for their school experience.

And, as in most of the previous home session records for Year One, Jane indicated that Ms. Carter's verbal interaction with Jo-Jo was evident in no less than 91 percent of Home Session 45.

Ms. Carter responded almost fervently to Myrtle Crawford's interview questions when the latter visited at the end of Year One. Ms. Crawford asked her the same questions that she had put to Ms. Willard. Ms. Carter's responses were, however, somewhat different from Ms. Willard's. Jo-Jo played with others and watched TV, just as Carol had done. But, unlike Carol, "He daydreams, as if studying or communicating with nature for long periods of time," said his mother.

Ms. Carter took Jo-Jo most weeks to all the places named by Myrtle: stores, playground, family outings, visits to neighbors, churches, and to a library. In addition, Jo-Jo was taken by "another adult" to visit a local college and had played in the college gym. She read to Jo-Jo four or five times a week, and "someone else" read to him about once a week. She played with him about forty-five minutes a day; other adults played with him fifteen to twenty minutes a day.

Ms. Carter watched *Sesame Street* and *The Electric Company* on TV with Jo-Jo almost daily. Still, Jo-Jo's favorite TV program was *Mighty Mouse Cartoon*.

Jo-Jo was in no other preschool program aside from The Parent–Child Home Program. Ms. Carter, however, had been in a part-time school program for herself for a few months, leaving the children's care to their paternal grandmother.

Ms. Carter thought the Program was "very good" and, as did Ms. Willard, showed clear understanding of the Program's goals for children. She felt that she was given enough chance to participate in home sessions and said that what she herself had gotten out of the Program was: "I had lots of fun and learned how to communicate with my son better." She could suggest nothing to improve the Program.

She hoped that Jo-Jo would graduate from college and become a doctor.

There was apparently no hesitation in Ms. Carter's mind about enrolling for Year Two of The Parent–Child Home Program, starting again in October. However, a moment after saying so, she looked worried. She explained that she wanted to start looking earnestly for a job to get off of welfare or to start college. But what would that do to her participation in the Program? Ms. Crawford assured her that the Program would somehow adapt to her work or school hours. Her new Home Visitor would come after or before work, even perhaps on a weekend. They could talk about it again at the end of the summer when Ms. Crawford would come again to arrange Year Two of the Program for Ms. Carter and Jo-Jo.

Ms. Carter's face looked for a moment as if she were going to weep. Then she smiled, radiantly. "It's real important," she said. "Jo-Jo's learning, and I am too. He really knows what I teach him."

Myrtle Crawford recalled the written comment of a mother on an anonymous written evaluation of the Program: "What I have taught my two year old, he remembers very well."

This was, in fact, one of the major ideas behind The Parent–Child Home Program in promoting concept-building verbal interaction within the parent–child dyad.

Second Year of Parent–Child Home Program: October to June

Ms. Willard and Carol: Year Two

When September came, Ms. Willard could look ahead to October. She told Ms. Crawford, who visited her in September, that she had definitely decided to continue in the Parent–Child Home Program for Year Two. Myrtle noted some changes in Ms. Willard and in the arrangements of the apartment. The previously backless chair had acquired a back, or perhaps it had been replaced by a different chair. There was less debris on the floor and none on the kitchen table, which was visible from the living room. Ms. Willard was now wearing a dress rather than her usual bathrobe.

Later in the fall Ms. Willard's new Home Visitor, Nancy, wrote about Session 5 of Year Two:

When Ms. Willard opened the door, she said there was no heat and that she didn't think we should have the session. I said I didn't mind leaving my coat on. Ms. Willard started looking for the book. She couldn't find it. I said we could use another book [given previously]. They brought out *One, Two, Three for Fun*.

We sat on the couch. I talked about a couple of the pages and read the words. Carol didn't give any response to questions. I asked Ms. Willard to do the see-saw pages. She read the words and then pointed to the see-saw and asked Carol what it was—no response. Ms. Willard reminded Carol that she used the see-saw in the nearby playground.

I suggested we get up and play Ring Around the Rosy to warm up. Carol got up reluctantly and the three of us went around twice. Carol did not sing with us.

Nancy (who was, unlike her predecessor, Ann, a college graduate volunteer) judged that Ms. Willard's verbal interaction was present in 30 percent to 45 percent of Home Session 5, in spite of the probably discouraging effect of Carol's almost unyielding passivity.

Perceptibly more than in Year One, Ms. Willard not only followed the lead of the Home Visitor but sometimes initiated Program techniques she had observed or had read about in the guide sheets (one-page curriculum) that accompanied each new book or toy. After Session 9, Nancy wrote:

The Willards have their new oil burner that she had demanded, but it's working sporadically and needs to be checked.

Carol and her mother said they liked the book *Wonder of Hands*. We looked at the cover picture, and I put Carol's hand on top of mine to see the difference in size. Carol said more words than usual today. She was interested in the picture of the man changing the tire. She said "tire." Ms. Willard hasn't made a pie crust, Carol hasn't seen a rolling pin, but she said "pie crust." She hasn't been to the beach but has been in a pool for swimming and had played in sand at a park. Carol said "rabbit" and we talked about *Pat the Bunny*. She said "knee" when we looked at the hurt knee picture. Carol has used play dough. She said "sewing" and "guitar." Ms. Willard reminded Carol of someone they know who plays the guitar.

Ms. Willard says she can make string figures but doesn't have any string in the house. Carol has played dress-up and said "hat." She said "dog" and "cat." I reminded her of the cat in the barrel she had last week. She did a good imitation of the little girl laughing and clapping. I made a bird shadow. Carol counted the children playing Ring-around-the-Rosy. Carol said the girl was "going to bed." We pretended we were playing the piano. Carol said the mouse was a "rat." When her mother asked her which picture she liked best, she pointed to the girl trying on the hat.

Carol was eager to see the Three Bears Game. I said the plastic bag was for the pieces after they were pushed out. Carol immediately pushed out the bears, etc., put them all in the bag. She put the board, the bear book, and the bag of pieces back in the box, all ready to take to her nap after I left.

Ms. Willard's verbal interaction was judged to be present in 46 percent to 60 percent of that session, possibly spurred on by Carol's responsiveness. Thus Ms. Willard was active in more than half of Session 9 and in most other sessions in Year Two. This was considerably higher than the usual amount of her session activity during Year One; in fact, she doubled the amount of her Year One interaction with Carol in home sessions.

As she had done at the end of Year One, Myrtle Crawford came around at the end of Year Two to ask Ms. Willard some questions, pretty much the same ones she had asked the year before. Ms. Willard's answers were not much different either, except that Carol now watched TV less often. However, Carol's mother was more emphatic and explicit in her response as to what she herself had derived from the Program: "Yes—I did get something, a lot. I learned to sit down and give some attention to her, like reading to her and listening to her."

Ms. Carter and Jo-Jo: Year Two

By the end of August, after she had completed Year One, Ms. Carter had not yet found a job or decided about taking college courses. When Myrtle came to see her about continuing for another year in the Program, Ms. Carter expressed surprise and pleasure upon hearing that the Program staff thought that she was ready to dispense with a Home Visitor in Year Two (a rare Program practice used with parents who had shown unusual competence in Year One).[2] She was now competent enough in Program techniques to conduct home sessions with her own child, without more help than the toys and books and their guide sheets. In fact, she had practically done so during most of the Year One home sessions, and the Home Visitor had faded more and more into the background. Therefore, the Year Two books and toys would be dropped off to her each week, along with

---

2. This technique of omitting home sessions during the second year for selected families is no longer used by The Parent–Child Home Program.

their guide sheets, and she would not have to have a Home Visitor, unless she wanted one.

Ms. Carter was glad to accept. The new Year Two arrangement would allow Jo-Jo to have the Program materials, and she would have the guide sheets to remind her of how to use them with Jo-Jo. That would also make it easier for her to find work or begin college (if she could find the means for it). Buoyed up, it seemed, by the staff's confidence in her, and by her own sense of accomplishment, Ms. Carter was able to find a part-time job doing clerical work. Jo-Jo's grandmother filled in with childcare.

The Program's contact with Ms. Carter during most of Year Two was through the delivery of the Program books and toys, along with their guide sheets. A Home Visitor brought the toys, books, and guide sheets to her on the usual weekly Program schedule. Ms. Carter signed for receiving them; they exchanged pleasantries and then said good-bye.

Ms. Crawford visited Ms. Carter after Year Two ended to conduct a final interview. Like Ms. Willard, Ms. Carter responded to the questions much as she had done in the previous year, except for her answer that Jo-Jo watched less TV. She liked the drop-off Program and said, "I got a lot of pleasure from Jo-Jo's enjoyment of the books and toys." From her replies, she seemed to have continued her frequent interaction with Jo-Jo outside the home sessions.

It was evident that she derived at least equal pleasure from another piece of news she had been saving to tell Myrtle. She had just won a need-based scholarship to nearby Molloy College and was about to enroll full time.

Myrtle Crawford couldn't contain her pleasure either. She didn't know just how much Ms. Carter's decision to try for the scholarship and to start college had to do with her Program participation. Mentally, however, she chalked up what she felt to be another score point for The Parent–Child Home Program.

Evaluations after the End of The Parent–Child Home Program

Ms. Willard, with Carol, and Ms. Carter, with Jo-Jo, returned to the Program office four more times for evaluations after the Program was over. This was so that the Verbal Interaction Project, Inc. (a name later changed to The Parent–Child Home Program, Inc.)—the nonprofit research group whose director, Phyllis Levenstein, had founded, directed, developed, and conducted the model Mother–Child Home Program (the original name of The Parent–Child Home Program)—could measure the extent to which the Program had accomplished its goals.

The children's first evaluation had been in the August before the Program began, when they were both two years old. Jo-Jo and Carol were given the same cognitive evaluation, although at a level containing more challenging tasks, immediately after the completion of the Program, when they were almost four years of age. This time each sat beside the mother instead of sitting in her lap. For this second evaluation, both mothers had agreed to be videotaped in ten minutes of play with their children. (Details of the videotaping and its results are explained in Chapter 5 and in the Appendix.)

Before entering The Parent–Child Home Program, Jo-Jo's IQ score was 91, and Carol's was 93, far enough below the national norm of 100 to predict future educational problems. However, after their two Program years, at age four, Jo-Jo's score was 105, and Carol's was 109, far enough above the norm to predict normal school achievement.

The Parent–Child Home Program had apparently had built a foundation for these two children through two years of carefully fostered, conceptually rich verbal interaction with their mothers for their cognitive development and future school success.

2.

Poverty in the
Twenty-First Century

Parental Love Fights Back

The Problem

The Parent–Child Home Program was devised as a way to help parents and their small children to use the tools of education and improved self-esteem to climb out of poverty. This is still the main goal of the Program, and it is just as essential in the United States of the twenty-first century as it was four decades ago.

Much has changed in this country since the time The Parent–Child Home Program was first conceived in 1963. At that time, poverty was highly visible and highly worrisome, and solving the poverty problem was widely viewed as a legislative and social priority. During the next two decades, the United States witnessed an explosive expansion of what the Swedish economist Gunnar Myrdal dubbed the "underclass," made up of chronically unemployed people such as Ms. Willard and Ms. Carter, lacking in marketable skills, who often became long-term recipients of welfare assistance (Myrdal, 1962). At the time the first edition of this book was published in 1988, the welfare rolls had expanded exponentially: The number of Americans receiving assistance from the chief welfare program, Aid to Families with Dependent Children (AFDC), had grown from 2 million in 1950 to 11 million in 1980, 6.6 percent of all American families (Murray, 1984). Although most of those receiving welfare assistance were doing so temporarily, tided over by welfare checks from the end of the breadwinner's unemployment benefits to the beginning of his or her next job, many families' place on the AFDC caseload seemed disturbingly permanent (Patterson, 1981).

Just a few years later came welfare reform, the Personal Responsibility and Work Reconciliation Act (PRWRA) that Bill Clinton signed into law in 1996. It can be tempting to believe that the face of American poverty has changed radically since the first edition of this book, between PRWRA; the War on Drugs; President George W. Bush's promises of investment in public education; the fall in urban crime; the Earned Income Tax Credit, which raises the net income of low-wage workers; and the growth of the African American middle class.

Unfortunately, all this has failed to transform the lives of the poor strikingly for the better. Considerable and highly politicized controversy surrounds the net effect of welfare reform. One key measure of its success, the poverty rate for single mothers, was, according to government statistics, fairly stable at about 45 percent from 1966 until 1994 but has fallen off since then, reaching 36 percent in 2004 (U.S. Census Bureau, 2004) and suggesting benefit from the PRWRA. On the other hand, it can be argued that the official poverty rate takes into consideration only cash income, not food stamps, Medicaid, or other benefits that are less available to working people who succeed in earning incomes just above the poverty line. This means these women's resources have increased less than the drop in the poverty rate might suggest (Loprest, 2001).

Judging from measures of resource adequacy rather than of income, it seems that true neediness may have fallen since welfare reform—a little. The Agriculture Department's Food Security Survey, for example, reports that 17 percent of single mothers said in 1985 they had to limit the amount of food they ate; the number tightening their belts had fallen by 2003, but only to 14 percent (Winship & Jencks, 2004). In 1999, 46 percent of former welfare recipients said that at times they didn't have the money to pay their rent or utility bills (Loprest, 2001). So in the welfare reform era as before, as pointed out by Lawrence N. Powell, professor of history at Tulane University, "Too many poor families now approach the end of the month with bare pantries" (Powell, 2004, p. 6).

Unemployment, drug use, and crime remain serious issues in the America of the third millennium, as detailed in the following sections of this chapter. And rates of high school graduation, the specific goal targeted by The Parent–Child Home Program, may actually be lower than they were at the time this book was first published: According to the 2004 rankings from the National Center for Education Statistics, 68.4 percent of public high school freshman had graduated within four years, as compared with 72.9 percent in 1990 (United Health Foundation, 2005).

Although poverty has largely disappeared from the front pages and the political agenda in the United States, it flourishes nonetheless. Most measures of socioeconomic disadvantage are similar now, some twenty years after the peak of welfare dependency, to what they were when The Parent–Child Home Program was born in the 1960s, and some—drug abuse, incarceration, single motherhood—are higher. The poverty rate among American families, which had been 10.0 percent in 1968, was 10.2 percent in 2004—and double that (22.8 percent) among African Americans (U.S. Census Bureau, 2004). Though the term *underclass* has rightly fallen out of favor as denigrating, the poor urban populations described by Myrdal and by Ken Auletta, the political scientist turned journalist who wrote *The Underclass* in 1982, are still with us, perhaps even more than they were in the 1960s and 1970s (Jargowsky & Sawhill, 2006). Television images of the aftermath of Hurricane Katrina put the spotlight briefly on them in 2005, before the often surprised eyes of the American people and of the world.

Social problems are not unique to poverty, as attested by the rates of youth incarceration and drug use among the middle class, not to speak of white-collar crime. But the intensity, prevalence, and intermingling of multiple serious problems permeate certain impoverished city neighborhoods more than anywhere else. In the tangle of those social problems, some are especially conspicuous:

Long-Term Unemployment

The lack of paid employment is the most obvious cause of poverty. According to *Risking the Future,* an important 1980s report on teenage pregnancy and motherhood (National Research Council, 1987), 16 percent of sixteen- to nineteen-year-old young white men and 41 percent of young black men were unemployed. These rates have not improved since. Although adolescents frequently say they are dropping out of school in order to work, the unemployment rate among teenaged high school dropouts (40 percent in October 2004) is actually twice as high as the rate among their age mates who finished high school without going on to college (U.S. Bureau of Labor Statistics, Division of Labor Force Statistics, 2005). What explains these high rates of unemployment among noncollege-bound men who have left high school and are supposedly ready to take jobs?

For one thing, many of the unskilled and semiskilled jobs that could once be counted upon to absorb young people lacking a high school diploma have been eliminated by technological advances. Though the bursting of the Internet bubble in 2000 gave graphic proof that an education does not guarantee permanent work, there are generally abundant job opportunities for corporate lawyers and other knowledge-intensive occupations—"little comfort to the unemployed high school dropout" (Herbers, 1986, p. 24). The current overall official unemployment rate of 6 percent is about the same now as it was in 1996 and is higher than it was in the 1960s when The Parent–Child Home Program was created. It is true that more single mothers are working now, but the number of single mothers who hold paid jobs rose only from 62 percent to 70 percent after welfare reform, hardly a quantum leap (Jencks, 2005).

Furthermore, the jobs available to undereducated Americans are increasingly unattractive. The double-digit unemployment of the 1970s and 1980s was overcome largely by the creation of vast numbers of dead-end, unskilled service jobs: flipping burgers at McDonald's for the minimum wage. For high school dropouts, the job options are not only poorly paid but often highly regimented, demeaning, and unstable while bringing long commutes, high frustration, and little or no prospect of advancement (Ehrenreich, 2001).

The blow to self-esteem represented by the long-term unemployment of formerly employed family heads cannot help but damage family relationships. Unemployed fathers sometimes compensate either by withdrawing psychologically or by abusing the women and children in their families. Unmarried young men who are not burdened by the responsibilities of family life and have never held a job are no less rudderless. Lacking the self-respect that might come from satisfying work, some use as a major source of personal pride the fathering of children they cannot support either financially or psychologically. The cost of this is often suffered by the women who bear their children and by the children themselves.

Criminal Alternatives to Jobs

The flip side of unemployment is the seductive pull of "the street," with its glittering peer-approved alternatives to legal jobs that are poorly paid, boring, and hard to find. Hustling is one such alternative: Hustlers find their way adroitly through the labyrinths of the street's underground economy selling drugs, stolen goods, and themselves. Conspicuous among them are the pimps and drug dealers who for decades have served as glamorous role models for certain subgroups of young male school dropouts.

Violent crime serves as another alternative to working at a job and commonly becomes a life career. Although appalling numbers of young criminals die at the hands of their rivals or are caught in the cross-fire, and despite high incarceration rates and the increasingly harsh sentencing of even the extremely young, teenagers are aware that they still have fairly good chances of getting away scot-free with lucrative violent crime. This is one more factor that makes ordinary employment less than interesting.

More and more young people, especially men, are entering the criminal justice system, even after the much-publicized decreases in violent urban crime during the 1990s. Ten years ago it could be said that on any given day, one of three black men in their twenties was in prison, on probation, or on parole (Mauer & Huling, 1995). This figure is unlikely to be lower today, since the total number of people under the supervision of the correctional system in the United States went up by an amazing 32 percent between 1995 and 2005 (Glaze & Bonczar, 2006).

Psychological studies have found criminals to have serious gaps in their cognitive and academic achievement, especially reading disability. Juvenile criminals commonly show two additional deficits: an inability to anticipate the possible future consequences of their acts (except for a blind confidence in their own ability to evade the law) and an indifference to the suffering of others that may, in some cases, be related to having spent their brief lives in severely dysfunctional families.

Drug Abuse

Drug use seems to be endemic to American (and not only American) society, although the specific patterns of drug use shift over time. When The Parent–Child Home Program was being developed, the greatest concern was from heroin, and when the first edition of this book was being written it was "crack" cocaine. Despite hopes raised by successes in antidrug campaigns during the 1980s, drug use has fallen very little since 1995, and it has spread from the urban ghetto into suburbs and small towns where it was unheard of some years back. According to the U.S. Department of Health and Human Services, nearly 35 million persons over twelve used an illicit drug in 2003, and another 17 million illicitly used prescription drugs. Of young adults aged eighteen to twenty-six, 7 percent had used cocaine that year, 29 percent marijuana, 2 percent methamphetamine, and 4 percent "ecstasy" (Substance Abuse and Mental Health Services Administration Office of Applied Studies, 2005). The insistence on an ever more punitive prohibitionistic approach to the War on Drugs has succeeded only in intensifying the alienation of young drug users from society and further increasing their chances of being turned into true criminals through drug-related entry into the prison system.

Dropping Out of School

Given the focus of The Parent–Child Home Program, it is worth repeating that nearly one in three public high school freshman will not have graduated four years later (United Health Foundation, 2005). In the low-income neighborhoods of large cities, the percentage is much higher; low-income teenagers appear to vanish from the school scene as soon as they are legally of age to do so, and sometimes even before. Dropout rates for African American and Latino adolescents have been reported to be as high as 50 percent (Greene, 2001).

The 2002 No Child Left Behind Act rewards schools in proportion to their pupils' graduation rates and their success on standardized tests. One unfortunate consequence is that accurate estimates of high school graduation rates have become harder to come by. School systems now fudge their statistics upward to avoid being penalized (Schemo, 2003; Swanson, 2004)—for example, by removing the names of truant youngsters from the registration records (Hartocollis, 2002). There is even suspicion that disadvantaged youngsters are being pushed out of high school, either by direct counseling or by being expelled for minor offenses and never readmitted, as administrators attentive to their schools' test pass rates try "to get rid of those who may tarnish the schools' statistics by failing to graduate on time" (Lewin & Medina, 2003, p. 1)

Many teenaged young women who drop out of school have a child within a year.

> Although some are undoubtedly pregnant at the time, it also seems likely that many young women who drop out become pregnant within several months after leaving school. . . . Early childbearers are more likely to have reduced educational attainment than later childbearers. . . . Do high school dropouts catch up? . . . . The answer is generally no. (National Research Council, 1987, p. 126)

A young man rarely drops out because of his girlfriend's pregnancy, but the underlying motivations may at bottom be shared by both male and female students: profound dissatisfaction with school, deepened by the humiliation and sense of failure engendered by their own poor academic achievement starting in the earliest school grades.

The implications of leaving school before graduation are dismal for any hope of young people climbing out of poverty. Dropouts are twice as likely to be unemployed as high school graduates are, and twice as likely to report no income at all; when they do work, they earn half the income (Greene, 2001; National Institute for Literacy, n.d.; U.S. Bureau of Labor Statistics, Division of Labor Force Statistics, 2005). As of 1997, 63 percent of the young children of high school dropouts were living in poverty, versus 29 percent for the children of high school graduates—and only 3 percent of children of college graduates (National Institute for Literacy).

The Feminization of Poverty

Close to half a million teenagers give birth every year in the United States, largely unmarried mothers from disadvantaged backgrounds—60 percent of teen mothers are poor at the time they give birth—and more than 100,000 are under eighteen years of age (Moss, 2004). Although somewhat lower than a few years back, our teen birth rate is still the highest in the developed world, twice as high as England's and four times as high as France's (Moss, 2004). And the percentage of children born to unmarried mothers has risen steadily from 7 percent when The Parent–Child Program began to 37 percent in 2005 (Hamilton, Martin, & Ventura, 2006). An ever-increasing percentage of first-born children are born to teenagers and are fathered by young men who either disappear or take only minimal responsibility for their own children.

In the United States, as in the rest of the world, poverty is increasingly female. Half the families living in poverty are headed by females, and two of every five poor individuals are unmarried women and their children (U.S. Census Bureau, 2004). Among single mothers, one in three has income below the poverty line.

Complex and controversial links connect the stresses of poverty, family structure, and the social problems of the American poor. Some, of course, see the very formation of single-parent families as a cause of family dysfunction, especially when the parent is very young. Daniel Patrick Moynihan, a champion of this point of view, commented in his 1986 book *Family and Nation* (p. 168): "A family is formed when a child is born. When an unwed teenager gives birth, a broken family is formed." Since the family is the basic social unit for society, bad news for the family is bad news for society.

In the years since the first edition of this book, the American household has evolved still further away from the traditional family. Cultural norms have shifted, and the importance or even the value of a two-parent family, no longer taken for granted, is a subject of considerable debate. But whatever the exact makeup of the unit that includes child and adult caretakers, it is still surely true that the family, "more than any other force . . . shapes the attitude, the hope, the ambitions, and the values of the child" (Moynihan, 1986, p. 32).

Data suggest that children raised by a single parent are more likely to drop out of high school, more likely to have a child before age 20, and more likely to be at loose ends in their early 20s, even above and beyond the considerable effect of low income (McLanahan & Sandefur, 1994). For disadvantaged young women who are struggling to maintain their children and themselves, some of them additionally hampered by depression and poor self-respect, increasing societal acceptance of single parenting does not keep life's problems from mounting up.

Young Single Mothers in the Age of Welfare Reform

The dilemmas of young single mothers have, unfortunately, survived welfare reform. Two consequences of teen pregnancy are that a teenager's failure to finish high school is likely to be permanent, and that she is likely to have additional children as an unmarried mother. Both of these will handicap her ability to work at a job and make her more prone to seek support from Temporary Assistance for Needy Families (TANF) or other forms of public assistance. Looking for a job means encountering and overcoming some difficult practical problems:

1. If the pregnancy occurs in early adolescence, it curtails the young mother's high school, or even junior high school, education. She often has to drop out not only before she acquires saleable skills but also before she even has a chance to learn some of the elementary entry-level skills needed for any job, such as reliability, punctuality, and respect for supervision and job standards.
2. Many single mothers have no extended family willing or able to look after their babies and toddlers. They hesitate to entrust their children to unlicensed strangers to enable them to work at jobs that can free the family from poverty, and decent, affordable day care is not easy to obtain. Although subsidized child care has expanded under welfare reform, facilities are not universally available, and their quality is often mediocre (Fuller, Kagan, Caspary, & Gauthier, 2002).
3. Some single mothers without job skills enter work-training programs mandated by welfare reform, especially when appropriate child care is made available—or when adolescent siblings can care for the young ones, at a cost for their own schooling and their own lives. Many who enter such training programs complete them and retain their learning. But when the training is over, private sector jobs are conspicuously absent or are so limited in terms of pay or conditions that the mothers find themselves unable to support themselves and their children.

Children at Risk

In contemporary America, for the first time in history, "a person is more likely to be poor if young rather than old" (Moynihan, 1986, p. 112). The odds of being poor are twice as high for preschool children (20 percent) as for the elderly (10 percent) or for nonelderly adults (11 percent) (U.S.

Census Bureau, 2004), putting the children's future achievement at risk (Duncan & Brooks-Gunn, 2000).

Furthermore, the poverty rate for children in female-headed families is four times that of children in other families (54 percent versus 12.5 percent) (U.S. Census Bureau, 2004). These children are often at additional risk physically, emotionally, and intellectually. As babies, they may be at risk for long-term health and developmental problems, especially if their mothers are in the youngest age groups, which have the highest rate of pregnancy complications. As they grow older, they may suffer from neglect, and have an increased risk of frank abuse. The intellectual stimulation necessary for the child's academic achievement may be severely limited, partly because of the young mother's educational limitations. Among all the family-structure factors with a negative impact on children's cognitive development, "mother's education has been shown to be most significant" (National Research Council, 1987, p. 135).

Children of poor teenage parents are at risk for having social behavior problems and problems of self-control (National Research Council, 1987). Many such parents, especially if they are young single mothers, can hardly cope with their own problems, and with welfare reform, it is even more difficult for them to be present to their children than before. These children must sometimes shift emotionally as well as physically for themselves, with dangers for the children and ultimately for society that can hardly be overstated since, as Moynihan (1986) says (p. 38):

> Family life not only educates in general but its quality ultimately determines the individual's capacity to love. The institution of the family is decisive in determining not only if a person has the capacity to love another individual but in a larger sense whether he is capable of loving his fellow men collectively. The whole of society rests on this foundation for stability, understanding and social peace.

Mental Health Problems

The attitudes and mental health of parents living in poverty, and especially of young single mothers, are inexorably challenged by reality-based problems growing out of their struggle to raise their children and make ends meet. This can lead to depression and hopelessness, which risk creating in turn a state of passivity that causes these parents, often hardly more than children themselves, to lack motivation for beneficial change. This listless state of just drifting along (Jayakody & Stauffer, 2000; Polansky, Borgman, & DeSaix, 1972) affects the quality of their parenting and, consequently, worsens their children's behavioral and cognitive outcomes (Jackson, Brooks-Gunn, Huang, & Glassman,

2000). Lack of self-confidence and self-esteem can in turn further weaken their motivation to change their lives, feeding a vicious cycle.

The Remedies

The barriers faced by impoverished children, intensified by the special difficulties of single-parent poor families, have long been recognized by researchers from various disciplines (e.g., Bee, et al., 1982; Bower, 1963; Burgess & Conger, 1978; Kohn, 1977; Sameroff, 1978; Sameroff & Seifer, 1982). When parents are driven to depression and low self-esteem by their lack of access to practical and emotional support for child rearing, their children's development may be particularly stunted intellectually and emotionally. In the terminology of Parent–Child Home Program theory, the intellectually and emotionally supportive parent–child network developed by these parents with their children is often too rudimentary to support the children in their school tasks. The resultant educational disadvantage of poor children in early grades becomes failure to finish high school, and winds up as the prospect of more or less permanent membership in the disadvantaged classes.

Welfare Reform

Of the remedies that have been proposed for ending this cycle of poverty and its accompanying tangle of pathology, the most draconian has surely been welfare reform. The 1996 Personal Responsibility and Work Reconciliation Act—toughened up still further by the administration of President George W. Bush—revolutionized the welfare system by abolishing the Aid to Families with Dependent Children (AFDC) program, replacing it by Temporary Assistance for Needy Families (TANF); delegating the design and administration of all aid to the states; instituting strict and near-universal work requirements; and setting a five-year lifetime time limit on receiving public assistance. Its impact has yet to be fully grasped, especially since in the best available studies, many clients had yet to run up against the five-year cutoff limit.

We frequently hear how the welfare rolls were cut in half between 1995 and 2001 (they have remained steady since then (O'Neill, 2006)) but hear less often that they have declined only to the levels that seemed so high in the mid-1960s when The Parent–Child Home Program was conceived. The number of American families receiving AFDC or TANF was 3 million to 4 million through the 1980s, 5 million at its peak in 1992, and just under 2 million in 2005, 0.7 percent of all Americans, higher than the 0.5 percent in 1968. In 2001, 26 percent of non-Hispanic blacks received some amount of cash assistance, food stamps, or Supplemental Security Income (Substance Abuse and Mental Health Services Administration Office of Applied Studies, 2004).

It is still not entirely clear what has happened to the families that once counted on welfare to help make ends meet. About two out of three single mothers on welfare did manage to enter the workforce in the first years after AFDC was abolished (Loprest, 2001), but usually in minimum-wage jobs that yielded little or no improvement in family economic resources considering that they frequently meant the concomitant loss of benefits such as Medicaid and food stamps. Some other former welfare recipients have fallen between the cracks into a resourceless abyss. Many are unable to work because of caretaking responsibilities or to their own disability (one-third of welfare leavers are not working because of health reasons (Loprest & Wissosker, 2001) but are no longer considered eligible for TANF. Others become discouraged trying to negotiate the increasingly difficult process of obtaining what benefits are still due them. The result is that in 2005, 50 percent more single mothers than in 1995 told the Census Bureau that neither they nor anyone else in their household had worked or received welfare during the previous year (Jencks, 2005). And the five-year cutoff for TANF looms for many more.

The net impact on children of what Clinton hoped would be "the end of welfare as we know it" is still a matter of debate. Among adolescents, the Next Generation Study has suggested the PRWRA has had deleterious effects on truancy, school performance, and drug use, especially when there are younger siblings in the house who need looking after (Gennetian et al., 2002). Toddlers lose hours a day with their parents when their mothers go from welfare to work (Chase-Lansdale, Moffitt, Johnman et al., 2003), and if the mother's work is full time, her toddlers seem to perform less well on cognitive tests (Bernal, 2005). For school-aged children, some studies have found cognitive and behavioral development to suffer when mothers leave welfare to move into the workforce (Zaslow et al., 2002), whereas others have found neither great harm nor great benefit (Chase-Lansdale et al., 2003).

The bottom line seems to be that welfare reform has been neither the disaster that some had feared nor the godsend others had hoped. In practice, as Jason DeParle points out in *American Dream: Three Women, Ten Kids, and a Nation's Drive to End Welfare* (DeParle, 2004), it didn't change most people's lives much at all. He said of one of the women whose life he traced in his book:

On welfare, Angie was a low-income single mother, raising her children in a dangerous neighborhood in a household roiled by chaos.

She couldn't pay the bills. She drank lots of beer. And her kids needed a father. Off welfare, she was a low-income single mother, raising her children in a dangerous neighborhood in a household roiled by chaos. She couldn't pay the bills. She drank lots of beer. And her kids needed a father. (DeParle, 2004, p. 321)

Preschool Education

Welfare reform is, fortunately, not the only arrow in our quiver. The mediocre school achievement of low-income children, which hobbles their ability to escape from poverty, has concerned educators and other behavioral specialists for many years. In the 1960s, the federal government, as part of its War on Poverty, began large-scale financial support for programs in every school system that enrolled large numbers of poor children. These Title I programs usually focused on remedial efforts such as eight-year-old Vincent Willard's special class for slow learners.

Preschool educational television programs such as *Sesame Street* and *Around the Bend* were also launched in the 1960s, with the idea of preventing school problems before they started. With the same preventive aim, the federally funded Project Head Start took its tentative first steps under the loving tutelage of Edward Zigler and others, and child development researchers had already begun to conduct longitudinal research on carefully designed pre-preschool programs for disadvantaged preschoolers. Forty years later, interventions during early childhood with the specific aim of reducing the achievement gap between poor and middle-income pupils have become a significant part of the landscape of strategies for addressing poverty in the United States: notably, The Nurse–Family Partnership during infancy; Parents as Teachers, Even Start, Early Head Start, Home Instruction for Parents of Preschool Youngsters, and The Parent–Child Home Program for toddlers; and preschool and Head Start when the child nears school age.

Some of the earliest among the researchers of early childhood education—Kuno Beller, Martin and Cynthia Deutsch, Ira Gordon with Emile Jester, Merle Karnes, Louise Miller, Francis Palmer, David Weikart, Edward Zigler, and the first author of this book—pooled their short-term and long-range results in the Consortium for Longitudinal Studies and published their individual research in the book *As the Twig Is Bent* (Consortium for Longitudinal Studies, 1983). The combined findings were also published as a research monograph by Cornell University professors Irving Lazar and Richard Darlington (Lazar & Darlington, 1982). Many of the Consortium programs had already been described earlier in *The Preschool in Action*, edited by M. C. Day and R. K. Parker (Day & Parker, 1977).

Parental Love Fights Back

One Consortium program included in *The Preschool in Action* was The Parent–Child Home Program, known at the time as the Mother–Child Home Program (Levenstein, 1977). This program shared the goal of preventing educational disadvantage with others in the Consortium, but it broke entirely with the classroom model followed by most of them. The Consortium programs developed by Ira Gordon (Gordon, 1977) and by David Weikart (Perry Preschool) (Weikart, Bond, & McNeil, 1978) were also partially home-based, as were several nonconsortium programs of the time, including Earl Schaefer's (Schaefer, 1969), precursors of later entirely home-based programs such as Parents as Teachers and Home Instruction for Parents of Preschool Youngsters.

In addition to the innovation of being home-based, The Parent–Child Home Program broke new ground by enrolling particularly young children and by continuing for the particularly lengthy period of 20 months. The pre-preschool age of two years was chosen as critical for the development of language-based cognitive skills. It involved their mothers—for example, Ms. Willard and Ms. Carter—and later their fathers as playful teachers of their own children in their own homes, using books and toys as curriculum materials. The mainspring of the Program was an age-old motive force: parental love.

Although there is much joking and a good deal of sentimentality about parental love (Mother's Day comes close to being a religious holiday in the United States), it is universally the most powerful and lasting of all infatuations. Whenever a parent is the primary person taking care of a young child, exposed to the interactional feedback and intense emotion that this nurture generates, there is likely to be a close bonding of parent to child and child to parent.

Because of this bonding, parents are willing to act as nurses and as civilizing agents for their children. Parents' love for their young is the lure that leads little children to conform to whatever type of civilization prevails in their societies. The basic patterns by which people meet the demands of their particular cultures are laid down by parents, usually by mothers, in children's earliest years. As with all their child care, it is usually done for love alone. Seldom does any society pay a penny for the long work hours and exhausting labor that parents contribute in the course of bringing up their children.

This applies as much to children's preschool education in the home as to their cultural–emotional socialization. In America, as throughout the world, parents are usually baby's first teachers of intellectual skills. For several years, they are the child's most important one. They are as much responsible for getting the child ready for school learning as for preparing him or her for any other aspect of civilization.

Parents, of course, hardly ever think this out ahead of time. They just do what comes naturally in their interactions with their babies and toddlers. For most, doing what comes naturally turns out to be just the preparation their children need for classroom learning once they enter school. These parents take the time and exert the effort to encourage their young children's conversation and, if they have the resources, to provide them with attractive educational books and toys. They know from their own education and from their life experience, or are able to learn quickly (as Ms. Carter did), how to stimulate interests and ideas in even very little children. Using the term coined by The Parent–Child Home Program, such parents can be called *Strivers*. They are to be found among impoverished parents as well as in other groups.

To be a Striver, as we saw with Ms. Carter, neither a college education nor a middle-class income is a prerequisite. But in most cases, it takes a special effort for low-income, poorly educated parents to become Strivers. They are handicapped not only by their lack of money but by all the obstacles that poverty raises, including health and mental health challenges, chaotic lives, and inadequate resources. One of the most pervasive and insidious of such problems for low-income parents of limited education is the combination of low self-esteem and depression. The two join to deepen or cause other problems such as inertia and a lowered ability to care for themselves or for their children. Consequently, *most* middle-income, college educated parents are likely to be Strivers, and *many* disadvantaged parents like Ms. Willard are what the Program calls *Hesitaters*, prevented by the paralysis of poverty from finding the strength and the motivation to move toward taking charge of their lives.

Hesitaters could theoretically act as Strivers with regard to their children, but they are often too bogged down in their own problems and too depressed to heed their children's intellectual, emotional, and sometimes even physical needs. As a result, Hesitaters' children tend to have major school problems like those of Vincent, Carol Willard's older brother. These problems are often thought to be typical of all low-income children but in actuality are most characteristic of those whose parents are Hesitaters.

The children of Strivers, even though they may be from equally disadvantaged origins, are more likely to achieve good school performance and therefore have a better chance of eventually escaping from poverty. Further, their parents will reach out for any program that promises to help them to help their children. Point a Striver in the right direction and parental love will go to work. If a parent-education or a preschool or pre-preschool program of almost any kind is offered to Strivers, they will enroll—although this doesn't guarantee that they will stay enrolled if the program does not seem to be living up to its promise.

Impoverished Hesitaters are least likely to join parenting or early-education programs even though they are the parents, and theirs are the children, who most need them. Yet they love their small children as much as Strivers do. Because they do, it is possible to persuade Hesitaters to put their parental love to work on behalf of their pre-preschool children's intellectual development, provided the program they are offered has a number of basic features designed to appeal to all parents and especially to the most disadvantaged:

- It approaches parents as free, valuable individuals, respecting their dignity, independence, and right to privacy.
- It requires no minimum level of education from the parent.
- It is voluntary and explicitly nonintrusive yet perseveres in reaching out to parents without exerting pressure.
- It has built-in incentives, which may include no-cost, attractive program materials: books and toys.
- It is minimal, with no mandatory tasks or difficult concepts.
- It is nonembarrassing and sensitive to parents' needs.
- It respects and, wherever possible, incorporates features of families' cultural/ethnolinguistic differences from mainstream culture.
- It makes the parent the main member of the program team, whose other members, including professionals, take a back seat as early as possible within the program.
- It involves parents' easy participation without leaving their home.
- Its goals are limited.

Because The Parent–Child Home Program fulfilled these conditions, it was able to win the commitment of Ms. Willard, a Hesitater. It also captured the lasting interest of Ms. Carter, a Striver, so that she could be supplied with curriculum materials (books and toys) and with some child-rearing guidance to support her efforts at preparing her son for school. Both Strivers and Hesitaters could be served.

One important intuition of the Program was that its role in fostering the parent–child network would also be supportive of parents' development. The Parent–Child Home Program can serve as a vehicle for improving the mental health of the parent and indeed of the whole family through the parent's improved self-confidence. Subsequently, it can provide him or her with an entry-level job as a Home Visitor within the Program and thus enhance future employability for other jobs.

Mental health is a vague and ambiguous label used to mean a state of well-being, a feeling of relative harmony with the world and with oneself, that engenders attitudes and behaviors tending to produce a similar state in significant others who are likely to be close family members, in particular one's children. As we have seen, the mental health of very impoverished parents can be so impaired that child neglect becomes a consequence of their problems. Yet many studies have shown that beneath some parents' seeming indifference usually lies deep affection, especially in the years before the child starts to be drawn more to peers and to playing in the street than to a relatively unresponsive parent.

The Parent–Child Home Program taps into the reservoir of love inherent in the parent–child bond. Love serves both as a motivation for the parent to enroll and stay with the Program and as a powerful motivation for the child's learning to learn—and to take joy in learning. Since childrearing falls disproportionately on women, this strategy utilizes one of poverty's greatest weaknesses, its feminization, as a strength against its pathological effects in a kind of psychological ju-jitsu.

As a deliberately minimal method that was planned to strengthen the parent–child network with each passing year as a bulwark against school failure, The Parent–Child Home Program dares to hope that it might contribute to interrupting, for some, the cycle of poverty. It proposes to start small changes in the lives of severely disadvantaged parents and children at a time in the children's lives when slight improvements in family dysfunction can widen in a few years into changes significant for the child's academic progress.

At the same time, the Program hopes that fostering the frequent, happy interaction between parent and child in two of the child's most formative years will have the effect of fostering mental health in the child. It can aid him or her to develop into a happy, sociable human being, a bit readier to meet the challenges of school; to empathize with the feelings of others; and to resist the temptations of drugs, of dropping out, and of the criminal lifestyle.

Ultimately, it is hoped that parents' pride in their visible accomplishments with their children will raise their own self-esteem and ability to cope with the everyday world. The Parent–Child Home Program can provide a path from living room into classroom for the child and from living room into a new realm of self-competence and self-confidence for the parent. Although not a panacea for all social ills, the Program aims to give children and parents a boost onto the first rungs of the ladder leading upward toward escape from poverty.

3.

"Show, Not Tell"

The Parent–Child Home Program Method

T he Parent–Child Home Program was founded on the proposition that a low-income child's best preparation for school, like other children's, is a cognitively and emotionally supportive parent–child network that starts in pre-preschool years. This network's three main cables are the parent's verbal and nonverbal nurturing, the child's intellectual growth, and the child's social–emotional growth. They are connected by strands of reciprocally reinforcing behaviors leading from parent to child and from child to parent.

The Program first surmised, and later demonstrated, that such a network can develop from positive interaction, especially verbal interaction, with a beloved primary caregiver. The interaction that builds the parent–child network, Program founders theorized, will contribute to the parent's dignity and self-esteem as well as to the child's school readiness. The Program converted this theory into practical action by helping both child and parent to access educational and economic opportunities and move out of poverty.

A Thumbnail History of the Program

The Verbal Interaction Project began The Parent–Child Home Program, originally known as the Mother–Child Home Program, as pilot experimental research in 1965 (Levenstein & Sunley, 1968). The Verbal Interaction

Project, first attached to the Nassau County Family Service Association, a private social agency, later became an independent nonprofit corporation affiliated for a period with the State University of New York at Stony Brook and eventually changing its name to The Parent–Child Home Program, Inc., in 1998. Its mission was to develop a pre-preschool, emergent literacy, school-readiness program; to research the effects of the program; and then to teach others how to replicate the program if the research showed that it was effective. Aside from a few generous gifts from individuals, the initial research and training activities were funded by federal and private foundation grants awarded through competitive proposals. Grant awards to the Verbal Interaction Project between 1967 and 1982 totaled almost $3 million.

In 1969, the original Mother–Child Home Program on Long Island, New York, began to serve as a model for sites across the country. By 1984, training had been provided for eighty-four replication sites scattered among sixteen states, Bermuda, and Canada. Local funding became difficult to obtain during the 1980s, and by 1985 only eighteen communities were still operating replication sites. Since the later 1990s, however, the Program has expanded enormously, with 150 sites operating in 2007.

During more than forty years of continuous operation, the Program has continued to evolve progressively. A change from professional to mostly nonprofessional Home Visitors, an expansion from one to two years, and revision of the curriculum to minimize didacticism were based on results of research at the model program (Madden, Levenstein, & Levenstein, 1976; Madden, O'Hara, & Levenstein, 1984). Among the strategies used by replication sites to meet their local needs are providing appropriate books and toys to families speaking languages from Spanish to Vietnamese, providing evening and weekend home visits to working parents, organizing parents' groups, and extending the intervention through the summer school holidays.

Among the many thousands of families who have been served by the original program site and its replications, the vast majority has been low-income and all have had children at risk for educational disadvantage. They have come from many ethnic groups—African American, Latino, Russian, Southeast Asian, Haitian, Native Canadian Indian, Caucasian, and others—living in a variety of geographical settings: Appalachian Mountains, rural communities, Louisiana bayous, suburbs, inner cities, small towns. Yet within this rich mixture of families served by the Program, two main categories of parents emerged: the *Hesitaters* and the *Strivers*. Ms. Willard and Ms. Carter, the mothers in Chapter 1, were chosen to represent these two groups for this book.

The Parent–Child Home Program aims to bring to all of the Ms. Willards and Ms. Carters special curriculum materials and guidance in using the pre-

preschool hidden curriculum of parent–child interaction found commonly in middle-income homes. It offers to parents not only the quality books and educational toys they do not have, but also and, most importantly, some joyful ways of weaving the interaction around these objects into every aspect of their relationships with their children, of strengthening a parent–child network that is cognitively and emotionally supportive for both parent and child.

Four decades after the Verbal Interaction Project first pilot-tested a tentative version, the mission of The Parent–Child Home Program's National Center under executive director Sarah Walzer is dissemination. It assists school systems, social service agencies, community health centers, public libraries, and other organizations across the country and beyond to establish Program sites, assuring that they will be true replications in every aspect of the Program's four major ingredients: curriculum, curriculum materials (books and toys), Home Visitors, and supervision by site Coordinators, each of whom oversees staff serving up to fifty to sixty families.

Overview of The Parent–Child Home Program

The Program consists of a minimum of ninety-two home sessions, typically scheduled over just under two years, to the homes of children and their parents when the children are two years old (Year One, also called Program I) and three years old (Year Two or Program II). The visitors are called *Home Visitors* to emphasize their nonteaching, noncounseling role with parent and child. They are trained to promote a parent's *positive parenting* and to show the parent, during play sessions with the child in their own home, how to interact verbally with the child to enhance the child's conceptual and social–emotional development. The play-oriented interaction is centered around books and toys that are attractive to both parent and child and are gifts to the family. The parent is free to adopt the behaviors modeled by the Home Visitor, or not, as he or she wishes. There are no assignments or homework.

At most replication sites, the Program visits parallel the school year, starting in the fall and ending at the end of May or in early June, observing local school holidays, which easily achieves the minimum of twenty-three weeks required in each of the two Program years. The parent–child pair (called a *dyad* in The Parent-Child Home Program, to indicate that parent and child interact with each other as a mini–social system) is visited twice a week for half-hour home sessions. The Home Visitor brings a new book or toy to the first session of the week and models techniques for conversation, activities, and other interactions around it. The second home session is used to review the book or toy introduced at the first session, and may also include some *extension activities* around the curricular material of the week. The extension activities could include arts and crafts, songs or finger plays, or the incorporation of previous curricular materials.

In each of the two years twelve books and eleven toys, selected to meet particular developmental, language-building criteria (including the opinions of parents and Home Visitors, who have an opportunity to rate and comment on the materials annually), are presented to the parent to use with the child. One week a book is brought, the next week a toy, in the same order for every child in the Program.

The main focus of the Program is on the parent rather than the child. The Program has a very light touch designed to convey respect for the parent consistently as the most important and indispensable person in the child's life. The parent is therefore required to be present at every home session, with the goal that over time, it will be the parent who really runs the home session and not the Home Visitor.

The operation of each Parent–Child Home Program replication site is supported by an extensive technical manual, which includes all the administrative forms needed to implement the intervention, sample curriculum guides, and materials for training Home Visitors. The Parent-Child Home Program National Center also provides a Coordinator's training manual, a Home Visitor's training manual, and a guide to the Program's management information system. All these materials are provided as part of the two-year training and technical assistance package that all replications must purchase from the National Center. Aside from the training package, the average annual all-inclusive cost of the Program for a replication site is approximately $2,500 per family per year.

The Parent-Child Home Program Method

First Program Ingredient: Curriculum

Chapter 1 shows how the Program's curriculum was unobtrusively conveyed by the Home Visitors to the parents, using the examples of home sessions with Ms. Willard and Carol, and with Ms. Carter and Jo-Jo. The Home Visitors' written records of their home sessions do not reveal all the subtleties of their own modeling of the curriculum and cannot fully convey their relaxed approach to child and parent. All Home Visitors are trained to model the three kinds of parenting behavior that make up the Program's curriculum: *verbal interaction techniques, positive parenting behavior,* and *fostering the child's social–emotional competence.*

Curriculum Element Number 1: Verbal Interaction Techniques

The first part of the three-part curriculum relates mainly to nurturing the child's intellectual growth through conversation with his or her parent. It promotes parent–child talk around the books and toys that have been provided. This encompasses the Program's techniques to stimulate the verbal interaction between parent and child—the most visible aspects of the curriculum.

The verbal interaction techniques were made more tangible to Ms. Willard, to Ms. Carter, and to their Home Visitors through the guide sheet that accompanies every book and toy. Each guide sheet is complete in itself as a "curriculum," for it is a one-page summary of the main intellectually stimulating part of the Program's version of the "hidden curriculum." The Home Visitors receive a guide sheet for each week's new book or toy. They also receive copies of the same guide sheet to give to the families.

Two guide sheets used with Carol and Jo-Jo can serve as examples, one for a toy (the school bus) and one for a book (*Ask Mr. Bear*). The little yellow school bus looked very much like the real thing and even had some interesting passengers who could be lifted out and manipulated. *Ask Mr. Bear* was a picture book about small Danny's quest among some animal friends to find a birthday present for his mother, which was finally suggested by Mr. Bear (a hug).

The Home Visitors gave the guide sheets to the mothers when they brought the school bus and *Ask Mr. Bear* for Carol and Jo-Jo during the first year of the Program, when the children were two years old. Ms. Willard and Ms. Carter were welcome to keep their guide sheets in a special folder provided by the Home Visitor or to discard them, as they wished. The Parent–Child Home Program staff never questioned what the mothers did with them.

Each guide sheet contains a general list of verbal interaction techniques to use with both books and toys, the core of the verbal interaction curriculum. Next to every technique on the list are examples taken from the book or toy related to that guide sheet.

The examples for the school bus and *Ask Mr. Bear*, which the Home Visitors named, and encouraged the children to name, were:

They Named	About the School Bus	About *Ask Mr. Bear*
Labels:	BUS	GRASS
Colors:	YELLOW BUS	GREEN GRASS
Shapes:	SQUARE WINDOW	ROUND WHEELS
Sizes:	LITTLE CHILDREN	TALL TREES
Relationships:	UP THE STAIRS	IN THE CENTER

Categories:	CHILDREN	ANIMALS
Numbers:	THREE GIRLS	TWO BIRDS
Causation:	"IF YOU PULL THE BUS, THE HEAD WILL MOVE."	"WHEN DANNY LOOKED FOR MR. BEAR, HE FOUND HIM."

On the guide sheet for the book, there was practical advice for how the Home Visitors (and thus Ms. Willard and Ms. Carter) could read *Ask Mr. Bear* with Carol and Jo-Jo:

- Invite the child to look and listen.
- Sit next to the child or with the child between the Home Visitor and the parent.
- Show and read the title page of the book.
- Show and describe how to turn the pages and treat the book.
- Read to him or her in a clear, easy voice. Don't go too fast.
- Stop at most illustrations.
- Invite the child to tell about personal experiences: "Can you hop too?"
- Ask questions about the illustrations to help the child reason things out: "Why is Danny sitting on the step instead of playing?"
- Encourage the child to join in on familiar words.
- Enjoy the book yourself.[1]

For the school bus, as with the other toys, there were many additional techniques listed on the guide sheet, including suggestions on how to model for children ways to describe their actions:

General: "The children are climbing into the school bus."
Matching: "The girl in the red dress should go in the red seat."
Fitting: "The round child fits into the round seat."
Sounds: "Listen to the bus as it rolls along."

The guide sheets also include suggestions for how to encourage children to think about what they are doing, to be reflective, as they play with the toy:

- To get their attention: "Make the bus driver watch the road!"
- To make a choice: "Will you put the children in from the top or through the bus door?"

---

1. Similarly, Melanie Klein said that play therapy could be effective only if the sessions were authentically enjoyed by both child and therapist.—SL

- To have self-control: "Slow down or the bus will crash!"
- To remember experiences: "Have you seen a real school bus?"
- To pretend: "Let's drive to the children waiting for the bus."
- To do things in the right order: "First stop the bus. Then let's have the driver put out the Stop sign."

Three kinds of general reminders are also included on all the guide sheets used for the books and toys in the two Program years. The Home Visitors and parents are reminded to:

- Encourage the child to talk: Ask him questions, listen to his answers, answer his answers.
- Encourage the child to want to learn: Praise her when she does well, try to ignore her mistakes, help her when she really needs help.
- Encourage his curiosity and his imagination.

These general suggestions are the same for both books and toys. They are there to remind Home Visitors and parents of the most fundamental features of the parent–child verbal interaction.

Curriculum Element Number 2: Positive Parenting Behavior[2]

For the second part of the curriculum, the Home Visitor is trained to model, as often as she can do so appropriately, twenty items of positive parenting behavior. Usually, the positive parenting behavior is directly related to the books and toys but occasionally it is not.

1. The Home Visitor *responds verbally* to the child's verbal or perhaps nonverbal requests for her attention.

   She uses words to show that she is aware of what the child wants and that she will either grant his request or not. In either case, she is careful not to ignore his bid for attention. For instance, the Home Visitor said, "Yes, I see the dog," when Carol pointed or exclaimed, "Dog!" while looking at a book illustration; or "Not now; mommy says you'll be eating lunch soon," when Jo-Jo indicated that he was hungry and wanted a cookie.

2. She *verbalizes affection* toward the child.

   She uses words to express a feeling of warmth toward the child. For example, she said, "Jo-Jo, it's fun to build block towers with you."

---

2. Some of the material in this chapter may be presented in more detail than might interest a portion of readers. We have tried to help their reading by setting off some of the more supplementary or illustrative paragraphs in a smaller type font.

3. She clearly *verbalizes to the child the expectations* she has of her.

She puts into words exactly what she wants the child to do or not to do so that the child is sure about what she really wants. For instance, instead of just saying generally to Carol, "It's time to clean up," she said, "It's time to put the blocks back into the block can!"

4. She *verbalizes her approval* of the child.

The Home Visitor praises the child in words. She makes comments that let the child know that she likes what he is doing or refrains from doing. For example, she said, "That's it!" or "That's good!" when Carol did start putting the blocks back into the block can.

5. She tries to *converse with the child.*

That is, she tries to conduct conversations with the child. She responds to the child's utterances (whether or not they are questions) with a question or with a comment on what was said. The conversation might be more of an accompaniment to a child's actions than an actual verbal give-and-take. For example:

Jo-Jo: "Green!"
HOME VISITOR: "Yes, it's a green block. And something you're wearing is green too. Maybe you can tell me what it is."

Or, for example:

CAROL: "I'm building (tower of blocks) up, up, up!"
HOME VISITOR: "Yes, up it goes, up, up, up!"
CAROL: "Gonna crash!"
HOME VISITOR: "Bang!"

6. She *verbalizes the reasons for the child's obedience.*

She explains why it is necessary for a child to perform or desist from performing a particular action. For instance, when the Home Visitor suggested that Carol put the blocks back into the can, she added: "So the pieces won't get lost."

7. She *tries to enforce her instructions* to the child.

She continues an attempt to get the child to comply when she directs him to perform or not perform a particular action. She doesn't let the directive drop without trying to follow through with it. For instance, the Home Visitor would tell Jo-Jo to bring a toy for review from his toy chest, wait for him to bring it, and then repeat the directive a few times before giving up on it.

8. She *discourages the child's overdependence.*

She does not help a child with tasks that she knows the child could do for herself. For instance, when Carol asked her to put her shoe on, the Home Visitor told her to do it for herself. Or when Jo-Jo gave her a puzzle piece to fit in for him, she returned it and suggested he do it himself.

9. She *encourages the child to understand the reasons* for her instructions.

She tries to demonstrate pleasure, rather than impatience or boredom, when a child shows curiosity about the pros and cons of a directive. For example, when Carol asked why it was time to put the blocks away, she patiently gave the explanation in a way Carol could understand: "We have to put the blocks away because it's time for lunch."

10. She tries to *show respect for the child's reactions* to a directive.

She takes into consideration the child's ideas and feelings, and she listens to what she has to say. She might either change the directive or stand firm with it, but the child has a chance to express her feelings or thoughts about it. For instance, when Carol indicated that she didn't want to gather up her blocks and thus delay playing with the truck, the Home Visitor said: "OK, I know you want to play with your truck, but first you have to put the blocks away."

11. She actively *encourages the child's independence.*

She suggests activities the child is able to do for himself. For example, she would say, "Now it's your turn to decide what you will make on the magnetic form board. Find the pieces for it yourself."

12. She tries to *train the child for self-direction.*

She gives the child information, in a way he can understand, that enables him to carry out age-appropriate tasks without any help. For instance, the Home Visitor showed Jo-Jo how to turn the pages of a book without tearing them. Or Carol's Home Visitor showed her how to put blocks on top of each other for good balance.

13. She *expresses some warmth toward the child.*

The Home Visitor shows by her facial expression or some small act that she feels affectionate toward the child. She smiled, touched Jo-Jo's or Carol's head or even hugged the child (but hugging was left mainly to the mother so as not to intrude on the parent–child relationship).

14. She tries to *satisfy the child's needs,* whether signaled verbally or non-verbally.

She is alert to the child's request for something he needs however the request is shown *(signaled)*: by a child's words, facial or vocal expression, or actions. She tries to make sure that the need is real, rather than a passing whim, and then tries to satisfy it. For example, when Carol began to rub her eyes, yawn, and seem weary, she suggested that the home session draw to a close. Or when Jo-Jo pointed at something in a book illustration and looked at her with a questioning expression, she would name whatever he had pointed at.

15. She tries to be *comforting to the child.*

She sympathizes by word, expression or act with a child's distress and makes some attempt at consolation. When Carol seemed sad, the Home Visitor would divert her attention by reading to her or (more likely) suggesting that the mother do so, or she would divert her attention by pointing to a toy.

16. She *uses positive reinforcement* a great deal.

In other words, the Home Visitor praises the child verbally or shows nonverbal approval for behavior she wants to encourage in the child. For example, she smiled and nodded and told Carol she had done a good job when Carol cleared the floor of blocks in preparation for playing with the truck. Or she clapped her hands when Jo-Jo fitted a puzzle piece into the right place.

17. She *refrains from scolding* the child.

She never uses nagging, hurtful words, or yelling, no matter how exasperating the child might be. For instance, when Jo-Jo started to throw a block at his sister, she said, "If you throw blocks at Dee-Dee, you might really hurt her. Let's build with them instead."

18. Her directives *gain the child's attention.*

She makes sure that the child is listening to her request or instructions. She does not accept the child's appearing not to notice what is being said. For example, she would say, "Carol, are you listening? I said it's time to put the blocks back into the block can."

19. She *persists* in enforcing directives.

She not only tries to get the child to comply, but continues the attempt until the child actually does so. Example: She told Jo-Jo to bring the school bus, the toy chosen by him for review, from the toy chest. She then waited for him to bring it and kept reminding Jo-Jo to bring it until he actually did bring it.

20. She is *firm* with the child.

> She usually takes a definite position, and she stays with it, in giving a directive to the child. She tries not to waver or give an impression of uncertainty. Example: The Home Visitor told Carol it was time to end a home session (Ms. Willard having shown her readiness) and brought the session to a close, even though Carol protested. Or she told Jo-Jo he was not allowed to throw blocks at his sister and physically prevented him from doing so when he persisted (took the block out of his hand and put all of the blocks away).

No Home Visitor could show all twenty items of positive parenting behavior during any one home session or possibly even over a few months. It is hoped, however, that they can all be demonstrated to the parent several times each during the first and second Program years.

Some Striver parents were already practicing many of the positive parenting behavior techniques and seemed to need less demonstration. Their intuitive skills supported the positive parenting items' selection in the late 1960s from what The Parent-Child Home Program's founder—this book's first author—had learned about parenting in almost twenty years as a mother and as a clinical psychologist, teacher, and social worker. Her own experience was greatly augmented by that of her staff members and by a study conducted by Dr. Diana Baumrind of the University of California at Berkeley (Baumrind, 1967). Dr. Baumrind found that parenting practices like most of the *positive parenting twenty* were carried on by the highly educated, middle-income parents of four year olds observed to be well-functioning in nursery school. Similarly, parent-participants' positive parenting skills correlated significantly with their children's social–emotional competence at the age of four. More important, many of these skills were found to form a supportive network for Program graduates' school competencies when they reached first grade (see Chapter 5).

Very likely the positive parenting twenty are sensible ways for all parents to interact with their children. They are likely to be as appropriate for six year olds, eight year olds, or twelve year olds as they were with two year olds and three year olds.

Curriculum Element Number 3: Fostering the Child's Social–Emotional Competence

The major aim of the third part of the curriculum is to help children develop not only intellectually but also in their attitudes toward social relationships; toward their inner selves; and toward the world of work, play, and ideas. In short, this Program goal, achievable mainly through the practice of positive parenting, is to foster children's social–emotional competence. That competence at any age level, starting at about the age of two years, should be such that each Program child:

1. Is *emotionally stable*

   a. Seems generally happy and content
   Gives an impression of being satisfied and even happy most of the time. Seems tension free, and negative feelings such as sadness, fear, anxiety generally appear to be minimal.

   b. Is spontaneous without being explosive
   Can freely express strong positive or negative feelings but knows when and where to stop an outburst. Appears to exercise sufficient control over emotional behavior to avoid overintense extremes inappropriate to the situation.

   c. Seems free of sudden, unpredictable mood changes
   Moods (happiness, sadness, anger, and so on) usually obviously related to the situation at hand. Reactions follow a rather stable pattern. It is thus possible to forecast what emotional behavior will be under most conditions.

   d. Tolerates necessary frustration (such as awaiting a turn at a game)
   Can control the need for immediate satisfaction of a wish, whether involving physical, emotional, social, or cognitive satisfaction. Appears to understand that at times has to wait to get what he wants and is willing to wait when has to do so.

2. Has a *willing attitude* toward tasks

   a. Is attentive and concentrates on tasks
   Focuses with eyes and ears quietly, first as a task is explained and then in carrying through its accomplishment. Appears to be intent on reaching the goal set by the task and is not easily distracted by outside sights and sounds.

   b. Understands and completes tasks without frequent urging
   Seems to understand directions and goes about what has to be done in a self-directed manner. Continues a task until it is done, at a fairly steady pace, with only occasional pauses. Does not have to be reminded frequently to finish.

   c. Enjoys mastering new tasks
   Shows pleasure in mastering a new activity. May show or express a sense of accomplishment (efficacy) at completion of the task.

   d. Initiates nondestructive, goal-directed activities
   Shows independence and sometimes thinks up and begins activities that will not hurt others and will have some constructive aim, however limited.

The activity may not involve much creativity, but it does demonstrate initiative and direction toward a goal.

3. *Thinks ahead*

   a. Is well organized in work or play
      Thinks through ahead of time the materials or activities needed and then uses them to go ahead with accomplishing the task or play in orderly sequence. Appears to be reflective about the task.

   b. Expresses ideas in language
      Uses words or sentences to convey thoughts instead of just gestures, tone of voice, or facial expression.

   c. Is creative, inventive
      Uses materials or ideas in original ways that may be different from those initially intended. The results may be interesting, attractive, or even exciting.

   d. Seems to know the difference between fact and fantasy. If "makes believe" in play, clearly understands that the pretending is a game, a fantasy. Seems firmly based in reality.

4. *Cooperates* in social situations

   a. Refrains from physically aggressive behavior toward others
      Does not direct physical force against people around. Is able to channel hostility into appropriate angry language or other nonphysical activity.

   b. Can put own needs second to those of others
      Understands that at times others have rights that transcend own. Shows consideration for the physical, social, and emotional requirements of other people around.

   c. Follows necessary rules in family or school
      Complies with directives devised for social group harmony at home or school but feels free to question the general necessity for a particular rule.

   d. Is cooperative with adults
      Is generally willing to follow the suggestions or directives of responsible adults, without arguing, objecting, or balking

5. Is responsibly *independent*

   a. Seems self-confident, not timid
      Is not shy in social interaction. Initiates interaction or responds to others with little hesitation. Appears to value self and does not seem to fear people or tasks.

b. Accepts or asks for help when necessary
Permits or requests help from adults without seeming to need help for everything. Usually tries, at least briefly, to understand or master the task before asking for help.

c. Protects own rights appropriately for age group
Tries to defend self or property from physical attack by others without overreacting or carrying hostilities beyond the actual attack.

d. Refrains from unnecessary physical risks
May enjoy physical challenge, as in sports, but does not expose self to danger without good reason.

These skills, closely related to the positive parenting twenty, echo most parents' goals for their children's social–emotional competence. They add up to children being happy, civilized, and intellectually well functioning young human beings, whether they are age two or eight or even teenagers well along the way toward maturity.

Second Program Ingredient: Books and Toys (Curriculum Materials)

The curriculum materials that comprise the second core ingredient in each Program year are one or more storage containers for the books and toys, followed by twelve books and eleven toys. All are of good quality, sturdy, attractive, and available at most toy and book stores. They are gifts from the Program for the family to provide a focus that is enjoyable to both child and parent in sparking verbal interaction between them.

To put it more simply, the books and toys supply parents and children with natural, intrinsically interesting subjects for conversation. The Home Visitors use the books and toys to model and encourage verbally oriented reading, conversation, and play activity within the parent–child dyads.

By furnishing picture books and playthings as gifts, The Parent-Child Home Program puts the stamp of approval on what is sometimes considered an unnecessary luxury by harried low-income parents: conversation between parents and child playing together and enjoying their play with each other, and time reading together with their children. In fact, an important reason for providing the families with books and toys that remain with them permanently, as if they were indeed school curriculum materials, is to ensure that the dialogue will continue between home sessions and long after the intervention is over.

Another reason for making the books and toys the focus of The Parent-Child Home Program's verbal interaction is that they provide a stepping-stone from the infant world of perception and action to the adult world of words. The books are profusely illustrated and thus have a rich potential for stimulating conversation. They are an inviting introduction to literacy and a bridge to school. Often children bring Program books to show their kindergarten and first grade school teachers.

A different set of books and toys is used with each age group, one for two year olds and one for three year olds, for a total of a minimum of forty-six books and toys over two years. After the presentation of a storage container, a new book or toy is brought for the child each week, one week a book and the next a toy.

The first of the week's two sessions is centered around the new book or toy. The second is a review session at which the new book or toy is again the center of attention. Sometimes the child brings out material from earlier in the Program. Whatever interests the child is the subject of that session. The books and toys are brought in the same order for every child in each year of the Program, so that the demonstrations of verbal interaction techniques around them in the weekly Home Visitor staff meetings can be applicable to the work of every Home Visitor.

It should be emphasized that although the books and toys may be educationally valuable in themselves, and the books serve as a bridge to future reading and school, their main value in the Program lies in their providing an abundant source of possibilities for verbal interaction between parent and child. In fact, their Parent–Child Home Program acronym is VISM, for verbal interaction stimulus materials.

The list of books and toys used by local replication sites may change from year to year in response to new materials coming on the retail market and to ratings of the books and toys by parents and Home Visitors on how much the children liked them. All books and toys chosen must fit the criteria developed by the Program; within those criteria the local sites can identify those books and toys that work best for their families.

Criteria for Choosing Toys

- Verbal
  Should induce or permit verbal interaction

- Perceptual
  Strong primary and secondary colors
  Possibilities for size discrimination
  Simple geometric shapes in variety but not confusion
  Form fitting possibilities
  Spatial organization possibilities
  Simple sounds when manipulated by the child

Varied and pleasant tactile qualities

- Motor

  Allows for large and small muscle activity

  Possibility of much manipulation

  Challenge to finger dexterity

  Development of specific motor skills

  Outlet for diffuse motor discharge (banging, pushing, etc.)

- Conceptual

  Possesses possibilities for imaginative play

  Challenge to problem solving

  Self-rewarding activity

  Gender and ethnic neutrality

  Promoting sociability

  Purpose understandable and interesting to a young child

- Other

  Safe

  Durable

  Low anxiety potential for child

  Easy care for parents

We want a toy to be very rich in perceptual and motor stimuli so that we can name these stimuli in various ways to the child and verbalize around them. The verbalization will have much more meaning for the child when he is actually encountering the experience of sensory motor stimuli, like the experience of Helen Keller who for the first time grasped the symbolism of the word water when the water gushed on her hand from the faucet. The richer the experience with sensory motor stimulation, the more opportunities there are for enrichment of verbal and language growth.

Criteria for Choosing Books

- Content

  Geared to child's age and interests

  Interesting to parents

  Widens child's experiences

  Leads to associations with child's experiences

- High literary standards
- Language simple, with some repetition
- Illustrations large, colorful, profuse, rich source of conversation
- Attractive to both sexes and any ethnic group

- Low anxiety potential
- Durability
- Reading level within ability of most Program parents

Third Program Ingredient: Home Visitors

The Home Visitors are The Parent-Child Home Program's demonstrators of books, toys, and parenting behaviors, such as those who came to the Willard and Carter homes. They are usually paid paraprofessionals, people from the same community as the participant-families, and often former Program parent-participants, who may have less than a high school education. They may be volunteers, students, or AmeriCorps members. All Home Visitors are trained together in an initial sixteen hours of training and in weekly two-hour Home Visitor staff meetings throughout the intervention. They are trained not to be a friend, counselor, or teacher but to *model* for parents how to use the three parts of the curriculum while playing and talking with their children about the books and toys.

All Home Visitors are trained and supervised in the same groups, whether paid, volunteers, or students, allowing for potentially valuable interchange of life experience. The Home Visitors meet weekly during each Program year in twenty-three staff meetings with the Coordinator. They learn the verbal interaction techniques for each new book or toy, studying the guide sheets for them and putting the guides into a cumulative *Home Visitor's Handbook*. They also get support and counsel for any problems they may have faced in home sessions and noted in their home session records. The Coordinator is able to be of special help because she herself has recruited all the families for the intervention, has interviewed every parent, and has introduced the Home Visitors to the parents, as Myrtle Crawford did for Ms. Willard and Ms. Carter. Each Home Visitor also has individual supervisory conferences with the Coordinator, near the beginning and near the end of the Program year, focused around an audio or video tape recording of one home session or the Coordinator's in-person viewing of a session.

Home Visitors need have little more than the knowledge and attitudes that they will learn from the Program itself. They must start with a certain degree of flexibility and warmth toward children and parents, and be non-judgmental and knowledgeable about the community the families live in. They may have a wide range of education, from below high school and up, and need not have any previous vocational preparation for the job.

Thus the Home Visitor does not need to enter The Parent-Child Home Program with any particular skills. However, by the end of her first year in the Program, she is expected to be demonstrating competence on fifty skills divided among four major areas and formally rated by Home Visitor and Coordinator together in their individual conferences:

- The Home Visitor's Program knowledge and work skills
- Her attitudes toward her parent–child dyads
- Her dependability
- Her ability to use supervision constructively

The Home Visitors are not expected to acquire counseling or teaching skills. In fact, they are carefully trained to *abstain* from direct teaching and to *resist* the temptation to counsel parents even when their advice is sought. The sixteen-hour initial training and the weekly staff meetings provide Home Visitors with the skills and information they need to bring the Program into families' homes. Limiting the Home Visitor's role to doing The Parent–Child Home Program activities with the families also protects the families from a "service overload" that they might consider too demanding or intrusive. Home Visitors are, however, taught to alert the site Coordinator to parents' requests for help (which are sometimes unspoken). The Coordinator then immediately visits or contacts the parents to explore whether they indeed wish help, either directly from her or from a community agency.

These modest requirements for the position of Home Visitor hardly reflect the diversity and strengths among the Home Visitors in practice. Their differences sometimes appear through their individual ways of describing home sessions.

The following examples from the notes of various Home Visitors in the original model program on Long Island illustrate their diversity:

Yolanda spoke little—speech not intelligible except for single words. Mother does not comprehend either. Child quite infantile: throws or drops pegs wherever hands are rather than putting them somewhere convenient for next usage; goes to get bottle; self absorbed in solitary play with little use of suggestion, direction, or social play. Learned mechanics of toy very quickly and enjoyed toy manipulation. Mother joined Home Visitor in describing child's activity, was inventive in using wagon stick to point out longer from shorter pegs. Home Visitor made clear there is no expectation from child's performance, reassured mother re child's "poor" performance.

Gary didn't like to use the hammer, he just wanted to push it down with his finger, but he did repeat everything after me like his colors, and what he was doing, and he enjoyed seeing the pegs coming out of the round hole, like "guess what coming out next." He is also getting to be very close to me, looks happy to see me when I come in. Mother seems to be very interested in what Gary is doing, like she always asks him the color after me if he doesn't repeat it.

At this session I introduced Ann to the color-roll wagon. She was very excited about it. She wouldn't look up when I tried to show her anything so I began describing what she was doing. She counted the sticks, built a tower, and rolled the blocks. After playing for about 20 min., she ran and got *Pat the Bunny* and read it to mother and me, she also played her music box and sang to me as I left.

Sammy was fantastic—in comparison to what had gone before, he practically made a formal address regarding page 1 of *Good Night Moon*. Identified phone, stars, moon, rug, light, window, "light on." He then climbed up on a stool and turned the living room light on. He and I noticed that the pink blanket was the same color as his, and "talked" about how the toy house roof protects everyone, like his roof. We all had a wonderful time, and I hated to leave. I'm always so glad when he says a word, but he is so unintelligible much of the time that I'm not sure how to respond to what he's saying. (I'm slowly getting a little more attuned to him, I hope.)

We started out reading *All Fall Down*. Tommy wasn't talking today, which he usually doesn't talk much just every now and then. Today I decided to talk less and play more. In the story I called a cat a boy, then Tommy said "no, no, that's a cat!" And I continue things like that, and I discovered that he knew what the following is: dog, cat, flowers, girl. The lady with the carriage he called a Mommy and he knew man and boy. It was very funny when I called the snow, ice-cream falling down. Tommy just laughed and laughed then, said that's not ice-cream, that's snow, silly!

I debated whether or not to review the rubber puzzles. My decision was difficult simply because, as a creature of habit, I have reviewed all of the toys and books. Candy seemed to have had mastery of the puzzles the first time we played. However, I did want to see if she had retained the names of the shapes. It was and has been extremely exciting for me to watch Candy in her learning process. She did retain a great deal and the session was very relaxing for mother and child alike.

Ruth was very happy today. She played and laughed every time she name a color and she knew it was right. She clap and yell, she was very very funny. I ask about the new baby and she talked about something else. Each time she did something right and I said "very good" she would say "yep, very good!"

Trained social workers with master's degrees (Helen Roth Adelman and Arlene Kochman) were chosen to be the first Home Visitors (then called Toy Demonstrators) in 1967. Their professional skills were used, paradoxically, to test out the acceptability to parents and the workability of employing untrained people in the role, people who might not even have an undergraduate college degree. They deliberately confined themselves to nonteaching, noncounseling behavior during home sessions while observing the parents' acceptance of their simply modeling the curriculum. The parents seemed to welcome this role limitation, thus opening the door to the use of paraprofessionals as Home Visitors. Nevertheless, the complexity of the Program's apparently simple delivery system does require a college-degreed person to direct it as a site Coordinator. The social workers who pioneered the Home Visitor role became the Program's first Coordinators in the years that followed.

Fourth Program Ingredient: Program Coordinator

The Coordinator carries responsibility for the total operation of a Parent–Child Home Program site, often establishing it as a brand-new function within a sponsoring agency or school system.

As background for the job, the person chosen to be the Coordinator has achieved professional status in a field closely linked to the method and goals of the Program, perhaps education, nursing, psychiatry, psychology, or social work. Either as part of his or her own professional training, or in addition to it, the Coordinator must be family oriented, that is, knowledgeable and caring about interpersonal behavior, values, and attitudes in families. Within that framework, the Coordinator is able to be responsive to families and to teach that responsiveness to the Home Visitors. The Coordinator should also be prepared to work with relative independence while remaining within the philosophic and structural framework of the sponsoring organization.

A site Coordinator (for brevity to be referred to as *she* since most, in practice, are women) can work with an assistant Coordinator or by herself. Her main job is to pull together the three other elements of the intervention—Home Visitors, books/toys, and curriculum—to form a smoothly working and effective whole. Her tasks are manifold and sometimes not easy. After she has been trained at a training institute run or authorized by the National Center, she enrolls the parent–child dyads, recruits and trains the Home Visitors, and purchases the Program books and toys. In the course of their training, Coordinators are provided with a large kit of technical aids for running a Parent–Child Home Program site. These include a technical manual and all the forms needed to operate the Program, videos and manuals for training home visit staff, and a manual for using the Program's management information system. The Coordinator also serves as a Home Visitor for at least one family and often more in the first years of the Program.

The Coordinator is known to all parent-participants. She has made the initial recruiting visit to them, has introduced the Home Visitor, and returns at midyear for a home interview. She gives every parent a chance to speak his or her mind about any aspect of the Program or relations with the Home Visitor. During the introduction of the Home Visitor to the family, the parents are invited (in the Home Visitor's presence) to get in touch with the Coordinator whenever they wish to do so. Thus the ongoing nature of the parents' relationships with both Home Visitor and Coordinator is clearly defined. If the parent continues on to become a Home Visitor, this previous experience with the Coordinator is an asset in her future working relationship with the Program.

The Coordinator seeks and heeds the wishes and opinions of parents in regard to their participation in the Program. When Home Visitors report verbal or nonverbal signals suggesting that a parent may want help of some kind, the Coordinator visits the parent at once. If the parent does wish aid with a family problem (possibly relating to a child's schooling or medical, emotional, or legal questions), the Coordinator provides information, gives advice, or contacts or connects the family with appropriate community agencies that can provide the needed services.

A Sampler of Home Sessions

No two home sessions are alike, and few reach an ideal standard. But, although they are enormously varied, each has within it some element of the ideal. Moreover, some common emphases have emerged among the many thousands of home sessions described by Home Visitors:

Individuality of Children in Home Sessions

Earl was happily excited and enthusiastic when I arrived, told me he had made a Christmas wreath in preschool and showed it to me. His speech requires close attention; the words are imperfect but he seems to have a vocabulary large enough to express himself when he wants to. Usually he speaks very little—one or two words at a time, but today he used whole sentences. "I made a Christmas wreath." "I made it in school." "We used pine cones."

Simone did the puzzle twice with me. She stuck to it, enjoyed it thoroughly—learned with each try and seemed determined to master it completely as I left, refitting each piece over and over.

Eduardo knew every picture in the book. He called the bear a teddy. He named the rabbit, telephone, clock, etc. When he named the telephone, he pretend to talk to the rabbit. He said, "Hello rabbit, are you there? Do you see that balloon and big rabbit sits in the chair?"

Keesha was very sleepy today. As soon as we all sat down in the living room, she lay down on the rug and looked as if she was ready to go to sleep. This happened once before, so I decided to do as I had the last time. I suggested to Ms. Hopkins to let her rest. We chatted for about 15 minutes, then Keesha woke up and we began our session.

Most of Teresa's board-game pieces were lost and she insisted that she get a new one. She wanted me to go home and get her some more pieces for the game. She started crying and her grandmother got after her. I told her to get a book and I would read to her. She said "No" and went into the bedroom. Her grandmother couldn't get her to come out.

Rakim greeted me with bubbling enthusiasm, and tried very hard to tell me several things during the session. I was unable to understand (his mother made no attempt) but he was very earnest about trying to communicate.

For the first time since the program started I was unable to do anything with Kim. She threw the drum at her mother and then she wanted to put on her new coat. I believe that was the problem. I started singing and she kind of cooled down. The session ended much better than it started.

Viviana was good today, really great, fit circle and square by herself. She talked and talked, fit pieces in the spaces like a champ, turned mat around to put pieces in the right place, she mix the colors, knew green and blue, triangle. Viviana didn't like rough sides, place all the pieces on the smooth sides. Was very happy while working with her Fit-a-Space puzzle pieces, jump up and down when she did them all right.

Striver and Hesitater Parents in Home Sessions

Great session! Tyler and mother both asleep when I arrived but got up right away and Mrs. B. apologized quite profusely for being asleep. Tyler brought out Mail Box, assorted blocks, peg bench and *Mother Goose*. He talked a great deal more, imitating or repeating what I or mother said. Used blocks with big holes as a spy glass, mother did too. She read a couple of rhymes also. At end Mrs. B. apologized again for sleeping. We discussed her fatigue a little—natural as a result of working at night. She seems much more relaxed about sessions—very cooperative. We all had fun.

The mother spent a large amount of time with Simon in filling the boxes and naming, as well as counting, the toys. He named only a few and we had the usual detour of his madly wheeling the car back and forth and making motor noises. Ms. Deacon carefully counted the pegs and named their colors and explained the game very well, keeping it extremely simple and step by step. She seemed to enjoy the idea of the game's long term value and being a group activity.

We reviewed *Good Night Moon* today. Mrs. Haywood seems to have a very high expectation of Carla. Carla simply wanted to leaf through the pages and identify the familiar objects over and over again. Mrs. Haywood seems anxious about this. She began picking up the incorrect answers but did try to correct rather than reprimand Carla.

When I arrived mother and child had just woken up. Mother gave us the two telephones and sat down on the couch by us and began falling back to sleep. When I asked for the toy dishes, mother told me that the child had made such a mess playing with the dishes in water, that she told the child that the man had come and gotten the dishes (which she had really put up in the closet). So we weren't able to play with them. Anna didn't want to play with the telephones by themselves. I think she was kind of upset by not being able to play with the dishes.

Again, Ms. Rodriguez's reading and usage of the book was great. I really had very little to add, except to get her back to the book itself when she would overdo one page with Juan. He liked it enormously and said many, many things, including "Chick come out of the egg" and "On top of his head." Ms. Rodriguez's was excellent in stressing what was happening and continually asking, "What will happen now, Juan?" She confessed to some "self-conscious" feelings, as she put it, in reading, and I assured her that she is well ready to read, play, and enjoy herself with Juan.

Child delighted with School Bus. Still mixes up colors and guesses, but cheerfully repeats all info Home Visitor gives. Easily matches children to same color seats. Delighted with dramatic play. Named all children and fed and took back and forth to school. Mother was silent—enjoyed Nancy's pretend play with a smile and slight embarrassment.

The story had been read to Cassy during the week so she now could understand it, whereas when she first received it, she seemed unable to comprehend the sophistication of Peter's feelings toward his sibling. However, during this session today she really seemed able now to grasp the idea and even related her own experiences as they related to the book, *Peter's Chair*. Mother and Cassy virtually did the whole session.

We didn't spend the whole time with *A Letter to Amy*, since Michael didn't seem too involved with it (he was tired). The important thing to me about this visit was Mrs. Walker telling me that Michael was a) more interested in *Letter to Amy* than he let on when we first read it and b) he memorized the action and objects in the pictures fairly quickly and insisted on telling Mrs. Walker the story, rather than vice versa. I was really pleased to hear not only of his initiative but of her recognition and pride in what he is doing and in letting him do it.

Twins in Home Sessions

The twins seemed to enjoy this toy very much. Angela repeated words after their mother and me, and she answered questions, but Alexandra wouldn't say anything. They both built towers out of the blocks and sticks, but Angela had more trouble because she just couldn't leave the stick on the floor when placing a second block on top of the first. Every time the blocks would fall down the girls would put them into the wagon and take them for a ride. In fact, that's the only thing that Alexandra would say: "Blocks going for a ride now!"

Mother had been teaching the girls how to set the table with the tea set, where to put the knife, fork, and spoon. They had also been eating their real food out of the dishes. Angela wasn't feeling well, she had a very bad cold. It didn't make her any less active, though. We talked to each other on the telephones, each pretending we were someone else. We had a party, the girls cooked chicken. Afterwards they washed the dishes, and mother and I dried them.

Mother wasn't at home, but Grandmother was there to be in the home session. The twins were very verbal. After I read the book, each one read it back to me, first Alexandra and then Angela. They told me what Peter was doing on every page. They tended to copy what each other said. Grandmother did more listening than talking.

Fathers as Home Session Participants

Dad and Carlos welcomed me for the review of *Corduroy*. Grandma and Uncle were also there, and I greeted them, but they did not participate in the actual session. Carlos immediately sat next to his father and told the story to his Dad in his own words, using the illustrations as a guide. Dad smiled and encouraged Carlos throughout. I also encouraged him and asked a few questions to remind him about what happened next in the story. Carlos appeared to be very proud of himself and his Dad was proud also. Grandma occasionally poked her head in from the kitchen to listen, and at the end we all exclaimed, "Bravo Carlos!"

Justin brought out his rubber puzzles. We put the pieces together and he did a very good job. Then I give him the book. We sat together on the floor and his father read the book and show him the picture of Peter's high chair and Peter when he was a baby. Then Justin show me his own crib and his high chair. He told me to get in the crib but I told him I was just too big. Then it was time for me to go, and for the first time he didn't want me to go.

Brothers and Sisters in Home Sessions: Helpers and Hinderers

Lisa thrilled with the toy Barn. She allowed her mother to finish fixing her hair while her brother Zachary and I opened up packages and set up figures. Then Lisa started to play. As usual her play was rather frantic, shoved every figure in Barn as Zachary named them for her. Sister Wendy spent most of the time feeding the animals, filled the trough with "cereal" and fed them. Lisa repeated names—tried to manipulate animals' limbs. Zachary pleasant, warm, good to his sisters.

Chantra and her mother were ready with the Earth Puzzle. Chantra was eager to "perform." She and her sisters had really been working with the puzzle during the week. The mother commented on how well the girls played together. In this family it seems that the girls have a tremendous learning influence on each other, i.e., the older children really teach Chantra quite a bit in their play.

When I entered the Whites' apartment, the TV was on and the girls (Linda and her sister Carolyn) were watching a show. Ms. White quickly told Carolyn to go into her room because Linda's teacher had come. The 5 year old did not make any effort to go. In past sessions when Carolyn was there, a tug of war ensued between mother and child. This time I took the initiative and asked Ms. White could Carolyn stay, providing she helped Linda play and did not grab the toy from her. (Carolyn is the middle child and I believe she feels just like the one in the middle.) The Knock-Out Bench was a huge success with both of them!

Tracy took the book, as always, and turned the pages. Andrea, her baby sister, was restless and distracting to Tracy, and after a few minutes Tracy was ready to forget the book. The mother sat with us, Andrea on her lap, and she loved the story and pictures, found them amusing, and wished Tracy would appreciate the book. When Andrea howled, she told Tracy that Andrea looked like the little bird in the book with his beak wide open.

The toy was moderately successful. I believe this can be attributed to the fact that there were too many distractions, i.e., the older sisters wanted to take over, which Alyssa resents bitterly. Mother stepped in and was able to interest the big girls in another activity (outside play). Unfortunately, when everyone had finally settled down, Alyssa was just too upset from the preceding events to be able to enjoy the toy.

Jeremiah's six-year-old sister was present. Ms. Grant wanted her away but we helped her join in, and she helped Jeremiah pick up cues from me, teaching him.

Books in Home Sessions: Listening, Looking, Talking

Nicole likes the books very much. *Good Night Moon* she enjoys. She likes to put her hand on the picture of the fire and say "Hot!" She repeats if you ask her to.

Tramont sat very quietly and listen to me while I read the book to him, then I invited Mrs. Summers to read to him. Mrs. Summers asked Tramont was the kitten and dog the baby bird's mother? He said no. And when she got to the cow, he took the book and said, No, Mommy, that's not his mommy. And he turn to the back of the book and show us the baby bird's mother! I asked Tramont where is his mother. He put his hand on his own mother.

Mother read the book for the first time. She did well with the book but still constantly spoke of how bad Yvette is. So quite naturally the child acted up. Hitting the book and giving the wrong answers to questions. Yvette said the Mailbox was a garbage can. But when her mother went along with her and said that Peter was mailing the letter by putting it into the garbage can, she corrected her mother by saying, "No, he's putting the letter in the Mailbox!"

Nancy asked her mother for *Wake Up Farm*. She doesn't usually ask for a book to read. I ask her to read the story to mommy and me. So she did. On the cover she pointed out everything. Then she showed us Daddy with the milk pails. She says "He's going to put milk in the baby's bottle." She says "The chickens are hungry!"

Bobby talk very much during the session. He wanted to know why Peter Rabbit didn't eat before he went out to play. He named some colors, but he didn't keep his mind on the book because the TV was on. His older sister was in and out. Mother wasn't too pleasant. When asked to show his mother the book, he told her everything he heard me say, like: Snow falls on Peter's head. Peter's mother took his clothes off for a bath. Why didn't Peter have on his shoes?

Viviana didn't say a word when I read the book to her. I kept reading it over and over again—but not a word. When I told her to take the book over to Grandma and show it to her, she told her Grandma almost everything I had read! I praised her, and we clapped, she said, "Thank you!"

Toys: Playing and Talking in Home Sessions

Roberto loved the Mail Box but he seemed to have a hard time fitting the block in the holes. He tried very hard, but he hated the idea of stringing the blocks like beads, he said blocks didn't go on a string. He worked very hard with the Mail Box—naming colors, mailing letters. Talked about the big Mail Box on the street and how he could climb on one. He knew the shape of some blocks and kept repeating "triangle" over and over.

The School Bus was not new to Tony, as one of his friends had this toy before he did. He loved it, and so did his mother. He pulled it, played with the stop sign, loved giving names to all the children. He put them in the right color seats without my suggesting it. Ms. Brown was delighted, and again impressed. She says she didn't realize all the possibilities the toy offers when she saw it at a neighbor's house.

Derek concentrated for 20 minutes on the Magnetic Board. His main focus was on creating birthday cakes, but he allowed me to start a boy, and he helped with the parts (he's got a fairly good conception of body and facial parts). He also made a circle from two halves, and a square from two triangles. In addition he tried to stick the magnets on to everything but the Board. He named almost all the objects on the Board. After 20 minutes, he was messing up the pieces and had lost interest.

Gerald listened for a while to the reading of the book. Then he got down and got out the Magnetic Form Board, and we played with that. He showed me how to make a fish, and that you eat fish. He also made items which he said was me and his mother. Mrs. Lee made a boat and told him what colors she used.

The Toy Barn: A Favorite Toy in Home Sessions

Terrence was very happy to see me, he took me by the hand and said, "Come on in, teacher!" I gave him the Barn and he said, Thank you. I told him it is a barn and I went on by telling him each piece I took out to put together. I told him what it was, he seem to be very happy. He named every animal after I did. Knew the dog, horse, chicken, cow. He didn't know the sheep. We put the barn together and pretend to feed the horse and the cow. Mrs. Johnson said she was very tired but she sat and watch.

The mother thinks that the Barn is too complicated for the children to learn all the things in it. I tell her, as with all the toys, at first it isn't easy but children learn faster than we sometimes realize. May played well with the Barn and the animals and people. She said, "The mother cooks and the daddy works."

Pamela ran for the Toy Barn with great excitement when I arrived. The *Wake Up Farm* book was already on the table. We put the Barn on the table and started with the book, showing her how the Barn looked a lot like the barn in the book, etc. Loves the noises of different animals. Still has trouble knowing the name of some of them—the pig, cow, horse, sheep. After going back and forth between barn figures and the book, we played with the Barn. Incidentally, her five year old sister Cammy came over to the table and stood and watched during this part of the session—even pointing out which figure was the cow, the horse, etc., to Pamela. She stayed with us until Mr. Nolan called over to her and asked her to get something. As we played with the Barn, Pamela wanted to play the "Farmer in the Dell," with the farmer figure picking out each animal as we sang. I try to get her to pick the right figure. She loves the song, loves all songs. Ms. Nolan seems to enjoy the singing too, and although she doesn't join in with the actual song, she helps Pamela pick the right animal.

Bilingual Home Sessions

Lisa vacillates between repeating English words for objects in book (*Good Night Moon*) and saying a Spanish word if I give the English word. Child delights in "telephone" and "curtains." Loves seeing bunny go to sleep. "Shh, bunny is sleeping!" she whispers, holding her finger across her mouth. I name colors, objects, body parts. Lisa tirelessly leafs through book. Sister Rochelle looks on and repeats also.

Maria at first shy with me, naturally. Carried the book to mother. Told me to sit (in Spanish). Smiled with joy when we played "This Little Piggy" and "Ring Around the Rosy." Repeated cat, dog, boy, girl in Spanish and in English. Mostly enamored of pictures in front of book. Not interested in words. When Mother left room, Maria ran after her. I explained to Mrs. M. about staying. Father came in and sat in on session, astonished at Maria's saying English words. I don't think English is ever spoken in the home, only when I come.

Carmen as usual repeated color names for mother but seemed to make no real connection of word to color. Her mother asked me to write the English names of objects, shapes and colors on a piece of paper for her.

Elvira identifies many objects by name as she leafs through the pages. She seems to use English and Spanish interchangeably in naming. Comments, though, are always in Spanish.

Mellisa knows why Peter's building fell down and exclaims "Dog!" in Spanish. She does not seem to comprehend story content, but she does get Peter's joke on his mother (shoes under the curtain) and knows a baby is in the lacy crib.

Yalira was very distracted today. Her mother at my suggestion pointed out pictures, mostly spoke to her in Spanish. Yalira wanted only to kiss the mother and baby in the book and did so continuously. Then her mother had to start cooking lunch. Yalira got a blanket, climbed into the play pen with the baby, and went to sleep.

The three girls, the mother and I sat around the table together, Rita on my lap and Vera on her mother's, and we read the book. The girls are beautiful—interested but shy— very little English. The mother is wonderful. She uses Spanish and English in describing books and uses illustrations to help the girls use the English words, which they do. She is patient and gentle with them. Rita responds less than Vera, who is more verbal and seems more outgoing. The mother said the program is wonderful, perfect for her family. They are learning so much, she is working with them and loves it.

Family Problems Reflected in Home Sessions

Illness

Mother had epileptic attack since last visit. Aunt apparently helps. Anna was dressed especially well. Aunt dressed her. Mother seemed ill—absented herself from part of the session. As a matter of fact, she just walked in and out, did not join in on floor. Mother would like to discuss her ills. Mother mentioned that everyone was surprised that "Anna didn't read her book to me." Very little verbalization on Anna's part. Apparently she has been exposed to colors and concepts. Shapes and textures appear strange. Liked playing as ice-cream man with truck. Delivered ice cream to mother seated nearby.

Child had just awakened and had a fever last night that necessitated a trip to the hospital emergency room. He was listless and only half listened while tapping with a stick. I sang and asked the mother for the *Mother Goose* book but ended the session early.

Mother, Steven and Erik were all suffering from flu or colds (particularly mother) and I feel that I did not use good judgement in holding this session. But mother seemed to expect and want it, perhaps partly to let her sister-in-law observe. Erik related well to the book and responded better than usual, but Steven was restless and inattentive, went to the kitchen to get food and just wandered around the room eating crackers, carrying the book with him. Would not sit on Mommy's lap nor allow her to read the book. He was miserable, wailed a little for no obvious reason; finally, toward the end of the session, Annabelle (the sister-in-law) captured him, held him on her lap did what Mommy would do, pointed out the pictures to him, whispering in his ear as I read, and talked with Erik and Lucinda. She is apparently more verbal than Mommy but will be moving out in the morning. Steven did not say a word, so far as I remember. This session was ATYPICAL.

Emergency Needs

Tiffany and Kyle listened to the story. Tiffany liked it and practically read it back, word for word, to her grandmother's great pleasure. She said that Tiffany is ready to read, points to words and asks what they are. The mother is still in the hospital and the grandmother's strength is beginning to wear out. Her own doctor told her to get away for awhile and she needs someone to care for the kids eight hours a day. She will speak to the hospital social worker this afternoon about this need. If they cannot help her, she will talk to our Coordinator, who will try to help her come up with some alternatives to care for the children.

Child's Atypical Behavior

It seemed very hard to get through to Rena with *Peter's Chair* today. I read the book over and over before Rena said any colors. Then she said "green." Usually when I would ask "What color?" she would say "count." If I said "red," she would say "Three." If I said "Orange," she would say "Eight." Each time, for a color, she would say a number. I spoke to the mother about it, and the mother said the child was doing it to be funny. But it has happened too many times for it to be funny.

Mother's Grief

Mother participated only a few minutes in the session. She not only needs rest but is still depressed over loss of the baby. She told me of the whole unhappy event (stillbirth) and that she is on a lot of medication to build herself up after this ordeal. She wanted the session to continue. Diego was excited by the telephones and we immediately "called each other"—he then phoned his mother and spoke with her about having a party (make-believe).

Multiple Problems

Child silent except for word "truck." Ignores directions and suggestions. Solitary manipulation of the toy. Only three trucks and the garage minus the tires were left to play with. Mother was rather withdrawn, preoccupied. House messy. Father has removed self. Mother has trouble organizing herself and coping with children and housework. Seems exhausted. Asked me to come at 2:30 P.M. instead of later when the other children will soon be home.

The mother was stretched out on the couch falling asleep. The house was in complete disorder. Destiny has been ill, rather lethargic. Showed me her School Bus, all the people were missing. Destiny said LaShawn took *Snowy Day* outside and gave it away. All her other books are gone. She took me into the room she sleeps in to try to find the children which belong to the Bus. The room is incredible, so much junk, impossible to find anything. Debbie said she is going to hold on tight to her new book (*All Falling Down*) so she has it!! She likes it but prefers books "with more story to it," however she loved the pictures and seemed to grasp the concept of falling down. She took the book to her mother, who had fallen asleep, woke her to read the book to her. Mother said, "Wait till I wake up" and did—and did read!

Successful Program Graduates as Adults

By now, many Parent-Child Home Program children have attended college. Brian Gordon was one such child, who enrolled in the prestigious Massachusetts Institute of Technology (MIT). Since his competence when he became a teenager was obvious to MIT, a few of his home sessions when he was three and a half years old may be of particular interest. His imagination, creativity, verbalization, and sociability were so evident in home sessions that, to provide a full description, his Home Visitor's notes on him at the age of almost four years were unusually lengthy and detailed.

Home Session 30: Book, *Are You My Mother?*

Both Brian and his mother were ready and eagerly waiting for me. They both were outgoing and friendly and volunteered many comments. Brian was very observant and verbal. He was very knowledgeable about the birth of baby birds though he occasionally called the baby bird a chicken. Brian knew most of the objects and relationships. When I said the baby bird looked up and then the baby bird looked down, and pointed to the picture, he was puzzled. He called the steam shovel a tractor. Otherwise he was well informed. He mentioned that the half-drawn nest was broken. When the little bird was running fast, he remarked that he had learned to fly because his feet were off the ground.

Home Session 33: Toy—Musical Instruments

Brian was very enthusiastic and cooperative throughout the session. Younger brother Danny was quiet and insisted on watching most of the time. I felt that Brian showed a great deal of imagination and initiative and a willingness to pick up and amplify suggestions. He used the drum to beat out rhythms in great variation with the stick ends, the middle of his fingers, alternating sides, etc. He danced to the beat and marched to the beat and discussed and participated in various types of parades—marching, waving a flag (scarf), pushing a large truck and pretending he was a Superman balloon. He also invented a game which involved hitting the drum before his mother moved it out of the way. He and Danny talked about the parades they would have when Danny received his drum. Their mother is imaginative and obviously enjoys Brian. She participated very effectively verbally and physically. She is very friendly and seems to enjoy talking about a great many things.

Home Session 35: Review

Brian was outside when I arrived. When he came to the door and saw me, he playfully hid. When I asked what he wanted to do, he said he'd like to build a castle. He built a tall tower, and then we all built one together, seeing how high we could make it. He decided to go get the School Bus, and while he was gone, his mother took one of the children "to see if he would notice it was missing." This action seemed significant in view of the fact that she has expressed concern about how much Brian teases. Brian discovered where the child was, he told his mother he didn't want her to do that any more. Brian became involved in imaginative play, taking the Bus children on a trip to a mountain which they climbed and slid down.

Home Session 36: Toy—Magnetic Form Board
Brian unpacked the Magnetic Form Board and asked how to detach the forms from the sticks. As he detached them, he matched them with comparable shapes on the board. He made a castle with wheels, a wagon, a train, Peter, buildings, trees, cheese (in wedges and in oblong pieces), stairs, a rocket, the moon, Humpty Dumpty (he insisted that H.D. had to have legs), various kinds of hats, etc. He tried sticking the magnets to each other and tried sticking the sticks to the board. The mother played with the forms and made suggestions and asked questions throughout the session.

Home Session 40: Review
I have noticed that Brian carries on more mature conversations with me which are not always related to the VISM. He doesn't tease like he used to and relates to both his mother and me in a more mature manner. Brian has been playing a great deal with the Toy Barn. The children from the School Bus were all in the Barn. Brian was interested in manipulating the legs of the animals and took a great deal of care to balance them on two legs, then at my suggestion he stood them on their heads. We decided to have a show with performing animals. The children were all lined up as the audience and Brian provided the voice for the ring master. Without any instructions as to what he should say or how he should say it, he sang out "Presenting the one and only dancing dog!" Though he is very receptive to suggestions, he has many imaginative ideas and a great deal of self-confidence. He corrects me if he thinks I'm wrong. For example, he told me "That's not a lamb, it's a sheep." He seems to have a very comfortable relationship with me and his mother.

Home Visitor Frustrations and Negative Reactions

Osbaldo's brother Cessy is impossible. He threw things, tried to break toys, cursed, etc. When I praised him for being able to stand animals on their heads (after their mother yelled and threatened to hit him) he showed O. how to do same thing. O. tried to listen to the book, to show his mother the pictures and compare them to the toy barn animals. But he gets caught up in Cessy's acting out and session is not as valuable to him as it could be.

This game is just a bit too much for Nancy. I wasn't able to play it with her. She wants to take all the toys out of the boxes. We just talk about the objects and let Nancy do as she wanted. She wouldn't let me touch any part of the game. Every once in a while she would give me one of each.

The book appears rather colorless and when I first brought it out Darin looked depressed and then darted away to find something else to play with. After we persuaded him to have a look, it turned out to be the most successful book so far and we all had a lovely time.

In 2007 The Parent–Child Home Program inaugurated an alumni program for adult Program graduates. Two years earlier, the Board of Directors had added its first member who had been a child in the Program. Julian Gomez, whose mother was a single parent immigrant from Columbia, graduated from The Parent-Child Home Program and went on to have, like Brian, a successful academic career. He graduated from college and law school and is now working for a New York City law firm. When he and his mother reflect back on the Program they particularly talk about how it empowered his mother and got her involved in his education. Julian even complains jokingly that when he was in elementary school, his mother would call the school and tell them they needed to give him harder work because his homework was too easy and he was finishing it too fast.

Like Julian and Brian, many other Parent–Child Home Program participants have gone on to successful careers. Their success can be attributed to three key factors:

1. The Program's gentle touch allowed their natural abilities to blossom in a timely fashion so that they entered school ready to learn and ready to be successful students.
2. The very act of entering school ready to learn put them on the road to success, because children who experience failure early on in school are more likely to continue to fail.
3. Their parents discovered their important role as their child's first and most important teacher and became empowered to be their child's academic advocate and support as the child continued through school.

The Parent–Child Home Program's short-term goals of cognitive/literacy growth for children and increased verbal interaction skills for parents may seem narrow when compared with the large number of stated goals in some other home-based programs encompassing a multiplicity of services. Yet these narrow aims, which permit a relatively simple and easily monitored method, may in the end be the most important factor contributing to its success.

4.

Underpinnings

The Theory behind
The Parent–Child Home Program

*"If I have seen further . . . it is by standing upon
the shoulders of giants."*
—Sir Isaac Newton

The Parent–Child Home Program was not conceived in a vacuum. Earlier work by an august series of "giants" inspired and laid the basis for this unassuming yet effective program for very young, economically disadvantaged children and their parents. The Program's apparently simple method for preventing educational disadvantage rests on a complex theoretical and empirical interdisciplinary foundation involving concepts related to cognitive, attachment, and social issues and owes debts to thinkers and investigators in anthropology, philosophy, psychology, and sociology.

The ideas and data culled from selected thinkers in laying the groundwork for the Program highlighted the differing and often interwoven roles in the child's intellectual development of optimum age periods for intervention, of sensory–motor development, of play, and, above all, of language exchanged within early family relationships. The Parent–Child Home Program's simple, nondidactic method and carefully selected goals are rooted in these sources, appropriately translated into procedures that provide both intrinsic and extrinsic motivation to the young child and the parent who form together the interacting dyad so crucial to the cognitive–conceptual development that must precede a child's literacy and academic competence.

Language and Cognitive–Conceptual Growth

Most fundamental to the creation of The Parent–Child Home Program was an understanding of the critical role in a toddler's intellectual development of parent–child exchange of language. Human beings' most distinctive attribute is their capacity for abstract conceptualization and for its symbolization through language. The child's conceptual development through the acquisition of language is the short-term goal of The Parent–Child Home Program.

The Parent–Child Home Program's concepts on language date back to Edward Sapir, the father of psycholinguistics. Sapir described language as a vocal expression of the human tendency to see reality symbolically, unique among animals, translating perceptions into a abstract system (Sapir, 1921). According to his theory of the origins of language, speech grew out of primitive vocalizations of the *abstract attitude* built into humans, sounds that summarized numerous concrete perceptual encounters between early man and the environment. It is conceivable, he speculated in one example, that people developed special grunts to summarize and symbolize the many characteristics of stones appropriate for chipping into tools.

Equally central to The Parent–Child Home Program's underpinnings are the writings of the philosopher Ernst Cassirer. Elaborating on Sapir's theory, his classic essay on symbolism (Cassirer, 1944) offered further evidence for the symbolic nature of language, ranging from conceptual differences between the Greek and Latin words for *moon* to the comprehension of the word *water* by the blind and deaf Helen Keller when she felt the pump's water splashing on her hands. He considered human beings unique among animals in our capacity for conceptual/symbolic thought, calling humankind the "animal symbolicum."

Neither Sapir nor Cassirer, however, stressed the role of social interaction as a prerequisite for the full development of language as emphasized by Sapir's Russian contemporary Lev Vygotsky (1897–1934) and by later psychologists Jerome Bruner and Irving Sigel.

Bruner, dean of American psychology, devised a valuable step-by-step framework for understanding the development of language symbolization in children (Bruner, Olver, & Greenfield, 1966). He divided a child's mental representation of the world and all it contains into three steps: the *enactive* (body charades used by the infant to indicate wishes—for comfort, for food, for being picked up—prevailing into the middle of the child's second year); the *iconic* (the predominance of mental images, which may persist among poets and primitives into adult life); and finally the *symbolic* stage.

At the symbolic stage, children who formerly learned and employed words solely as labels for immediate experience (only Fido, the dog they were petting, was *dog*) begin to use words to generalize the common attributes of many such experiences. Fidos of all shapes and sizes have similarities that may be summarized as a concept and symbolized by the word *dog*. The children are at last able to use words as verbal symbols of concepts. Bruner theorized that the child's growing skill in the symbolization of concepts by language probably depends on interaction with other people around him or her. The social psychologist Roger Brown called this interaction the original word game (Brown, 1958). Bruner commented that the original word game may become the human thinking game, a phrase that neatly encapsulates what may well be the most important underlying function of language: aiding people's ability to think, which may even overshadow its aid to human communication.

A similarly concise explanation was furnished by developmental psychologist Irving Sigel's *distancing hypothesis* (Sigel, 1964; Sigel, 1971; Sigel, Stinson, & Flaugher, 1991). Sigel suggested that young children must interact with others to learn the use of language to stand for increasingly distant referents (what the word refers to), to aid their intellectual development. The referents farthest from sight require the most abstract use of language. *Dog* can mean the dog actually with the child (no distance: a concrete label); dogs in general (dogs everywhere, a thousand miles away or in the next room, but distant from the child); or an abstract symbol that can be used to indicate a nasty person (a further step in symbolic abstraction), which can lead into a mounting hierarchy of similarly related symbols as the child matures.

The cognitive development theories of Bruner and Sigel are linked so closely to those of Lev Vygotsky as to make it possible to speak of their work as one combined theory of cognitive development dissecting the connections in children's intellectual development among language, conceptual thought, and social relationships. The ideas of these developmental psychologists had a profound influence on the creation of The Parent–Child Home Program, whose central concept is the promotion of conceptual thought by fostering conversation in the context of the toddler–parent relationship.

The power of social interaction, imitation, and love for facilitating learning and especially for children's linguistic development is a common thread in the work of all three thinkers. Physiological substrates of this power are now beginning to emerge, with the discovery of *mirror neurons* in nonhuman primates and similar mirroring systems in humans: When individual A observes actions (e.g., eating) or emotions (e.g., pain) in individual B, neurons fire in much the same brain areas for A as for B (Rizzolatti, Fadiga, Gallese, & Fogassi, 1996; Singer et al., 2004). If the same brain region that controls action also supports perception, it follows that imitation, which begins in the first weeks of life (Meltzoff & Moore, 1977), is primed to play a central role in early learning. This centrality validates The Parent–Child Home Program's emphasis on using a loving social context to enhance learning, and buttresses the Program's instructions to its Home Visitors: model, don't teach; show, don't tell.

Vygotsky touched on so many aspects of cognitive development in his short life that the philosopher Stephen Toulman dubbed him the Mozart of psychologists (Toulman, 1978). In the first extensive fragment of Vygotsky's work to appear (posthumously) in English, *Thought and Language* (Vygotsky, 1962), prefaced by Jerome Bruner, Vygotsky cited theory and some evidence for the efficacy of children's language as a verbal symbol system for abstracting and thus summarizing, as concepts, traits held in common among unlike experiences, as opposed to a toddler's compiling many concrete instances to convey a general concept. To convey both the brevity possible for these linguistic symbols and the need for the dialogue's subject to be of common interest, or at least known, to both members of the conversing dyad, he quoted a passage from *Anna Karenina* to illustrate that even the most basic of linguistic symbols—the letters of the alphabet—can communicate the most abstract concepts if two people have a shared core of interest. In Tolstoy's novel, the unspoken hope for love and marriage shared by two characters, Kitty and Levin, was conveyed by "CYLM?" ("Can you love me?") traced by Levin's finger on a table top and understood by Kitty. In The Parent–Child Home Program, books and toys are provided as the shared core of interest to both partners of the parent–child dyad.

After *Thought and Language*, which was immediately reflected in the theory and method of The Parent–Child Home Program, more of Vygotsky's essays appeared, in the United States as *Mind in Society* (Vygotsky, 1978), which emphasized the crucial role played by social interaction in the development of children's cognition; Vygotsky maintains that children's first utterances with peers or adults are for the purpose of communication, but that once mastered, those utterances become internalized and allow inner speech. He provides the even simpler example of a very young toddler pointing a finger, behavior that begins as a meaningless grasping motion. As people react to the gesture, the grasping movement takes on meaning and changes to the act of pointing, a gesture now representing an interpersonal connection between individuals. Vygotsky continues (p. 57): "Every function in the child's cognitive development appears *twice:* first, on the social level, and later, on the individual level; first, between people (interpsychological) and then inside the child (intrapsychological)."

According to Vygotsky, all the most basic cognitive functions (thought, language, and intellectual development) are formed within the context of social experience. Language is a crucial tool for determining how the child will learn to think because advanced modes of thought (i.e., concepts) are transmitted to the child by means of words. To Vygotsky, understanding the interrelations between thought and language is necessary for understanding the unfolding of intellectual development. Language is not merely an expression of the knowledge that the child has acquired; it is essential to the formation of thought itself.

For Vygotsky, thought and speech have different roots, thought being nonverbal and language being nonintellectual in their early stages. Their developmental lines are not parallel; they cross again and again. Yet, at a certain moment, when the child is approximately two, thought and speech meet. That is when thought becomes verbal and speech becomes rational. At first, a child seems to use language for superficial social interaction; but at around twenty-four months, language goes underground to become the foundation of the child's thinking. Once the child realizes that everything has a name, and lacks the name for a new object, he or she demands the name from parents or other adults. The early word-meanings that are acquired in this way become the embryos of concept formation.

In *Mind in Society*, Vygotsky's theory of the child's cognitive–conceptual development expands to include what he called the *zone of proximal development*: the difference between the child's capacity to solve problems on his or her own and the capacity to solve them with some assistance. It includes all the functions and activities that a child, as a learner, can perform only with the assistance of someone else. The adult who intervenes in this growth process for very young children should, in Vygotsky's view, be a beloved caretaker: generally, the child's parents, as the idea is interpreted in The Parent–Child Home Program.

Vygotsky's zone of proximal development has important applications in the Program. One is the idea that early human learning presupposes the presence of a specific social relationship (usually that between parent and child) and is part of a process by which children grow into the intellectual life of those around them. According to Vygotsky, an essential feature of learning is that it joins with a variety of internal developmental processes that can operate only when the young child is interacting with people in the environment. The idea of a zone of proximal development implies that the child's best learning is the learning that is slightly in advance of his or her current development. In the Program, the zone of proximal development is illustrated by the choice of increasingly complex books and toys presented in the home visits, when the child seems on the brink of more complex thought, as well as in more complex verbal interaction with the parent.

Play, which is the indispensable motivating feature that facilitates the inter-relationship of the main actors in Parent–Child Home Program home visits, also serves a vital role in the development of thought and language. "In play a child always behaves beyond his average age, above his daily behavior; in play, it is as though he were a head taller than himself. Play contains all developmental tendencies in a condensed form and is itself a major source of development" (Vygotsky, 1978, p. 102). This concept is echoed in pleas of University of Chicago psychologist Csikszentmihalyi for teachers to recognize the important role of intrinsic enjoyment in children's acquisition of literacy (e.g. Csikszentmihalyi, 1990).

Influence of Socioeconomic Status on Parent–Child Verbal Interaction

The exchange of language by meaningful others with a toddler is a prerequisite for the child to acquire the verbal symbols—words—for the conceptual thinking basic to intelligence, as Vygotsky emphasized. The young child's others are most likely to be immediate family members, especially his or her parents.

An essential component in the creation of The Parent–Child Home Program was the recognition of the profound effect on a child's family and on their interactions of influences related to the broader social system and its socioeconomic structure. In the American context, members of the lowest income strata are not only economically disadvantaged but, often, profoundly educationally disadvantaged. Recent twin studies have demonstrated that the cognitive disadvantage related to low socioeconomic status, however self-perpetuating it may be, is overwhelmingly related not to genetic factors but to environment (Turkheimer, Haley, Waldron, D'Onofrio, & Gottesman, 2003).

On the basis of theory and empirical research, it may be hypothesized that this educational disadvantage begins with low-income children's inadequate conceptual language foundation from their earliest toddler years, an inadequacy that might be prevented by an intervention to stimulate cognitive/conceptual verbal interaction between a toddler and emotionally close others: the child's parents or other primary caretakers. This comprehension of the influence of socioeconomic status, and the conjecture about the process by which it led to educational consequences, led to the 1965 creation of The Parent–Child Home Program (at the time, the Verbal Interaction Project/the Mother–Child Home Program), whose main mission was, and is, to prevent low-income children's educational disadvantage.

That 1965 hunch found interesting confirmation in the 1990's by a family observational study in the United States, Hart and Risley's systematic examination of the influence of socioeconomic status on children's early language and later school achievement. Those investigators first published their findings as a journal article (Hart & Risley, 1992) twenty-seven years after The Parent–Child Home Program had put into action an approach to prevent the educational disadvantage of economically disadvantaged children, based on an educated guess as to the influences of socioeconomic status on parent–child verbal interaction and educational accomplishment. Two subsequent books followed, expanding on different aspects of their subject (Hart & Risley, 1995; Hart & Risley, 1999).

The main purposes of the Hart and Risley study were to investigate the influence of social class on the number of words addressed by parents to their young children and to explore the association between the parents' language quantity on the toddler's later school achievement. The parents' words to the child and the child's to the parents, along with accompanying activities, were tape-recorded monthly in 1,318 one-hour sessions by trained observers who visited the forty-two subject families in their homes over two years, from the toddlers' age of ten months to when they reached age three. The families, all with both parents living in the home, fell into three socioeconomic status groups: six families receiving welfare aid, twenty-three working-class families with fathers earning an income near the national average through steady employment, and thirteen families headed by professionals earning a relatively high income. Nineteen of the forty-two families were African American. There proved to be marked quantitative differences among the three socioeconomic status groups: the average number of words spoken per hour in each group was 2,153 from professional parents, 1,251 from working-class parents, and 620 from welfare parents. As the authors point out, over the course of three years these differences add up to millions fewer words heard by a toddler whose family is on welfare.

These socioeconomic status-based differences in the numbers of parental words addressed to their small children were confirmed when word characteristics were compared, such as the variety of verb tenses and the number of distinct nouns and modifiers spoken. The differences were also reflected in the school achievement tests in third grade taken by the twenty-nine children who had remained in the area (69 percent of the original forty-two families), whose results ranged as expected from below average for children in welfare families to far above it for those in professional families. The authors' 1995 book contained details of their data and their conclusions about the implications for early educational interventions, whereas their 1999 book focused on the content of the parent–child verbal interaction, giving many examples of the speech addressed to children and of the children's own speech.

The seminal research that laid the groundwork for Hart and Risley's study, as well as for many previous examinations of how socioeconomic status-embedded parent–child interaction can influence children's linguistic and intellectual growth, was that of the British sociologist Basil Bernstein (Bernstein, 1961, 1965), who observed the types of language interaction that predominated in families of differing socioeconomic status. The contrasting cognitive development of middle-class and working-class children in Bernstein's early studies suggested that conceptually limited patterns of language in the families of British working-class children were linked to parallel limitations in the children's intellectual development.

Both in Bernstein's British studies and in American anthropological studies preceding Hart and Risley's work (e.g., Heath, 1983; Taylor, 1983) the language of parents in low-income families—whether British, European American, or African American—tended to be restricted, or *telegraphic.* A low-income mother says to her young child going out to play on a wintry day: "Your jacket, put it on!" A middle-income mother is more likely to say in an expanded way: "You need your jacket to keep warm on such a cold day; go find it and put it on!" If the child protests, the low-income mother may combine her restricted style of language with a reminder of her dominant status as a parent: "Do it because I told you!" This is likely to be her parental attitude into the child's later years too.

The differing language and interpersonal styles of these two mothers illustrate the way that the structure of the social system (e.g., the family's socioeconomic status) and the structure of the family (e.g., parental tendency to be authoritarian or egalitarian) shape communication and language of parents to children (Baumrind, 1967). In its turn, the extent to which family language is limited or expanded and the parental attitudes are authoritarian or egalitarian forms the thinking and influences the cognitive development of the child.

The influence of the family-mediated social structure on language and thought has also been demonstrated, although perhaps in less detail than in Hart and Risley's investigation, in a large body of empirical, statistically supported research that appeared between 1957 and the 1990s (Bee, Van Egeren, Streissguth, Numan, & Leckie, 1969; Belsky, 1985; Birns & Golden, 1972; Bradley & Caldwell, 1984; Bradley & Caldwell, 1976; Deutsch, 1965; Farran & Ramey, 1980; Findlay & McGuire, 1957; Goldberg, 1963; Golden & Birns, 1968; Gottfried, Fleming, & Gottfried, 1998; Gottfried & Brown, 1986; Kamii & Radin, 1967; McKinley, 1964; Phillips, Brooks-Gunn, Duncan, Klebanov, & Crane, 1998; Schacter, 1979; Siller, 1957).

As did Bernstein in Britain, a few American sociolinguistic researchers used anthropological methods through a combination of interviews and observations of actual family language and other interactions. Denny Taylor (Taylor, 1983) was a participant-observer of family literacy in six middle-class, two-parent, European American families within a fifty-mile radius of New York City, all with more than one child in the family. Four of the six families contained children three years old or younger. Shirley Heath (Heath, 1983) gave a more expanded account of family language, writing, and other interactions in three quite different social settings, all three in Gateway, a mill town of 50,000 people in the Piedmont region of South Carolina. She observed, recorded (by unspecified means), and compared family language, writing, and other interactions. Two families lived in working-class neighborhoods of Gateway. One she called Trackton, whose inhabitants were mainly rural rooted and African American. The people living in the other working-class neighborhood, Roadville, were European American and had been mainly mill employed for generations. She then recorded similar observations among *mainstreamers*, middle-class African American and European American families who made up the majority of the population of Gateway. Child rearing, oral linguistic competence, and written literacy in all homes were the family interactions that she especially observed and recorded. She thus included a broad scope of observations in families and then linked the consistent cultural differences she found among the family interactions to their children's widely differing preparation for school experiences, starting with preschool, with middle-class children's performance superior to that of children from working-class families. The differing family–cultural languages, attitudes, and values, including those with regard to literacy and education, affected not only the children's future school careers but also the attitudes of their teachers. Few quantitative data were provided in the reports of these anthropological studies, in the tradition of the anthropologists of the last century who studied the Samoans or the Hopi.

American psychologists Robert Hess and Virginia Shipman similarly systematically tested socioeconomic status influence on parents' language with their young children, using the technique of involving the mothers of African American middle-class and poor children in game-like problem solving. They found support in their resulting data for a trenchant conclusion: "The structure of the social system, and the structure of the family, shape communication and language; and language shapes thought and cognitive styles of problem solving" (Hess & Shipman, 1965, p. 870).

Social–Emotional Setting for Early Cognitive Intervention

Whatever constrictions on concept-building verbal interaction might be observed in low-income families, research into socioeconomic influence on language and thought has detected no significant differences in the amount of warmth and affection between parents and children among high-income, middle-income, and low-income families. The tendency of low-income parents to use restricted language and authoritarian attitudes with their young children, rather than person-to-person attitudes and expanded language, is a difference in interpersonal style, not in affection.

Parental love exists regardless of social class. Strong attachment between parent and child develops through the parents' everyday caregiving to the child from infancy through childhood. Whatever the parents' verbal and behavioral patterns may be, that attachment is crucially important to mental health, according to studies of the mental–emotional impact of family relationships on children and adults (Ainsworth, 1963, 1973; Bowlby, 1951; Sroufe & Sampson, 2000). But as Bernstein, Hess, Shipman, and others cited in the preceding section have shown, parents' use of expanded language and a person-to-person approach is more productive for their young child's intellectual and perhaps social–emotional development than restricted language and an authoritarian attitude.

When parents make conscious attempts to add intellectual stimulation to their relationships with their young children, the children consistently show cognitive benefits. Irwin reported years ago that mothers' reading stories to their young children resulted in toddlers' improved speech development (Irwin, 1960). Many other studies have supported these findings: (Bus, van Ijzendoorn, & Pellegrini, 1995; Freeberg & Payne, 1967; Gordon, 1969; Karnes, Teska, Hodgins, & Badger, 1970; Laosa, 1983; Levenstein, 1970; Moore, 1968; Norman-Jackson, 1982; Schaefer, 1969), especially for the kind of *dialogic reading* that has been encouraged by The Parent–Child Home Program since long before the term was coined by Grover Whitehurst (1994). Recent evidence from families participating in Early Head Start suggests that children's cognitive gains from book reading do not depend on the mother's education or her own cognitive abilities (Raikes et al., 2006).

Social–Emotional Roots of Cognitive Development

The close connection between early learning and parent–child attachment was delineated by the developmental psychologist Urie Bronfenbrenner in a well-documented review of the effects of early deprivation on humans and animals (Bronfenbrenner, 1968) and has received ample empirical verification since (Bus & van Ijzendoorn, 1988). Earl Schaefer (1970), a University of North Carolina psychologist, suggested that early home education within the context of mutual affection between toddler and parent be given a name connoting its primeval nature: *Ur-education.* Implicit in this idea is

Schaefer's belief that the parent–child emotional relationship forms a vital base for the parent and toddler's verbal–cognitive exchange. In short, intellectual stimulation can best benefit the pre-preschool child when it is embedded in the attachment between the parent and child within the familiar setting of their own home. The interaction and associated activities are deeply satisfying to both, so strong is the motivation provided by what Bronfenbrenner was fond of describing as the irrational and unconditional affect called love. These concepts are integrated into the basic theory of The Parent–Child Home Program.

Parent–child interaction can be reinforced by *props*, Harvard Professor Courtney Cazden's label for objects such as books and toys that encourage conversation and provide extrinsic motivation for intergenerational conversation (Cazden, 1970, 1972). Developmental psycholinguists now speak of the props a little differently by broadening their attention beyond children's linguistic development to its context, including the physical objects in the environment where that development occurs (e.g., Bates, 1976).

Gordon Wells, former director of the University of Bristol's Centre for the Study of Language and Communication and of its longitudinal family language study, has pointed out the practical necessity for a context that interests both parent and child, if the child is to make maximum use of the parent as teacher: "It is difficult to over-emphasize the importance of strategies that increase the child's motivation to converse. Those [parents] whose children were most successful were not concerned to give systematic linguistic instruction but rather to ensure that conversations with their children were mutually rewarding" (Wells, 1985, p. 415).

By the time Wells was writing, The Parent–Child Home Program had already posited and incorporated into its method the necessity of offering a framework mutually rewarding to both parent and child, and that increases the child's motivation to converse within a context of interesting immediacy: play with toys and books. Program theorists also theorized that toys that offer problem-solving challenges can exploit children's intrinsic motivation to master the environment through play, resulting in a gain of self-confidence and in what psychologist Robert White (1963) called *effectance*, the feeling of competence that comes from having an effect on the environment and persons in it.

The creation of The Parent–Child Home Program acted on the insights of various investigators suggesting that the best time to begin taking advantage of verbal interaction between parent and child, within the context of their mutual attachment and of their mutual interest in play materials, is when the child is two years old (operationalized in the Program as sixteen to thirty months). It is generally agreed that during the second half of the child's second year, the capability for conceptual–symbolic thought develops, that thought and speech meet (Bruner, 1964; Piaget, 1952; Vygotsky, 1962), although Hebb argued that the learning of *percepts* and simple associations may begin even earlier (Hebb, 1949), mirroring Piaget's sensory-motor stage of *preoperational thought.*

Program visits thus are timed to begin as the infant is emerging into the period of what Cassirer called *reflective intelligence,* signaled and reinforced by his or her rapid language development (Bates, 1976; Levenstein, 1983; Nelson, 1973; Vygotsky, 1978). This period at about age two (cf. Bayley, 1965; Hebb, 1949; Vygotsky, 1978) coincides with the child's heightened attachment to his or her parents; with a greatly increased curiosity about the environment; with a growing skill at using *symbolic representation* (Bruner et al., 1966); with a developing sophistication in using arms and legs and hands; in short, with an explosion of rapidly developing skills and feelings.

Age two is also the time for optimum development of a parent–child network. By the age of about four years, children have already incorporated the main benefits of this revolution and become eager for experiences away from mother, father, and the family home—although not too far away. If parents have not been able to take full advantage of the period before the child reaches four to develop a strongly and mutually supportive parent–child network, a downward turn in cognitive development can be expected to follow (cf. Golden & Birns, 1968). Poverty or the structure of the social system (Hess & Shipman, 1965) takes its toll by constricting parents from helping their children avoid the resulting lag, which can gravely handicap their future academic achievement in the absence of help from a theory-based early intervention such as The Parent–Child Home Program.

Educator Benjamin Bloom's (1964) summary of the evidence, which included some of the studies cited in this chapter, indicated overwhelmingly that intervention to prevent this cognitive slowdown should occur between the ages of two and four years, which thus emerges as the optimal and critical period to prepare children for school learning. Even earlier, tremendous impetus had been given to the field of early childhood intervention research by psychologist J. McVicker Hunt's (1961) careful review of the role of environment in the growth of intellectual functioning, which promised new hope for preventing the personal tragedy and social problems so often posed by educational disadvantage. The implications were summarized by Meredith Phillips thirty years later: "Our results imply that we could eliminate at least half, and probably more, of the black–white test score gap at the end of the twelfth grade by eliminating the differences that exist before children enter first grade" (Phillips, Crouse, & Ralph, 1998, p. 275).

Partly as a result of the writings of Hunt and Bloom, federal and private funding was made available as part of President Johnson's War on Poverty in the 1960s and early 1970s for studying duplications in preschool classrooms of what developmental psychologist Bettye Caldwell (1967, p. 18) called the optimal learning environment for young children: "The child in his own home, within the context of a warm and nurturant relationship with his mother or a reasonable facsimile thereof."

Based on the theoretical and empirical data available in the 1960's, Parent–Child Home Program theorists concluded that the ideal location for carrying out an intervention program to prevent educational disadvantage should be not a duplicate or a re-creation of a child's home, but the home itself. Yet that was only part of the story. It seemed equally clear that small children's first *interveners* in their home should be not professional teachers but people who care deeply and enduringly about them: their parents. The program was therefore created on the theory that the intervention should take advantage of the attachment-oriented interaction already existing between parent and child, and that it should give the low-income parent the option of being the child's primary intervention agent. As Meredith Phillips (1998) points out, parenting practices have a powerful impact on children's cognitive development, so changing them may be to the key to improving cognitive skills.

The power of the concepts behind The Parent–Child Home Program is such that even a much more primitive forerunner of the Program was said to be efficacious, although the reports are somewhat anecdotal. In an Iowa state residence for the mentally retarded during the 1930s, sharp-eyed staff noticed that some of the young children who had been placed there seemed to blossom when taken under the affectionate wing of older inmates. They therefore randomized toddler inmates into intervention and control groups, the intervention consisting simply in encouraging young adult inmates and staff personnel to play and chat with the selected toddlers and letting staff take them home on visits. At the end of the intervention, the intervention toddlers were described as having lost their apparent retardation and to have become adoptable, and they are said to have grown up to be nonretarded, well-functioning adults (Skeels, 1966; Skeels & Dye, 1939).

Putting Theory into Practice: The Parent–Child Home Program

In creating The Parent–Child Home Program, its founders made a careful attempt to work out a delicate balance between enough structure to turn theory into operational reality and the preservation of the parent's autonomy and bonding with the child. Empirically backed theories of conceptual and more generally cognitive development, rooted in the development and use of language, were joined by lessons drawn from Sigel's original distancing program, an inquiry-based instructional approach to enhance the development of representational understanding, the awareness of the equivalence of different symbol systems (Sigel, 1964; Sigel et al., 1991). Language was targeted during the critical language-learning years, and toys, play, and a playful spirit were embraced as tools knowing that children at this age learn best through play.

The goals and procedures of The Parent–Child Home Program, leading up to its curriculum of dyadic verbal interaction, appear to be echoed in a brief paragraph from Urie Bronfenbrenner's 1974 review of early childhood education research: "In the early years of life, the psychological development of the child is enhanced through his involvement in progressively more complex, enduring patterns of reciprocal, contingent interaction with persons with whom he has established a mutual and enduring attachment" (Bronfenbrenner, 1974, p. 26).

Bronfenbrenner's sentence, which could serve as a synopsis for most of this chapter, can be translated into specific features of The Parent–Child Home Program:

- The early years of life are from sixteen months to four years of age.
- The psychological development of the child is enhanced by verbal interaction centering around program books and toys.
- The books, toys, and verbal interaction curriculum are progressively more complex as the child matures in the Program.
- Parent and child are encouraged toward patterns of reciprocal, contingent interaction: responses of parent to child and of child to parent.
- The persons with whom the child establishes a mutual and enduring relationship are, of course, his or her parents.

Bronfenbrenner's recipe for early intervention did not focus on the educator nor on his or her own psychological development. In fact, none of the theoretical or empirical studies so far discussed had much to say about the feelings, thoughts, and psychosocial functioning of the parent, in spite of the parent's crucial involvement as the child's first teacher, much less regarding the effect on the parent of the reciprocal, contingent interaction with the child. Yet one of the basic assumptions of The Parent–Child Home Program was White's concept of effectance. The Program conjectures that parents can derive feelings of effectance from seeing the impact they have on their child's development, both in the week-to-week Program procedures and long-term as they see their child's school accomplishments. Strengthening a low-income parent's self-confidence could be a goal as important as preventing his or her child's educational disadvantage. And this goal, in and of itself, has an impact on the child's future when it leads to more education, better employment, and better housing for the parent.

Out of the reciprocal interactions within the dyad can evolve a productive parent–child network that may be supportive for the parent as well as for the child. In actual Program operation, evidence of such a parent–child network at work has been provided by the demonstration of statistical correlations between positive parental behaviors and children's later school outcomes (Levenstein, 1986) (see Chapter 5 and Chapter 11).

The theoretical foundations described in this chapter may deepen our concern for the individual and societal costs of the self-perpetuating characteristics of American poverty, but they also hint at a way out: the possibility that The Parent–Child Home Program can set into motion a virtuous circle, for and by the parent–child dyad, with potential to improve the outlook for the future of both partners.

5.

How Effective Is
The Parent–Child
Home Program?

Individual Results: The Carters
and the Willards

In the first chapter of this book, we met Ms. Carter and Ms. Willard, the mothers of Jo-Jo Carter and Carol Willard. They were quite different from each other although both were receiving welfare assistance. Ms. Carter, the only one of the two to have graduated from high school, showed greater self-confidence, initiative, and interactive behavior with her child in home sessions, and a more positive attitude toward The Parent–Child Home Program at the start than did Ms. Willard. Ms. Carter was interested, even eager, to join the Program and participated actively in it from the beginning. Toward the Program's end, she began spontaneously to mention going on to college and becoming self-supporting. She was typical of the parents whom the staff had begun to call *Strivers*.

Ms. Willard was slower in her decision to join the Program, was silent and unsure in the first year's home sessions, and at first seemed to give her children little attention and to be oblivious to the clutter of her apartment. She progressed slowly in her Program participation, but she did progress; she was a typical *Hesitater*. Parents like her are far more numerous in The Parent–Child Home Program than the Strivers. In fact, the Program is directed especially to assisting Hesitater parents to assure future literacy and school achievement for their toddlers. Is it effective in doing so?

Effects of the Program on Jo-Jo Carter and Carol Willard

Jo-Jo and Carol had had two years of fun in The Parent–Child Home Program, and each had acquired a durable library of good books and long-lasting toys. But of course the Program's goal went beyond giving them happy times and enjoyable gifts; it was to provide a way to climb up from poverty through becoming ready to take advantage of public schooling, to achieve literacy and all academic skills. Did it accomplish this goal?

To begin to answer this question, we can track the progress of Jo-Jo and Carol from age two to the middle of second grade, examining six years of objective quantitative information from the children's performance on standardized tests with national norms. One type consisted of cognitive tests predictive of later school achievement ("intelligence tests"). Just before entering the Program, Jo-Jo scored 91 on an IQ test, and Carol scored 93, far enough below the national average to predict educational problems in their school years. After their two Parent–Child Home Program years, at age four, the children's scores were 105 and 109, predicting at least normal academic achievement. Cognitive tests were repeated every year after that until the middle of second grade at age seven when standardized reading and arithmetic tests were added; both children attained average or above-average scores on every test: reading, arithmetic, and cognitive. Both thus appeared to be well launched on a school career of literacy and normal academic progress. The Parent–Child Home Program had apparently built a foundation, through conversational partnership with their parents, for their cognitive development and school success.

Effects of the Program on Ms. Carter and Ms. Willard

During the six-year period of tracking the two children's progress, systematic Parent–Child Home Program records were also kept on their mothers by Home Visitors, observing the amount of parent-initiated parent–child conversation in every home session and systematically measuring various aspects of child and parent behavior, using validated instruments created by the Program for this purpose: the Child's Behavior Traits (CBT) for the child, and the Parent and Child Together, (PACT) for the parent (see Appendix). In addition, mother and child were videotaped, when they completed the intervention and one year later, during ten-minute structured play sessions with a toy train and a shapes puzzle. The number of times the mother attempted to converse with her child on these videos were tallied on another Parent–Child Home Program-created instrument, the Maternal Interactive Behavior (MIB) (see Appendix), by raters who did not know whether the dyad had been in the Program.

Jo-Jo Carter's mother demonstrated marked early and sustained increases in her verbal interaction with Jo-Jo in home sessions (rated by the Home Visitor after each home session on a scale running from 0 to 15 percent, to 91 to 100 percent of the time). Ms. Carter kept all but one of her home session appointments, and by the fourth session, she had begun to take the initiative, depending less and less on her Home Visitor for guidance.

Given the one-page curriculum guide sheets for each session, without any urging to use them, Ms. Carter apparently perused them for tips on how to interact with Jo-Jo. The videotapes of her play sessions with Jo-Jo showed that she had learned, according to the ratings of her verbal interaction, to be a sensitive, responsive teacher-playmate for her own child. She encouraged his questions and mutual verbal give and take. On the MIB scale, just after completing the Program, she interacted verbally with Jo-Jo 260 times in ten minutes, higher than the average of 228 for mothers in her cohort. She had a similarly high MIB score in a second video play session one year later. Ms. Carter's plan to start college reflected emergence from the mild depression she had seemed to be suffering at the beginning. This may or may not have been the result of her Program participation; the cause of a gain of this sort is hard to identify. However, there appeared to be a link between the confidence she displayed more and more during the home sessions and her taking this step to climbing out of her low-income status.

Ms. Willard, a Hesitater like most Parent–Child Home Program parent-participants, showed excellent cooperation with the Program from the first by her high rate of kept appointments, sixty-five of a possible sixty-nine home sessions. Despite this evidence of motivation to cooperate with an intervention intended to help Carol's future school performance, she seemed to ignore the curriculum guide sheets that were given to her as they had been to Ms. Carter. Her verbal progress in the Program was also less striking than that of Ms. Carter's. Indeed, from Ms. Willard's shy and almost wordless ten-minute videotaped play session with Carol immediately after the end of the intervention, it seemed that she had learned little about conceptual parent–child dialogue from The Parent–Child Home Program; the number of verbal interactions she had with Carol during that ten-minute videoed session was only 104, far below the program average of 228 or Ms. Carter's score of 260. Yet her home session verbal interaction with Carol increased from an average of 16 percent in Year One to 45 percent during Year Two of the Program, suggesting she was probably conversing more with her daughter when the video camera was not turned on. Further, improvement in her childcare and household management noted in her home session records suggested positive mental health effects of the Program, which did not appear in the quantitative data but which may have contributed to Carol Willard's good postprogram cognitive and academic test results.

Comment on the Carters and the Willards

Both of these children demonstrated significant literacy-relevant gains both immediately after completing the Program at about age four and also near the end of second grade, at about age seven. Those outcomes suggest that both Jo-Jo and Carol benefited from the intervention, cognitively and educationally, even though one had a Hesitater mother and the other a Striver mother. For these children, it seems, The Parent–Child Home Program was on its way to accomplishing its goal of preventing poverty-related educational disadvantage.

The positive effects on their mothers that may have played a role have been observed time and time again in the notes of midyear interviews with parent-participants, conducted and recorded by Coordinators:

> "Elissa's physical activity is now seen as meaningful rather than just misbehavior."
> "Father talks about 'do's' more than 'don'ts.' "
> "She said she has been able to relax more since the beginning of the program and see the fun side."
> "We had a 'Royal Tour' of the new apartment, which she had mobilized herself to find after first Program year."

Home Visitors' notes of home sessions supported the Coordinators' impressions:

> "Mr. Deacon carefully counted the pegs and named their colors and explained the game, keeping it very simple. He seemed to enjoy it."
> "Again Ms. Rodriguez's reading of the book was great—I really had very little to add." "Mother had been teaching the girls how to set the table with their toy dishes. They had been eating real food out of the dishes."
> "Both Brian and his mother were eagerly waiting for me. They both were friendly and volunteered many comments."

Group Effects: Testing Parent–Child Home Program Efficacy

Carol's and Jo-Jo's outcomes suggest that this nondidactic program can have positive effects on children's performance on cognitive tests and in the classroom, even if their mother's verbal interaction with them seems to remain modest. But can we be sure The Parent–Child Home Program can take the credit? Although they may seem typical to Program staff, the good individual outcomes of these mothers and their children are still only case studies—useful as illustrations, but insufficient to demonstrate the efficacy of the Program in achieving its goals. Every would-be social or educational program must address this issue when it obtains seemingly encouraging results. In any individual case, too many chance factors might have been the actual cause of the child's success, rather than the program that was taking place at the same time. What is necessary is to examine the outcomes in groups of program participants, rather than in individuals, to rule out extraneous factors as causes of the effect.

What this boils down to is the question: Will hard research data confirm that the program can really work for most of its intended population? Staff and participant enthusiasm is not enough; only systematic experimental evaluation, including comparison with control groups, can give an objective estimate of program effects. It is this kind of evaluation, not glowing testimonials, that provides valid evidence for the success of an intervention, the evidence needed before a program is approved for widespread use. Since its inception, The Parent–Child Home Program has insisted on seeking objective, statistically tested evidence of program effectiveness by measuring and comparing the progress of whole groups of Program and nonprogram mothers and children in addition to looking at the anecdotal experience of individual families like the Willards and Carters.

There have been dozens of papers describing systematic research studies of The Parent–Child Home Program among low-income populations. Most have been published in professional journals or as book chapters; a few are unpublished reports to funding sources and accrediting agencies. They have variously examined the intervention's short-term and long-term effects on child-participants, its effects on the interaction between parents and their children, and Program characteristics associated with better outcomes. The resulting body of evaluation research and scrutiny, which began to be published and presented at professional conferences a mere three years after the Program began as a pilot project, generally supports the positive effects of The Parent–Child Home Program on child-participants and parent-participants. For children, significant benefits were found in enhanced cognitive development immediately after completing the Program and in school achievement as long as twenty years later, whereas parents have been shown to increase their positive verbal, concept-building interaction with their children. The following section of this chapter summarizes this research. In Chapter 11, writings about The Parent–Child Home Program are listed chronologically and described individually in more detail.

A Summary of Parent–Child Home Program Research

Cognitive Outcomes

Early research efforts of The Parent–Child Home Program team concentrated on asking whether children's cognitive abilities were improved by the intervention. In the very first study, a small group of disadvantaged toddlers living in Freeport, a poverty pocket in wealthy Nassau County in New York, was offered a preliminary four-month version of the Program. Their scores on a verbal intelligence test turned out to rise by 17 points immediately afterward, whereas those of demographically similar control children dropped slightly (Levenstein & Sunley, 1968).

After these encouraging before-and-after results held up among several dozen more children, The Parent–Child Home Program team initiated a controlled experiment by tossing a penny to assign three local housing projects to different treatment plans: Parents of two year olds would be offered a developmental evaluation service alone, evaluation plus weekly gifts not meant to stimulate conversation, or evaluation plus The Parent–Child Home Program—initially lasting one year, in later groups lasting two years. Mothers were told that they would be informed of the results of their children's developmental evaluations and that their toddlers would be referred to community resources for help with any problems the testing revealed.

Between 1967 and 1972, invitations were issued to the parents of all the two year olds in each housing project. All Parent–Child Home Program and control families were socioeconomically at risk, with parental education no greater than high school and occupations no higher than semiskilled. In these studies, IQ scores of Parent–Child Home Program children were similar to controls' on pretest but significantly higher at the end of the Program (104.8 and 95.6, respectively), and they maintained their cognitive edge and normal IQ scores long after their home visits had ended, as late as age ten (101.9 vs. 93.6) (Lazar & Darlington, 1982; Madden, Levenstein, & Levenstein, 1976). The superiority of Program graduates held up when baseline characteristics such as baseline IQ and mother's education were taken into account in Irving Lazar and Richard Darlington's multivariate analyses for the Consortium for Longitudinal Studies (Lazar & Darlington,1982).

Bolstered by these data, The Parent–Child Home Program moved forward with disseminating its model to secondary sites away from the original one in Freeport. IQ gains of 10–16 points, similar to those in the model program, were documented in the first of these replications (Levenstein, 1976; Levenstein, Kochman, & Roth, 1973), in a replication site twenty years later (DeVito & Karon, 1990), and in the studies of an outside researcher who compared The Parent–Child Home Program with mothers' discussion groups and with a toys-only control group (Slaughter, 1983).

This body of IQ research has some limitations. The studies showing gains compare post–Parent-Child Home Program scores either with the same children's scores before the intervention, with demographically similar but nonrandomized comparison groups, or with control groups randomized according to location (*quasiexperimental*). These approaches are methodologically weaker than studies where each individual is randomly assigned to receive the intervention or not. Two full-scale attempts have been made to examine the effect of The Parent–Child Home Program on IQ using such a subject-randomized design, but both ran into methodological difficulties related to subject recruitment, resulting in pools of potential participants who came predominantly from ambitious and well-motivated families; both Parent–Child Home Program and control children in these studies proved to have above-average IQs on follow-up despite some initial gains favoring the Program (Madden, O'Hara, & Levenstein, 1984; Scarr & McCartney, 1988). Subtle problems of this sort hound the research literature in social interventions in general, such that seemingly minor variations in methods of recruiting experimental subjects can lead to important biases variously for or against the detection of program effects. Chapter 6 examines these issues in depth.

School-Readiness Outcomes

The goal of The Parent–Child Home Program is to eliminate educational disadvantage. If in the 1960s and 1970s studies of early intervention programs focused on children's scores on IQ tests, this was largely in the hopes that these scores would predict children's ability to cope with actual school tasks. As soon as program graduates began to reach school age, the measurement of academic performance took center stage, and here The Parent–Child Home Program shines: From kindergarten through high school, its graduates have consistently bested the performance of at-risk control or comparison groups and have often closed the achievement gap with middle-class youngsters.

Studies over three decades suggest that when they first begin school, disadvantaged children who have participated in The Parent–Child Home Program do not labor under the handicaps that would be predicted. In a study of South Carolina first graders, the scores of program graduates were as good as the statewide average for all students on the Cognitive Skills Assessment Battery, overcoming the achievement gaps that in comparison groups derived from being poor or African American (Levenstein, Levenstein, & Oliver, 2002). Parent–Child Home Program kindergartners in Pittsfield, Massachusetts, have recently been found to outscore not only graduates of other pre-preschool programs but also district youngsters as a whole on the Daberon Screening for School Readiness (Shiminski, 2005a); thirty years earlier, at-risk participants at the same replication site had approximated national academic norms in kindergarten (Bradshaw-McNulty & Delaney, 1979). In Buffalo, New York, Parent–Child Home Program graduates are reported to have higher Peabody Picture Vocabulary Test scores than their kindergarten classmates have, surpassing national norms (Alexander, 2005). And on Long Island, New York, LaRue Allen found that Parent–Child Home Program graduates from disadvantaged and predominantly immigrant families performed as well as their less disadvantaged and mainly native English-speaking classmates on most achievement measures in kindergarten (Allen, Sethi, & Astuto, 2007).

School readiness includes more than just cognitive achievement. Measures of social–emotional development or competence rated blind by teachers a year or two after the end of the intervention have also proved higher in Parent–Child Home Program children than in location-randomized controls (Levenstein, 1979b) and comparable to nondisadvantaged peers (Allen et al., 2007). These scales measure traits such as enjoyment of new assignments and toleration of frustration, which seem likely to predict future ability to deal with scholastic tasks.

Scholastic Outcomes

Parent–Child Home Program graduates succeed in elementary school. In the original model Parent–Child Home Program, participant-children did better in third grade on the Wide Range Achievement Test than did disadvantaged controls despite their equally limited preprogram cognitive scores, meeting national norms for both reading and arithmetic (Levenstein, O'Hara, & Madden, 1983; Madden et al., 1976). For reading, although not for arithmetic, these gains held up in fifth grade, and statistical adjustment techniques showed that attrition, maternal education, and baseline IQ did not account for the effects (Lazar & Darlington, 1982).

The Parent–Child Home Program replication site in Pittsfield, Massachusetts, has followed children still further through their school careers, tracking their achievement scores on the California Achievement Test. Disadvantaged children who had received the Program achieved reading and arithmetic scores that matched national norms in elementary school and middle school, outscoring other Chapter I (Title I) students on all tests and matching the performance of nondisadvantaged Pittsfield students on some (Bradshaw-McNulty & Delaney, 1979; DeVito & Karon, 1984, 1990).

When the first Pittsfield Parent–Child Home Program participants reached high school graduation age, fewer than 30 percent had dropped out—much better than expected—and 72 percent of The Parent–Child Home Program high school graduates went on to higher education (DeVito & Karon, 1990). A decade later the dropout rate of Program cohorts at the same site was reported in a juried journal to be even lower (15.7 percent for children who had completed the full two-year Parent–Child Home Program, 22.2 percent in *intention-to-treat* analysis of all youngsters who had had at least one home visit); the graduation rate of 84.1 percent for graduates of the full Program was significantly higher than the rate of a small group of subject-randomized controls and comparable to nationwide rates for nondis- advantaged, middle-income students (Levenstein, Levenstein, Shiminski, & Stolzberg, 1998). Even children who had received only one year of The Par- ent–Child Home Program had an edge over randomized controls. Still higher high school graduation rates have been claimed in internal reports from Program sites (Greene & Hallinger, 1989; Shiminski, 2005b).

The high school dropout rates in the Pittsfield article can also be com- pared with those of analogous groups in the same area who had had no contact with the Program. In 2006 (when the Pittsfield all-city dropout rate was 24.1 percent, no better than it had been ten years earlier), it was re- ported that 41.8 percent of all low-income students who began high school in Pittsfield dropped out before the time they should have graduated (an- other 12.2 percent were still in school the next fall) (Massachusetts Depart- ment of Education, 2006), with a definition of *low income* similar to criteria for participation in The Parent–Child Home Program. Exposure to the intervention thus appears to have halved the dropout rate for disadvan- taged youngsters.

Parent–Child Home Program participants are less likely to require placement in special education, less likely to be left back, and less likely to require further Title I services than comparison groups are (Darlington, Royce, Snipper, Murray, & Lazar 1980; DeVito & Karon, 1990; Royce, Darlington, & Murray, 1983; Springs, 1990), and teachers' ratings of Pro- gram students' social–emotional competence are age-normal at least through third grade (Levenstein et al., 1983). In a recent study of mainly immigrant families who had gone through the Program, most measures of parental participation in their education matched those of the children's classmates (Allen et al., 2007).

Parent–Child Home Program participants thus perform comparably throughout their schooling to national normative groups, surpassing disad- vantaged comparison and control groups, and there is good evidence that a disadvantaged child's chance of graduating from high school is improved by the Program to that of a middle-class student. Exposure to The Parent–Child Home Program therefore seems to fulfill its chief goal of closing the academic gap associated with socioeconomic disadvantage.

Family Outcomes

The Parent–Child Home Program uses the intrinsic love and playfulness of the parent–child relationship to catalyze the task of learning. Program creators theorized that strengthening the bond between parent and child is a way to lend power and durability to improvements in children's cognitive abilities beginning in the crucial early years of language. If the universal power of parental love can be exploited as a springboard for the child's cognitive as well as emotional growth, longer lasting results should be produced, among particularly vulnerable groups, than by working with the child alone or with the parent alone.

There is general agreement that parenting patterns contribute to the difficulties that disadvantaged children have in school. Some observers question, however, whether parents, and especially parents of low socioeconomic status, are capable of improving those patterns to a meaningful and lasting degree on the basis of even the best meant interventions. Studies of Parent–Child Home Program effects on the parent–child bond are therefore of broad interest.

The first studies that looked at The Parent–Child Home Program's impact on parent–child interactions used an in-house instrument, the CBT, to rate children's social and behavioral competencies. We have already seen the age-normal CBT scores of graduates of the model program when they reached first and third grades; much more recently, at three replication sites, CBT scores evaluated in parent–child play sessions have been seen to improve markedly over the course of the intervention (Business Partnership for Early Learning, 2007; Organizational Research Services, 2006; Rafoth & Knickelbein, 2005).

A limitation to simple before-and-after studies is that CBT scores might improve simply because of the child's growing older. An attempt to overcome this problem was to study positive interactions between mothers and their children using instead the PACT, which is less likely to be affected by maturation. On this scale, the families' Home Visitors rate parents' responsiveness, affection, consistency, and communication in relating to the child during home sessions, and the child's responsiveness. Striking postprogram increases on PACT scores have been shown in several settings over three decades, including in Pennsylvania (Rafoth & Knickelbein, 2005), in Seattle (Organizational Research Services, 2006), and among native Canadian Indians (McLaren, 1988).

The PACT has some limitations as a research tool: Home Visitor observers may be biased, and there is no way to rate control dyads (who have no home sessions). To overcome these problems, Parent–Child Home Program researchers devised a method for independent observers to score parent–child interactions on videotapes of dyadic play, the MIB.

On the MIB, the mean frequency of desirable kinds of speech are strikingly greater in Parent–Child Home Program graduates than they are in subject-randomized controls, with effects persisting at least two years after the intervention has ended (Madden et al., 1984). Program parents are more likely to reply to the child, verbalize their actions, or ask for information and are less likely to ignore a child's verbal or nonverbal request for attention (Madden et al., 1984). In a recent study from a replication site, using a similar system for rating videotaped play sessions, both verbal and nonverbal interactions were found to increase dramatically after The Parent–Child Home Program (Rafoth & Knickelbein, 2005).

Behavior-rating scales such as the PACT and the MIB have also allowed Parent–Child Home Program researchers to explore the workings of the parent–child network in more detail, especially with regard to the possibility of setting enduring changes into motion by an intervention program limited to early childhood.

First it was shown that interpersonal behaviors in the parent–child dyad, measured by the PACT, are strongly correlated with children's performance on the CBT (Levenstein, 1979b); verbal behaviors were the PACT items that most strongly predicted high CBT scores for their children. A limitation of this study was that a single observer (the family's Home Visitor) rated both scales.

A second series of parent–child network studies looked at PACT scores of Parent–Child Home Program participants in relation to outcomes at later time points. Parents' verbal responsiveness during the second Program year was found to predict not only children's IQ scores at the end of the intervention but also their skills on the CBT (independence, task orientation, emotional stability, and positive cognitive orientation) two years later (Levenstein, 1979b; Levenstein, 1986).

In the final set of studies, positive interactions on the MIB were shown to predict children's first grade cognitive skills, school performance, and emotional stability (Levenstein, 1986; Levenstein & O'Hara, 1983), demonstrating a long-lasting effect on the behavior of both parents and children and suggesting specific factors in their interaction that can have an impact not only on academic outcomes but also on the realm of social competence emphasized by Edward Zigler (Zigler, Haskins, & Lyon, 2004).

The specific parental behaviors that most predicted good outcomes included one that was strongly and positively influenced by The Parent–Child Home Program ("mother replies to child's vocalizations") and another that was relatively unaffected by the Program ("mother smiles or makes other positive gesture"). Correlations between MIB items such as "gives label information" or "gives color information" and children's school age competence were generally statistically nonsignificant or even negative, suggesting that it is counterproductive to bombard a child with a relentless barrage of information (Levenstein, 1986). When this became clear, during the early 1980s, The Parent–Child Home Program curriculum was modified to decrease the emphasis on labeling behaviors and avoid possible harmful effects of didacticism.

These studies indicate that The Parent–Child Home Program can improve parenting skills in such a way as to bolster the parent–child network, which nourishes the child's intellectual and social–emotional growth while it creates a foundation for later school achievement. They also issue a sharp warning that the early childhood learning that plays its part in weaving this supportive network functions best in a family climate of nondidactic spontaneity and joy.

Further indirect evidence that The Parent–Child Home Program fosters a cognitively nurturing parent–child bond comes from the finding that younger siblings of Program participants, when it came time for them to enter the Program themselves, scored eight points higher on their preprogram IQ tests than their big brothers and sisters had scored at the same age (Madden et al., 1976)—contrary to the usual superiority of first-born children (e.g., Sutton-Smith & Rosenberg, 1970). That pretest differential of eight points was the kind of result one would expect if parents transfer the skills they have learned during the intervention to the baby next in line, indicating that the Program succeeds in converting them to more effective parenting methods.

Parent–Child Home Program theorists were convinced from the outset that the intervention would be beneficial for parents as well as for children. Staff members often voice their impression that the Program improves parents' mental health (improved self-image, less depression), their motivation for literacy skills, and their involvement in their child's education for many years after the home visits have ended. These observations remain largely anecdotal (e.g., Gilinsky, 1981; Richman, 2004), but there are some research data hinting that participation in The Parent–Child Home Program can lead to improvements in the home environment (Rafoth & Knickelbein, 2005), can enhance parents' communication with teachers (Allen et al., 2007) and their self-confidence in relating to their children (Ginandes & Roth, 1973), and can stimulate parents to return to school and job training (Gomby, 2000).

Defining the Target Population

Since the goal of The Parent–Child Home Program is to close the achievement gap between poor and middle-class children, Program site Coordinators generally recruit participants who are considered to be at risk based on income, occupation, and education. But such formal criteria include a wide range of families. Research has suggested that it is relatively easy for special programs such as Title I federal aid to school systems to help the educational progress of moderately disadvantaged children, but that a hard core of those most at risk, whose families are the most difficult to involve, risk remaining untouched (Carter, 1994; Cross & Independent Review Panel, 1999). The Parent–Child Home Program has tried to go straight for that hard core, putting its focus on the most disadvantaged families of all, the ones its staff came to call Hesitaters. Instead of putting out advertising and waiting for families to sign up, which selects for Striver parents who are more strongly motivated or have demonstrated a better capacity to follow through, Program replication sites are encouraged to actively seek out the neediest families with small children. Special attention is paid to subject retention, a bane of most parenting programs, knowing that those same Hesitater families would be the most likely to drop out before gaining the Program's full benefit. Hesitaters and Strivers alike are capable of furnishing the family supports that, along with children's enhanced cognitive–conceptual growth, mediate the positive effects of The Parent–Child Home Program (cf. Reynolds, Suh-Ruu, & Topitzes, 2004).

Whereas Hesitaters are The Parent–Child Home Program's special target, the Program can also be of help to Striver parents, who are reasonably likely to do well if they are merely pointed in the right direction. But it is clear that The Parent–Child Home Program is not useful for all toddlers. In particular, several studies have shown that the intervention is likely to have little to offer children of relatively well-educated parents, who enter the Program with normal cognitive ability. In one subject-randomized experiment where more than a third of parents had attended college and two-thirds had a middle-class or upper-class income (Scarr & McCartney, 1988), children's IQ scores were normal (and similar between intervention and control children) both before and after the experiment. Confirming the relative uselessness of The Parent–Child Home Program for cognitively normal children, the Program's greatest impact on high school graduation was found to be among children with baseline IQs lower than 90 (Levenstein et al., 1998). Similarly, the Infant Health and Development Program (whose curriculum was adapted from the Abecedarian Project) and the Nurse–Family Partnership have achieved their strongest results in the families most at risk (Olds et al., 1999; Ramey, Campbell, & Ramey, 1999).

If it is wasteful to offer The Parent–Child Home Program to middle-class families and cognitively normal toddlers, research has also shown that offering it to children with severe developmental delay is futile (Levenstein et al., 2002). It seems that the best target group for the Program in terms of initial cognitive functioning is children who are not severely retarded but who have initial cognitive functioning below the normal range, with the goal of boosting that functioning over a threshold to levels that make school learning feasible.

Another aspect of the target population that has been examined by Parent–Child Home Program researchers is the lower age limit for children to benefit from the Program. A *downward extension* was pilot tested during the 1970s in children ten to fourteen months old. Program staff members reported that home visits were welcomed warmly by mothers, but that delivery was often disrupted by the babies' physical needs. These difficulties, in the absence of reliable outcome data and given some perplexity about offering a language-based program to children who are barely verbal, speak against enrolling children under sixteen months in the standard Parent–Child Home Program (O'Hara & Levenstein, 1979). However, piloting a modified version of the Program for the younger children continues to be a goal of the organization because the expertise that it has developed in effective home visiting, modeling positive parenting, and outreach to families could be valuable to families with younger children as well.

Reaching and Retaining Target Families

Parent–Child Home Program research has documented remarkable success in meeting its recruitment and retention goals, meaning that the Program continues to serve families with multiple strikes against them.

In 2005, 68 percent of participating families nationwide had annual incomes of less than $20,000 (in 35 percent of families, less than $10,000), 65 percent were single-parent families, and 30 percent were non–native-English speakers (The Parent–Child Home Program Inc., 2005). Most replication sites have maintained the original focus on recruiting Hesitater families, and the descriptive language used by researchers at various locations suggests that this policy has been successful. Participating children are variously described as being from "the most needy families" enrolled in the local WIC (Women, Infants and Children) Program (Becky Knickelbein, 2006, personal communication); as showing "a lack of mother–child contact or mother–child bonding . . . or a lack of awareness of the needs of an infant or a toddler" (Gilinsky, 1981, p. WC11); as "exceptionally high risk toddlers . . . referred to the PCHP by welfare social workers or by teachers of older siblings" (Levenstein et al., 2002, p. 337); as referred by family service agencies because of child neglect (McLaren, 1988); or as having a "particularly grim" educational prognosis (DeVito & Karon, 1990, p. 14). This active recruitment reaches clients more disadvantaged than the formal entry criteria of income, education, and job status would require. One of the strengths of The Parent–Child Home Program has been its ability to win the participation and the loyalty of the families who are usually the hardest for early intervention programs to reach and to hold on to—and the most in need of their help. Of note, the 40 percent dropout rate among the Pittsfield follow-up study's small group of randomized controls (Levenstein et al., 1998) is similar to the 41.8 percent among low-income students in the same school district (Massachusetts Department of Education, 2006), providing further reassurance that the families who agree to participate in The Parent–Child Home Program are likely to be representative of the local low-income population.

The vast majority of parents who are offered The Parent–Child Home Program agree to try it: 85 percent in five years of the original location-randomized model Parent–Child Home Program and 100 percent at locations as diverse as a New England mill town (Levenstein et al., 1998), a semirural South Carolina county (Levenstein et al., 2002), and the island of Bermuda (Scarr & McCartney, 1988).

Once they have enrolled, few families choose to leave The Parent–Child Home Program prematurely. In the original model program, only about 15 percent of dyads dropped out before the end of the first Program year and 25 percent over the full two years, usually because of moving away; 85 percent of home visit appointments were kept (Levenstein et al., 1983). At replication sites, from 85 percent to over 96 percent of families who remain in the area have been reported to complete the entire two-year intervention (Gomby, 2003b; Levenstein et al., 2002; Shiminski, 2005a). Researchers have examined the roles played by Home Visitor characteristics (Allen, Astuto, & Sethi, 2003) and by extended-family attitudes (Higgins, Krupa, & Williams, 2006) in retaining participant-families.

Parent–Child Home Program rates of acceptance and retention compare very favorably with the usual experience of home visiting programs (Gomby, 2003a; Rapoport, O'Brien-Strain, & The SPHERE Institute, 2001) and have remained high despite the intensified demands on single mothers' time brought by welfare reform. This shows once again that the Program has succeeded in making itself attractive to Hesitater parents. It may be speculated that this success stems from the Program's careful training of Home Visitors, its cultural sensitivity, a ludic spirit that makes the intervention fun for both child and parent, and—why not?—even with its offer of tangible gifts of toys and books (Guyll, Spoth, & Redmond, 2003).

When polled, virtually all Parent–Child Home Program parents endorse the Program enthusiastically. Of course, the words of "happy customers" should be taken with a grain of salt. More convincingly, parents have voted with their feet by enrolling in the Program, staying with it, and keeping their home session appointments. Those are the endorsements that really count—a home-based intervention program can succeed only if its target population opens the doors to their homes.

Replication Issues

After only a few years at its model setting, The Parent–Child Home Program began to experiment with expansion into secondary locations. Mindful that many apparently well-designed interventions work well in their original settings but fall down when an attempt is made to transfer them from the hothouse settings of research projects into real world locations, special care was taken to hone Parent–Child Home Program replication techniques to a fine science (see Chapter 7) and to monitor replications' outcomes from the onset. Results from several trial replication sites were studied carefully to confirm the exportability of the Program before the Verbal Interaction Project opened the door—always with safeguards for program standards—to training replication staff nation-wide (Levenstein et al., 1973).

The forty-year life of The Parent–Child Home Program has seen countless changes in American society; in the overall economic, political, legal, and social context of poverty (Chapter 2); and in the ethnic and linguistic makeup of our poor. It is therefore important to ascertain the durability of its intervention model and its ability to adjust to change.

The Parent–Child Home Program has been used in a great variety of settings and populations, and the populations studied in its published outcome research have variously been white, African American, Native North American, Hispanic, and African/Asian immigrant. Several research studies have been performed in the welfare reform era, and their key findings in terms of retention rates (Gomby, 2003b), effects on parental behavior (Business Partnership for Early Learning, 2007; Organizational Research Services, 2006; Rafoth & Knickelbein, 2005), parental enthusiasm (Allen et al., 2003; Rafoth & Knickelbein, 2005), and early academic outcomes (Alexander, 2005; Allen et al., 2007; Shiminski, 2005a) have been as good as those from previous periods. In practice, welfare reform has dictated fewer changes in Program practice than might have been expected. Expanded early evening and weekend hours is one example, and extension of the intervention through the summer months in some replications (instead of limiting it to the school year) may make it easier for working parents to get their fair share of home visits. It would seem from these data that The Parent–Child Home Program model has proved remarkably robust, evolving as necessary to fit the evolving societal/political context without losing its core characteristics or its efficacy.

Although even one year of The Parent–Child Home Program can be beneficial, two Program years have proven to be better for consolidating long-term gains (Levenstein, 1977; Levenstein et al., 1998; Madden et al., 1976). At the

Pittsfield replication site, an excellent population for examining this issue because none of the study families withdrew voluntarily from the intervention after reaching the one-year mark, high school graduation rates were significantly higher in children who had had two years rather than one year of the Program (82.9 percent vs. 60.7 percent) (Levenstein et al., 1998).

Data from Parent–Child Home Program research can also address the ongoing debate as to whether it is better for home visiting interventions to be carried out exclusively by professionals such as the Nurse–Family Partnership nurses (Olds & Kitzman, 1993; Olds et al., 2002), or whether well-trained paraprofessional Home Visitors may do just as well or even bring special advantages when delivering The Parent–Child Home Program model. The first Parent–Child Home Program Home Visitors were social workers, but by 1968 the transition had been made to a combination of unpaid volunteers, usually with four years of college but often without relevant professional training, and paid paraprofessionals, many of whom are former parent-participants, few with any education beyond high school. Research data showing Program efficacy have been obtained using chiefly nonprofessionals.

In research at the model program, no difference in outcomes was found between high school- and college-graduate Home Visitors (Levenstein, 1977). A recent study involving Parent–Child Home Program sites in several states found, similarly, that the educational level of the Home Visitors had no substantial effect on results; the relation between other Home Visitor characteristics and outcome variables varied from site to site, with former parent-participants and Home Visitors from the community showing particular success in connecting families to local resources (Allen et al., 2003). The similar efficacy of professional and paraprofessional Home Visitors in The Parent–Child Home Program may derive from several elements: Training is highly systematized and continuing (the initial training workshop is followed by weekly staff conferences and ongoing individual supervision); the role of the Home Visitor is strongly and explicitly structured rather than open ended; and the home sessions themselves have a strictly delineated structure, with all issues beyond the Program curriculum referred to the site Coordinator for resolution.[1] Differences in the age of child-participants in the kind of needs expected to be addressed by the Home Visitors are particularly relevant when comparing the experience of The Parent–Child Home Program with that of the Nurse–Family Partnership. The efficacy of nonprofessionals as Home Visitors has a meaningful impact on the cost, and hence the practicality, of replications.

---

1. Another reason paraprofessional Home Visitors perform so well in The Parent-Child Home Program may be that the two years of experience many of them have had as previous recipients of the Program corresponds to a psychoanalyst's training analysis.—SL

The Parent–Child Home Program and the Broader Scientific Community

Evaluations of The Parent–Child Home Program

The Parent–Child Home Program caught the eye of experts in the field early on. J. McVicker Hunt called it a "laudable example of program development" (Hunt, 1975, p. 303), and Urie Bronfenbrenner singled out for praise the Program's emphasis on the parent–child dyad rather than the child and the use of the parent as the direct agent of intervention, surmising that the depth of parental involvement would make the intervention particularly efficient and particularly long-lasting (Bronfenbrenner, 1974).

Four years after The Parent–Child Home Program began, a study conducted for the U.S. Office (now Department) of Education included it among the country's top ten compensatory education programs on the basis of demonstrated cognitive benefits, one of only two early childhood programs meeting its criteria (Wargo, Campeau, & Tallmadge, 1971). The Parent–Child Home Program was considered highly effective by the writers of most major reviews during the 1970s (Anastasi, 1979; Goodson & Hess, 1975) and was singled out by the National Institute of Mental Health as one of the five best programs in the country for fostering mental health of children in families (National Institute of Mental Health, 1978). When the Joint Dissemination Review Panel of the U.S. Department of Education included The Parent–Child Home Program in the National Diffusion Network's annual catalogue, *Educational Programs That Work* (from 1979 through its last edition in 1995), it judged that the Program had produced reliable short-term and long-term effects on children and their parents that could be expected to be generalizable to low-income populations in general. In the early 1980s, the final reports of the Consortium for Longitudinal Studies concluded that The Parent–Child Home Program had developed a reliable dissemination method as well as showing effects on parental behavior and children's school achievement, noting that the IQ scores of graduates of the model program not only were superior to those of controls but met national norms (Datta, 1983; Lazar & Darlington, 1982; Royce et al., 1983).

During the next period, The Parent–Child Home Program continued to draw favorable mentions (Barnett, 1995; Kamerman & Kahn, 1995) despite a gap of several years in the appearance of new research data and despite the limited number of replications, and in 1992 two program replications were singled out for the U.S. Department of Education's National Recognition Awards to exemplary programs to prevent school disadvantage. But it is particularly since 1997, with the rapid expansion of the Program's base of replications and the publication of new research evidence of effectiveness in the era of welfare reform, that The Parent–Child Home Program has drawn new attention from experts in preschool intervention (Manoil, Bardzell, & Indiana Education Policy Center, 1999; Segall, 2004). It is currently recommended as an exemplary research-based program by the Council of Chief State School Officers (Stebbins, 2006); is considered one of "the home visiting programs whose goals are most closely aligned with the school readiness focus of the California Children and Families Commission" (Gomby, 2003a, p. 13); is on the list of science-based programs approved for funding through the Safe and Drug-Free Schools and Communities Act Program (New York State Department of Education, 2005); has been endorsed by the Children's Trust Fund of Washington/Washington Council for Prevention of Child Abuse and Neglect as one of the top three evidence-based home visiting programs (Children's Trust Fund of Washington/Washington Council for Prevention of Child Abuse and Neglect, 2007); and was gauged a "wise investment" by the comptroller of the City of New York (Hevesi, 2001, p. 76). Characteristics particularly appreciated by recent evaluators have been The Parent–Child Home Program's cultural sensitivity, its emphasis on family strengths, and its ability to win and maintain the participation and even the enthusiasm of extremely disadvantaged parents who have few other resources.

The central Parent–Child Home Program organization has received grants from numerous private and public funders over the years. In the early period, the Carnegie Corporation provided many years of funding to the model program on the basis of what it called "careful, painstaking research" (Russell, 1979, p. 1), and more recent funders have praised its ability to give its graduates "the same potential for success as a child from a middle class family" (Rauch Foundation, 2003) and have proposed, "At four, they're ready for preschool. At twenty-four, they're ready for med school" (Business Partnership for Early Learning, 2007).

Parent–Child Home Program replication sites have received support from sources ranging from Even Start and Early Head Start grants to First Five grants in California, TANF funds, local school district funds, and foundation and corporate donations. In justifying their grant support, the Mailman Foundation refers to the "extraordinary results" of "this play-based, culturally appropriate, family-support program" (A.L. Mailman Family Foundation, 2006). The United Way of Long Island lauded its pioneering, strengths-based model (United Way of Long Island's Success By 6 initiative, 2005). The Massachusetts Department of Early Education and Care says it "has embraced the nationally recognized Parent Child Home Program (PCHP) model as an effective and innovative literacy and parenting program" (Massachusetts Department of Early Education and Care, 2007). And Pennsylvania's Department of Public Welfare calls it "a proven family literacy and parenting program" (Pennsylvania Department of Public Welfare, 2006), with one state representative commenting, "Pennsylvania can't afford NOT to provide funding for this high-quality program" (Richman, 2004).

The Parent–Child Home Program's intensive schedule, its timing at a critical period of childhood, its openness to and acceptance of cultural variation, its partnership with parents, its strategy of building on preexisting family strengths, its attention to maintaining quality standards in home visitor training and in replication, and its approach based on modeling rather than didactic instruction to maximize the chance that the cognitive curriculum of home sessions will spread to other moments in the child's daily life exemplify principles considered fundamental for high-quality early intervention programs (Gomby, 2005; Ramey & Ramey, 1992).

Home Visiting Yes, Home Visiting No?

Most of the programs developed to prevent poverty-linked school problems have been based in daycare centers or schools, but a few have been conducted in the homes of at-risk children. The Parent–Child Home Program pioneered this approach and remains convinced that verbal interaction with parental figures at home offers pre-preschool young children a golden opportunity to develop basic concepts necessary for cognitive growth, exploiting parents' privileged access and position to give them a crucial role in disadvantaged children's acquisition of literacy and school readiness.

Home-based interventions have been experiencing a boom in the United States, spurred by the publication of durable benefits from home visiting programs such as the Nurse–Family Partnership (Kitzman et al., 1997; Olds et al., 1998; Olds et al., 2004); Parents as Teachers (Pfannenstiel, Seitz, & Zigler, 2002; Zigler, Pfannenstiel, & Seitz, 2007, in press); The Parent–Child Home Program (Levenstein et al., 2002; Levenstein et al., 1998); and from mixed center-based and home-based programs such as the Perry Preschool (Schweinhart, Barnes, & Weikart, 1993; Schweinhart et al., 2005) and the Brookline Early Education Project—which in a recent report emphasized the importance of the home visiting component in its success (Palfrey et al., 2005). More than 400,000 families are being reached by home visiting programs every year, between Even Start, Early Head Start, Home Instruction for Parents of Preschool Youngsters, Parents as Teachers, Healthy Families America, the Nurse–Family Partnership, The Parent–Child Home Program, and others (Gomby, 2005). If the Education Begins at Home Act introduced in 2005 by Senator Christopher S. Bond (R-MO) and Representative Danny Davis (D-IL) becomes law (in 2007 the act was reintroduced in the House and Senate with additional sponsorship by Senator Clinton (D-NY) and by Representative Platts (R-PA)), this trend will increase enormously.

Enthusiasm has probably also spilled over from reports of long-range academic and behavioral benefits from purely center-based early-childhood intervention programs such as the Abecedarian Project (Campbell, Ramey, Pungello, Sparling, & Miller-Johnson, 2002) and the Chicago Child–Parent Centers (Reynolds et al., 2007). Most expert observers, such as Jeanne Brooks-Gunn and others, now agree that early intervention programs can help give disadvantaged children a better start in life (Brooks-Gunn, 2003; Haskins & Rouse, 2005; Nelson, Westhues, & MacLeod, 2003) and that at least some "of the benefits that accrue to children seem to operate through changes in parenting behavior" (Brooks-Gunn & Markman, 2005, p. 151).

But the very popularity of home visiting has intensified critical scrutiny, and the approach is controversial in some quarters. Although many reviews and meta-analyses have reported short-term and long-term benefits (Kendrick et al., 2000; Nelson et al., 2003; Rapoport et al., 2001; Sweet & Appelbaum, 2004), and although there is evidence that the home visiting approach may maximize the participation of the very disadvantaged in family interventions (de Souza, Sardessai, Joshi, Joshi, & Hughes, 2006), positive reports have been counterbalanced, in the minds of some, by mixed findings from some individual programs (Baker, Piotrkowski, & Brooks-Gunn, 1999; St. Pierre & Layzer, 1999; Wagner, Spiker, Hernandez, Song, & Gerlach-Downie, 2001) and by several reviews and meta-analyses from authorities including Jean Layzer and David Olds, suggesting that positive effects may be at best modest (Elkan et al., 2000; Layzer, Goodson, Bernstein, Price, & Abt Associates Inc., 2001; Olds & Kitzman, 1993).

A particularly sobering report on home visiting was published by the Packard Foundation in *The Future of Children* in 1999, a mere four years after its own enthusiastic review of the same subject. After examining six programs (which did not include The Parent–Child Home Program), Deanna Gomby and her colleagues concluded that overall they had shown relatively weak benefits in health outcomes, child development and behavior, child maltreatment, and maternal life course (Gomby, Culross, & Behrman, 1999). This report's clarion call stimulated the formation of the Home Visit Forum, a consortium that includes The Parent–Child Home Program along with five other nationally based programs (Early Head Start, Healthy Families America, Home Instruction for Parents of Preschool Youngsters, the Nurse–Family Partnership, and Parents as Teachers) and is funded in part by the Packard Foundation itself. Its mission is to increase delivery efficiency, develop practice benchmarks, and better define the role of home visitation, thereby addressing some of the 1999 report's perplexities (Home Visit Forum, 2006). The participation of The Parent–Child Home Program in the Home Visit Forum can be seen as part of a long history of collaboration with other compensatory programs to optimize outcomes and process research, beginning in the 1970s with the famed Consortium for Longitudinal Studies.

One expert observer, Deanna Gomby, recently expressed her opinion that the modest results often reported by home visiting programs are largely related to service quality and would likely be improved if the programs were more intensive, the home visitors better trained, and more attention paid to the content of the home visiting curriculum (Gomby, 2005)—all areas in which The Parent–Child Home Program is particularly strong.

Among the subjects of debate that are addressed by data from The Parent–Child Home Program is the issue of how the effects of early intervention may be mediated. The Program has been shown to increase parents' responsiveness to their toddlers, and the degree of that responsiveness has in turn been shown to affect children's cognitive performance, task and cognitive orientation, and social–emotional stability while children are still in the intervention and several years later (Levenstein, 1986; Rafoth & Knickelbein, 2005). Proponents of home visiting can also point to the Program as evidence for the lasting *emergent literacy* benefits of parents reading to toddlers (Bus & van Ijzendoorn, 1988; Raikes et al., 2006; Whitehurst & Lonigan, 1998; Whitehurst et al., 1999)

Goodwill is not enough to have children succeed in school, much less to eliminate poverty, whether our interventions are home-based or center-based. Some enthusiasts may be tempted to believe that the mere act of sending a well-intentioned visitor into a home will bring benefits. Experience shows that, on the contrary, this risks not only failure and waste of resources but also potential harm to recipients (Frasure-Smith et al., 1997). Home visiting programs demand particular vigilance in carefully defining the role of the home visitor and in maintaining standards of supervision and delivery (see Chapter 7 and Chapter 8). It might be concluded, conservatively, that the potential of parenting programs for contributing to antipoverty interventions in the welfare-reform era, whether alone or in combination with other elements, remains to be properly delineated and that guidelines and standards for home visiting are as yet imperfectly defined; The Parent–Child Home Program, one of the current home visiting programs with the strongest evidence for success, remains an active participant in these tasks.

Conclusions

The title of this chapter asks whether The Parent–Child Home Program is effective. We have summarized the highly suggestive body of evidence that has been gathered from 1965 to 2007 and have seen time and again that the Program has been reported to improve children's performance on cognitive tests, academic achievement, and high school graduation rates while achieving 85 percent to 100 percent initial acceptance rates among highly at-risk families and 75 percent to 96 percent rates of completing the entire two-year intervention.

Such long-lasting positive effects are not unheard of from interventions very early in life (Campbell et al., 2002; Garces, Thomas, & Currie, 2002; Olds et al., 1997; Olds et al., 1998; Reynolds et al., 2007; Schweinhart et al., 2005). In the case of The Parent–Child Home Program, several elements of its approach make long-term results particularly plausible. One is reflected in Bronfenbrenner's speculation that what he calls the momentum of the system could ensure enough continuity of parental verbal interaction into the child's future to support the child's academic progress long after the parents had terminated their connection with the Program (Bronfenbrenner, 1974). Another key element is the choice to intervene during a critical period when the young child is just emerging into the verbally symbolic mode necessary for intellectual development. Yet another factor driving durable positive outcomes is the demonstrated ability of the Program—by virtue of its respectful approach, its ludic spirit, and its light touch—to win the participation and the enthusiasm of even profoundly resourceless parents.

The Parent–Child Home Program research base continues to expand. Some investigative lines might be especially interesting to follow, particularly in the context of prospectively designed subject-randomized trials:

1. Evaluation of the mechanisms behind lasting Program effects (cf. Campbell, Pungello, Miller-Johnson, Burchinal, & Ramey, 2001; Pfannenstiel et al., 2002; Reynolds et al., 2004; Zigler et al., in press). Bronfenbrenner's hypothesis regarding parents' continued positive verbal interaction could be empirically tested by periodically gathering verbal interaction data on former program dyads for correlation with children's academic performance. Other verifiable mechanisms might include increased reading to the child, enrollment in preschool, parents showing more warmth and empathy toward the child, children showing interest in schoolwork (willingness to work on homework, etc.), parents' involvement with school, children participating in chores within the family, and some form of *inoculation* by the two-year intervention.

2. Formal investigation of Program effects on parents' lives (education, work, home, health, depression, self-esteem) and on child abuse/neglect.

3. Examination of nonacademic child outcomes such as criminal and antisocial behavior (Garces et al., 2002; Olds et al., 1998; Schweinhart et al., 1993).

4. Comparison of effects of the Program on parent and child in different ethnic, linguistic, and cultural groups and at different sites.

Consistent with the Parent–Child Home Program founding principle of ongoing scrutiny of its results and its method, individual Program sites are encouraged to gather systematic outcome data by administering assessments of children and parents or by videotaping, whether or not they have immediate plans to examine these data in a formal manner. Beyond this routine data collection, current ongoing research projects (several of which extend previous published studies) include investigations of recruitment, engagement, and retention under the auspices of the Home Visit Forum; a subject-randomized study of the school readiness and later performance of a largely Latino population of Parent–Child Home Program participants in Philadelphia; an outcomes and process evaluation of the Program at a cluster of sites in Seattle; a Brooklyn, New York, study of the impact of the Program on reducing the risks of abuse and neglect by strengthening protective factors; and longitudinal studies by the Massachusetts Department of Education, by the Pennsylvania Department of Public Welfare, and by a South Carolina school district tracking the performance of Parent–Child Home Program graduates throughout their schooling. Funding is being sought for a multi-site, subject-randomized study of the impact of The Parent–Child Home Program on Latino families. The Program's National Advisory Council of experts in various fields relevant to its mission, which had been inactive for several years, is currently being revitalized in part to promote high-quality research.

So how effective is The Parent–Child Home Program? Very. How far can it take its participants? It can start them off well on their road through elementary school, high school, college, and beyond, increasing the odds that the Program graduate will be able to accomplish the academic or job training it takes to emerge out of poverty into the life he or she chooses. The research base and record of implementation of The Parent–Child Home Program have imperfections but also considerable strengths. At the same time that we continue to encourage substantial investment in good research to document the Program's benefits and to identify ways to make it ever more effective and efficient, we can confidently disseminate the model as one of the best existing hopes for successful intervention that bridges the achievement gap for disadvantaged families. In 1999, when Dr. John Silber, then chair of the Massachusetts State Board of Education, asked lawmakers to think about adding money for Parent–Child Home Program replications to the state budget, he contrasted the short-term investment necessary for the Program with the potential costs of school failure by referring to the local state prison (Fitzgerald, 1999): "You can fund twenty-five kids in this program for one prisoner in Walpole."

6.

Methodological Issues in Intervention Research

Lessons from The Parent–Child
Home Program Experience

The Parent–Child Home Program has a strong record of research showing its benefits. We have summarized these studies in Chapter 5 and will present each of them in more detail in Chapter 11. But in the process of conducting subject-randomized experimental evaluations of Program effects, researchers have encountered a variety of difficulties. Since this experience is important for The Parent–Child Home Program and may bring lessons valuable for other researchers in the field, it is worth examining in some detail.

Experimental Intervention Research and Volunteerism

The gold standard for evaluating interventions is the true experimental design: Researchers divide a pool of subjects into intervention and nonintervention (control) groups, offer the intervention only to the former, and then statistically compare the outcomes of the two groups on well-validated measures of hypothesized intervention effects.

Two generally accepted criteria underlie this kind of research: First, the pool of subjects must have the main characteristics of the population intended to receive the intervention and must thus be a representative sample of that population. Second, the pool of subjects must be randomly assigned to intervention or control groups. This maximizes the likelihood that intervention and control subjects will be alike in all relevant ways and ensures that any differences between the groups are not systematic but are due to chance.

These two criteria apply to all kinds of trials. The chief thesis of this chapter is that in the special case of social or educational programs such as early childhood interventions it can be particularly difficult to achieve the first criterion, thus biasing research outcomes. The reason is that the simple act of volunteering to participate in a research study can select for subjects who, although sharing many characteristics of the target population, actually are unrepresentative of that population in important ways.

Rosenthal and Rosnow performed now-classic studies of people who volunteered to be subjects for various experiments (Rosenthal, 1965; Rosenthal & Rosnow, 1975). They concluded that sample bias was an inevitable scourge because volunteers for human research (as opposed to nonvolunteer subjects such as college students fulfilling class requirements) tend to be more intellectually alert, better educated, more willing to risk the unusual, and better motivated than nonvolunteers—and more likely to value and desire favorable evaluation by the researchers. Later work (e.g., Marcus & Schütz, 2005; Padilla-Walker, Zamboanga, Thompson, & Schmersal, 2005; van Heuvelen et al., 2005) has generally confirmed those ideas.

Most experiments on human beings use volunteers as their subjects, and self-selection of atypical individuals can at times pose a serious threat to the validity and the generalizability of their findings. When the intervention is aimed at young children, it is not the primary subjects but their parents or guardians who must be asked to volunteer for randomization into intervention or control groups. This means that the incentive for volunteering must lie within the adult. The likelihood that parent-volunteers will have the classic Rosenthal characteristics, with resulting sample bias, can cause special problems for experimental tests of an intervention such as The Parent–Child Home Program whose main ingredient—explained in simple terms to parents when they are recruited—is dyadic interaction involving the parent equally with the child in their two-person social system.

In a dramatic example of these effects, self-selection of parents and thus of their preschoolers resulted in sample bias that distorted the 1972 national early childhood norms of a widely used cognitive test, the Stanford-Binet Intelligence Scale. When the 1963 standards were renormed in 1972, the two-to-five-year-old preschoolers who were tested for this updating either were brought to the testing center by their parents or were selected by virtue of being in private nursery schools whose tuition was beyond the means of low-income parents. This produced a normative group capable of performing better on the IQ tests than the public school children who had been tested in 1963, without parental consent, to determine the earlier norms for their age levels. For example, the average test performance of the

1972 preschoolers, although placed arbitrarily at an IQ level of 100 (average) on the 1972 norms, would have been rated at 110 (high average) if judged by the previous 1963 norms.

Columbia Professor Robert Thorndike, the director of the 1972 norming, suggested one explanation for the preschoolers' IQ superiority: "There may be a tendency for parents of young children not in school to be less willing to permit a child to be tested if the child has not appeared to be an advanced or competent youngster, and for this reason there may be a tendency to get somewhat upgraded samples of preschool children. No clear evidence of this is available, but we do have some impression that in the initial sampling there was more loss of very young children from the designed sample than was the case of children of school age" (Thorndike, 1977, p. 201). In other words, parents who were proud of their preschoolers may have been more willing and motivated to allow their children to be tested or to bring them to the testing center.

The difference of ten points between old and new norms is not trivial and has had practical consequences: With the 1972 super-norms, based on the scores of children brighter than most preschoolers, young children's preschool Stanford-Binet IQs may seem to be low when the children are really performing adequately.

Experimental Research Evaluations of The Parent–Child Home Program

The implications of Thorndike's experience and of Rosenthal's observations are invaluable for understanding the significance and the limitations of four studies that have attempted to determine the effect of The Parent–Child Home Program on children using a true experimental research design. One of them found clear-cut evidence of Program efficacy, but the others had equivocal results. Careful examination of the possible contribution of methodological flaws to this discrepancy in these studies, integrated by further examples from the literature, can bring new insight to an important threat to methodological integrity: subject bias, a ghost that haunts experimental studies of parent–toddler interventions in at-risk populations.

Experimental Study 1: High School Graduation in Pittsfield[1]

This subject-randomized study found that among 123 young adults who had been eligible for The Parent–Child Home Program as toddlers, those

---

1. Levenstein, P., Levenstein, S., Shiminski, J. A., and Stolzberg, J. E. (1998). Long-term impact of a verbal interaction program for at-risk toddlers: An exploratory study of high school outcomes in a replication of the Mother–Child Home Program. *Journal of Applied Developmental Psychology, 19,* 267–285.

who had completed at least one year of the intervention were significantly less likely than nonprogram controls to drop out of high school, and the graduation rate for graduates of the full two-year Program matched the nationwide rate for middle-income students. These results held up in an intention-to-treat statistical analysis that included all youngsters who enrolled in the Program no matter how few home sessions they received.

The randomized control group for this study was created serendipitously. A group of mothers of at-risk two year olds had originally accepted The Parent–Child Home Program but had to be informed before the intervention began that they would be excluded because of a sudden reduction in available funds. When the funding was just as suddenly but only partially restored, the problem of which families to include again was solved in a fair way by randomizing the potential subjects: Half of the excluded families were assigned by chance to receive the Program, and the others were not. All the mothers randomized to The Parent–Child Home Program went on to enroll in it, whereas those still excluded formed a small strictly randomized control group.

Of key importance for present purposes is that the control group was created without the mothers having to volunteer for having only an even chance at receiving The Parent–Child Home Program. Randomization was performed among a group of subjects whose parents were recruited from the Program's intended population and all of whom had agreed to participate.

Experimental Study 2: *Far from Home* in Bermuda[2]

In this study, all parents of children aged twenty-four to thirty months in one Bermuda parish were invited to be randomized into Parent–Child Home Program and control groups. The children had age-normal IQs (averaging 99.5) at baseline, which rose to 106.6 and 103.1 in Program and control groups, respectively, two years later, a nonsignificant difference.

The study was flawed by an inappropriate choice of study population: Only one-third of the families were socioeconomically disadvantaged. Unfortunately, the number of controls (thirty-nine total, including all socioeconomic levels) was—according to the authors—too small to perform reliable analyses adjusting for socioeconomic level. The *Far from Home* research thus fulfilled one methodological standard, subject randomization, but fell short of the other: The experiment's sample must represent the population for which the intervention is intended. The socioeconomic status of the Bermuda sample was middle class in income, occupation, and education. Reflecting this, the

2. Scarr, S., and McCartney, K. (1988). Far from home: An experimental evaluation of the Mother–Child Home Program in Bermuda. *Child Development, 59*, 531–543.

children had normal IQ scores at baseline, suggesting that they had no need for a Parent–Child Home Program-type early childhood intervention program to prepare them for school success. Since the subjects were not drawn from an at-risk population, reasonably good cognitive outcomes were predictable with or without the Program. Nonetheless, the few significant differences in outcomes after two years all favored the Parent–Child Home Program group.

Experimental Study 3: The Human Factor as a Source of Bias in Group Assignment

One small unpublished attempt to evaluate Parent–Child Home Program outcomes using a subject-randomized design encountered another source of selection bias in studies of social programs: the human factor. The well-meaning staff members in charge of recruiting subjects at this site turned out to have unwittingly sabotaged the randomization process by, instead, selectively assigning the neediest children to the active intervention group so that the Program group had markedly lower initial IQ scores; posttesting showed age-normal results for both groups (described in Levenstein, 1992).

Experimental Study 4: *Home Again* at the Model Parent–Child Home Program[3]

In 1973 the investigators of outcomes at the model Parent–Child Home Program changed their methodology from location-randomized to subject-randomized experiments, assigning four successive cohorts of low-income families, mainly welfare supported and 85 percent African American, either to the intervention or to control conditions. The results they found seemed puzzling: Large Program effects were found on maternal interactive styles in videotaped observations, but there were no consistent cognitive effects on the children's posttest IQ scores, which were normal in all experimental and control groups (the Stanford-Binet's 1963 norms were used). By second grade, both Parent–Child Home Program and control children's reading scores more than met national norms, fulfilling for both groups the major goal of the Program—prevention of educational disadvantage.

Many years later, armed with greater sophistication as to the potential pitfalls of field research in impoverished populations, it is both possible and important to examine the extent to which the results of this subject-randomized experiment may have been flawed by the subtle effects of volunteerism.

---

3. Madden, J., O'Hara, J. M., and Levenstein, P. (1984). Home again. *Child Development,* 55, 636–664.

"Home Again," the 1973–1975 Cohorts

The mothers who were prospective subjects in the first three of the four subject-randomized *Home Again* cohorts were all Parent–Child Home Program eligible by low income, low occupational status, and limited education. They were interviewed in person and asked to volunteer for taking a chance on being either in a group of mothers whose children would receive the full Program or in a nonprogram group; they were told that their group assignment would be decided by something like the toss of a coin. All were assured that no matter what the results of the lottery, their children would receive yearly developmental evaluations and that they would be given the results. In 1973 and 1975, the control children received only pretest and posttest cognitive evaluations, whereas the 1974 controls also received gifts of the Program's toys and books (without Home Visitor sessions).

When the results of these three cohorts were analyzed, the posttest cognitive score results were similar for Parent–Child Home Program and control groups, and both groups in each cohort had IQ scores at or above normal (including, for one cohort, follow-up at age seven), predicting adequate school achievement and meeting the Program's stated goal for its at-risk participants.

Why did the posttest and follow-up scores of the randomized Program and control groups in these three cohorts both equally meet national norms? A pivotal observation is that the overall average rate for acceptance of entering the experimental lottery was only 54 percent in these cohorts, much lower than the 85 percent acceptance of The Parent–Child Home Program itself in earlier location-randomized cohorts. So the mothers who agreed to be randomized were self-selected, most likely for the qualities of volunteers—high motivation, intellectual alertness, openness to novelty—whether they were then assigned to the Program or to control groups. Self-selection of high-functioning families in the *Home Again* randomization sample is supported by the observation that the pretest mean IQ score of the 1973–1975 children, 91.4, was higher than the 87.5 in earlier years.

Another possible element in the mysteriously good results among the 1973–1975 control groups was suggested at the time by Dr. Donald Campbell, an eminent proponent of true experimental research (e.g. Campbell & Stanley, 1966) whom the Parent–Child Home Program research team approached for his thoughts. Campbell suggested that the *John Henry effect* (Zdep & Irvine, 1970) could have compromised the validity of the experiment: Knowing about the experimental conditions, the control mothers may have interpreted the study as a competition and might therefore have been exerting a special effort to have their children do well, like the mythical John Henry who famously succeeded in competing with a mechanical steam hammer before dying of overexertion.

"Home Again," the 1976 Cohort

The *Home Again* researchers set out to eliminate the John Henry effect among their fourth cohort of mothers by enrolling all the women who had received and accepted an invitation from the Welfare Department and similar agencies to enter their two year olds in the Early Screening program, a yearly vision-speech-developmental examination. Without their knowledge, and therefore without their volunteering to be research subjects, half the mothers who signed up for the Early Screening program were assigned via a randomization table to The Parent–Child Home Program and the other half to the control group. The Program and control families were demographically similar: No mother had more than a high school education or a higher than semiskilled occupation, 84 percent of families were both female headed and receiving welfare aid, and all were eligible for low-income public housing.

Every mother randomized into the experimental group was then invited to enroll in The Parent–Child Home Program as well as in the Early Screening program; all accepted. The control mothers participated, as they had planned, in the Early Screening program conducted at the Parent–Child Home Program Center (not identified as such to these mothers). Yearly evaluations of both groups continued through third grade, when reading and math tests were added.

The difference from the 1973–1975 *Home Again* cohorts was that in 1976 neither Program nor control mothers were informed of the other group's existence, nor did the control group know anything about The Parent–Child Home Program. These conditions seemed perfect for a longitudinal subject-randomized experiment testing the effects of the intervention without subjects being asked to accept a lottery, without volunteerism to introduce sample bias and without a John Henry effect pushing the control mothers to urge their children on.

The results showed large Program effects on videotaped maternal interactive behavior, measured by the Parent–Child Home Program's Maternal Interactive Behavior instrument (MIB) (see Appendix). The 1976 program group's MIB scores were significantly better than the controls' were not only just after the Program's end but also two years after completion, demonstrating that experimental group mothers had learned and assimilated the Program's maternal interaction techniques (Levenstein & O'Hara, 1983).

The Parent–Child Home Program graduates also did significantly better than controls on a Parent–Child Home Program-specific Program Achievement Test (Madden, O'Hara, & Levenstein, 1984), showing they had acquired specific concepts on the Program curriculum. And Program children had significantly superior Stanford-Binet IQ scores just after the Program (experimental group = 107.0; controls = 101.0). Clearly, the intervention was having some positive effect.

But the cognitive superiority of the experimental group did not last. Two to three years after the end of the intervention, in first and second grade, both Parent–Child Home Program and control groups had equal IQs and achievement scores, surpassing national norms in all cases. These scores were not just equal between experimental and control children and higher than in location-randomized years, but they were even higher than those of the three previous subject-randomized cohorts (Levenstein et al., 1983; Madden et al., 1984).

On analysis, it did not seem these results could be explained by selective loss of subjects to follow up. And since the 1976 subjects had been randomized without their knowledge among mothers unfamiliar with The Parent–Child Home Program but demographically eligible for it, it seemed that volunteerism and self-selection could not be involved.

But this assumption was erroneous. In fact, the pool of seventy-one mothers from which the 1976 Program and control groups were drawn had itself been highly self-selected. These seventy-one were the few who volunteered for the Early Screening program in the first place from among 415 mothers who were invited. This low acceptance rate seriously impaired the generalizability of the experiment.

To enroll in the Early Screening program, parents had to feel motivated to have their children tested and then to reach out actively by filling out an application form, mailing it, and bringing their child to the testing site. These actions took an unusual degree of initiative for an at-risk population and was especially atypical of the *Hesitaters* whom The Parent–Child Home Program particularly aims to help.

The initiative taken to have their children developmentally evaluated every year can be interpreted as *Striver* behavior, reflecting parents' hope and conviction that their children would score well, thereby validating their ambitions for those children and, incidentally, looking good themselves in the eyes of others—like those Japanese mothers who send their toddlers to "cram schools" so they will be on a track to attend Japan's best universities and eventually retire from first-rate jobs sixty years later (WuDunn, 1996). In other words, the *Home Again* research was sabotaged by the same phenomenon that had flawed the 1972 renorming of the Stanford-Binet: Parents were more likely to bring their children for testing if they were already proud of their toddlers' ability or determined to help them do well (cf. Thorndike, 1977). The act of stepping forward to enroll their children in the Early Screening program thus, once more, self-selected mothers with the hallmarks of experimental volunteers, from high motivation and self-esteem to a wish to impress others.

These characteristics are so atypical of the Parent–Child Home Program target population that only 17 percent of the mothers approached by the welfare agencies actually enrolled their children in the Early Screening program. Such a degree of self-selection indicates that the low-income mothers in the 1976 experimental cohort were even less representative of the Program's target population than those who had agreed to accept a lottery in the 1973–1975 cohorts.

Other characteristics of the 1976 cohort support the hypothesis that its members were predominantly Strivers. The pretest cognitive scores of the children who were randomized in 1976 (average IQ = 95.1) were even higher than those of the 1973–1975 cohorts, and the 1976 group of Program mothers were also observed to be unusually interactive with their children in the home sessions from the onset and throughout the intervention.

It can be concluded that although the subjects in this cohort were eligible for The Parent–Child Home Program according to standard demographic criteria, in actuality self-selection ensured that neither the Program nor the control groups were much in need of the content of any intervention, although results on the Program Achievement Test, on dyads' verbal interaction in videotaped play sessions, and on immediate postprogram IQ tests suggest that the intervention enriched both child and mother despite the children's good baseline cognitive ability.

One lesson from the excellent outcomes of the *Home Again* subjects is that the category of low-income, low-education, low-achieving parents hides very diverse subgroups—including an ambitious, upwardly mobile layer of the poverty population—and that recruitment methods can result in an unintentional "creaming" of the intended sample. The Parent–Child Home Program has long identified this Striver subgroup by their quick understanding and enthusiastic adoption of the Program's curriculum. The chief target population of the Program is the other type of parents, the Hesitaters, who would tend to remain mired in their low socioeconomic status without outside help. Strivers, who try actively to improve their children's chance of climbing out of poverty and have a reasonable chance to succeed with or without our intervention, will be over-represented in any experimental cohort whose selection method entails an element of self-selection.

Parent–Child Research in General: The Thorny Problem of Sample Bias

A larger issue raised by the *Home Again* experience is the difficulty, in the real world, not only of subject-randomized, controlled measurement of cognitive/educational effects of a home-based, parent–toddler early childhood intervention but of almost any research involving mothers and young children. The parents must speak for their children and be their surrogates in giving consent to participate and become volunteer subjects. Enrolling self-selected parents in voluntary interventions or research with their young children will result in a bias against detecting intervention effects when self-selected subjects are randomized in a strict experimental design. An important lesson of the *Home Again* study is that, roughly speaking, the lower the rate of acceptance of an intervention among at-risk individuals who are invited to participate, the higher the likelihood that the subjects will constitute biased samples not representative of the disadvantaged population to which the findings are meant to be generalized.

Similar considerations limit the generalizability of the many child psychology studies that recruit volunteer participants from much larger pools of potential subjects approached through schools, local newspapers, bulletin boards in public libraries, and similar sources (e.g., Bornstein, Haynes, O'Reilly, & Painter, 1996; Creasey & Reese, 1996; Feeny, Eder, & Recorla, 1996; Krevans & Gibbs, 1996; Lehman, Arnold, Reeves, & Steiner, 1996; Nucci & Weber, 1995).

One recent study provides an example of how self-selection can subtly affect sampling in observational, nonexperimental parent–child research. Loeb, Fuller, Kagan, and Carrol (2004) found that different types of childcare facilities serving welfare-to-work participants in three poor communities yielded different benefits, with preschoolers in center-based care showing better cognitive ability than children in "kith and kin" home-care settings. The researchers recognized that selection or self-selection may have led to more able mothers choosing, or more able children being placed in, center-based care, and they made some attempt to counteract this bias by analyzing only the 44 percent of their subjects whose mothers had not completed high school. But self-selection may also have provided another more remote link to maternal variables: The very fact of choosing to leave welfare support for work that yielded an average monthly income of only $1,008 may have selected for a group of upwardly mobile women, limiting the generalizability of the study to child care among other welfare populations more weighted toward Hesitaters. This means that even though 89 percent of invited mothers agreed to cooperate with research, the study may not have succeeded in escaping the pervasive effects of subtle bias from antecedent self-selection.

The Nurse–Family Partnership, a model of success among early intervention programs in demonstrating benefits using a true experimental design, recruited women from prenatal care facilities during their first pregnancy for a program of nurse visitations. Some 85 percent of subjects in their first study and virtually all the subjects in their Memphis replication were either teenaged, unmarried, or of low socioeconomic status (Kitzman et al., 2000; Olds, Henderson, Chamberlin, & Tatelbaum, 1986). The acceptance rates of

80 percent in Elmira and 88 percent in Memphis demonstrate that it is feasible to enroll high proportions of at-risk populations in randomized trials, decreasing the impact of self-selection. Olds did estimate, however, that 10 percent of the target population in the Elmira study was likely missed because of late registration for prenatal care (Olds et al.). This could affect the generalizability of the study since late or nonregistrants are likely to include many of the young mothers most at risk (Melnikow, Alemagno, Rottman, & Zyzanski, 1991).

Another important early intervention study, the Perry Preschool project, assigned families to program or control status using a complex procedure that included deflection from strict subject randomization by logistic considerations. Potential subjects were felt capable of participating fully in the intervention only if at least one parent was at home during the day and only if they had ready transportation to the day-care center. Many families with working mothers or without cars were therefore shifted to the control group, leading to systematic differences between the groups (e.g., 8.6 percent of experimental-group mothers vs. 30.8 percent of control mothers were employed) that may or may not have affected their results (Lazar & Darlington, 1982, Appendix A; Weikart, Bond, & McNeil, 1978, pp. 16–18).

Lessons for Research Design in Social/Educational Interventions

Biomedical scientists have rightly crowned the subject-randomized double-blind intervention trial as the gold-standard source of reliable information. A notorious recent example of the danger of trusting weaker research designs was the widespread conviction during the 1990s that female hormones ("hormone replacement therapy") could prevent coronary artery disease in postmenopausal women. Numerous observations seemed to confirm this hypothesis, but it melted away as soon as placebo-controlled experimental trials were performed (Writing Group for the Women's Health Initiative Investigators, 2002). A human factor had led to massive confounding: In the 1970s and 1980s, physicians prescribed hormones preferentially to patients who could successfully articulate their suffering from vasomotor symptoms and insist on relief. This meant that women taking hormones were generally similar to their doctors—well off, educated, slender, and nonsmoking, with healthy diet and exercise patterns—and thus, because of an unrecognized human factor, at particularly low risk for heart disease.

Even the results of randomized-controlled trials testing new drugs or other medical innovations, where personal characteristics would seem to be a minor issue, can be affected by the considerations we have been examining.

The giant *MRFIT* study of a multifaceted heart disease prevention program encountered a similar problem to the Home Again experiment: People randomized to the control group, learning about the prevention techniques through other means, took such good care of themselves that they had just as low a rate of heart disease as the experimental group (Multiple Risk Factor Intervention Trial Research Group, 1982). It has even been found that patients assigned to the placebo group in a research trial have better medical outcomes if they are assiduous in taking their sugar pill than if they don't take it as directed (Simpson et al. 2006). Cooperative behavior either might be a marker of better prognosis or might itself confer a protective effect (McDermott, Schmitt, & Wallner, 1997).

In trials of social interventions, sample bias resulting from self-selection can affect a wide variety of studies, if the characteristics that affect a person's choice to participate in a trial are potentially associated with outcomes. When the intervention under experimental scrutiny is aimed at young children and their parents, the methodological difficulties are even greater. And if the target population comprises the kind of impoverished, often depressed Hesitater parents who are least likely to volunteer for, or follow through with, any intervention that may be offered, a randomized controlled trial capable of demonstrating program effects can be extraordinarily difficult to achieve.

The Parent–Child Home Program's mixed results using the experimental method exemplify the difficulty of trying to measure the effects of a home-based, parent–toddler intervention by incorporating only the two standard research criteria of formal representativity and subject randomization. Subtle forms of volunteer self-selection by the parents of potential subjects' make subject-randomized research of social/educational interventions among profoundly at-risk populations prone to systematic bias in favor of the null hypothesis, increasing the likelihood of what is called a Type II error (failure to detect true effects). The most at-risk subjects may also be particularly likely to drop out if they are assigned to a control group, artificially inflating the performance of even well-randomized controls, so that negative experimental trials of early interventions must be taken with a grain of salt. "Attention, consumers of research: let the buyer beware" (Clark, 2000, summary, p. 6).

The difficulties with subject-randomized trials in this field may be even greater now than they were a few decades ago because, paradoxically, of the very success of the concept. Since early intervention to prevent educational disadvantage for disadvantaged populations has become more the norm than the exception in twenty-first century America, members of any control group are likely to be exposed to alternative interventions. This creates another bias in favor of a Type II error, making it still more difficult to obtain airtight evidence of the efficacy of the model under study.

The difficulties encountered by Parent–Child Home Program researchers and others in using the classic research design suggest the wisdom of adding several research guidelines for researchers who wish to evaluate intervention programs intended for disadvantaged populations. If disadvantaged subjects are asked to participate in a randomized trial involving a lottery for assignment to intervention or control groups, intense effort should be placed in recruitment techniques aimed at achieving very high participation rates to avoid the volunteerism pitfall. Only if participation rates are high is there a reasonable chance that subjects will genuinely represent the target population, over and above formal criteria such as years of education and employment status.

In real-world practice, a valid alternative to informed participation in a randomized trial may be to obtain the names of potential subjects and then, instead of inviting them to accept a lottery voluntarily, assign them randomly, without their knowledge, into two groups, offering the intervention to one group only. This approach may, however, raise some ethical issues related to informed consent.

Researchers working with disadvantaged populations may at times legitimately use nonsubject-randomized research designs, which, although less rigorous on a formal level, have the merit of allowing maximal recruitment of the neediest families who are the intervention's intended target. Some evaluations of early childhood interventions may thus track carefully the later academic and other outcomes in program children, comparing them with the performance of groups that are comparable but not randomized, watching out with an eagle eye for the possibility of Type I error (detecting apparent effects that in reality do not exist). Such designs, including location-randomized experiments (which Donald Campbell dubbed quasiexperiments) and the use of historical and concurrent comparison groups, have been the principal evaluation tools for such major early intervention programs as the Brookline Early Education Project and the Chicago Child–Parent Center program (Palfrey et al., 2005; Reynolds et al., 2007). Comparisons of this kind are particularly valid when attention has been paid to enrolling the Hesitater families most representative of at-risk populations—a recruitment goal easier to accomplish with severely disadvantaged parents if potential participants are simply offered a service than if they are asked to participate in research.

The Columbia University psychology professor J. McVicker Hunt, author of the influential *Intelligence and Experience*, after praising The Parent–Child Home Program for its "carefully researched development," advised long ago against using an experimental design for further testing of the Program: "[Levenstein proposes] testing the effects of the Project with a 'true' experimental design with one year's cohort randomized by subject rather than the quasiexperimental design in which controls come from different locations than do randomized subjects. . . . Such an additional effort places more emphasis on 'true' experimental design, which can never be more than approximated, than it deserves" (Hunt, 1975, p. 303).

A similar cautionary note was sounded in a recent social policy report to the Society for Research in Child Development that discusses alternative research methods: "Reliance on the experimental method can lead to inappropriate conclusions. . . . Public services are never randomly assigned, and their effectiveness may well depend on participants' motivation or belief in the service, as signaled by their choice to participate" (McCall & Green, 2004, p. 1).

A final lesson from the *Home Again* experience is its empirical confirmation of an informal observation of many students of the low-income scene: The poor, even the poor of color, are not a monolithic group (Phillips, Brooks-Gunn, Duncan, Klebanov, & Crane, 1998). It is important for social planners to recognize that there is an upwardly mobile segment of the disadvantaged population made up of people eager to find and follow up on any and all leads towards escape from poverty and its effects on their children.

7.

From Laboratory to
Real World

Successful Replication of a
Successful Intervention

Haste Maketh Waste—and
Sometimes Tragedy

Even sophisticated observers may think that the essential tasks for producing a new social program occur during its development: the creation and refinement of an idea; the carrying out of a model program; and the researching of the model's effectiveness. Once these steps have been accomplished, the program developer simply hands over the program to its new administrators in the real world and moves on to other projects—or at least so it seems.

Alas, it's not so simple. What was successful in the research setting may turn out to be a failure in the real world. Model programs are usually meticulously organized and implemented; their staff members are highly skilled and closely supervised; their physical settings are close to ideal; and funding is adequate to maintain their standards. If model program standards are not maintained away from the research setting, and the social program so carefully developed in the laboratory is diluted in its real world replications, the glowing preliminary results will be socially meaningless.

Examples of such diluted application have reached public attention. One is the struggle of many day-care centers to operate according to the standards set by the model day-care programs that have been carefully researched and found to have benefits for children. Day-care centers' excellence is likely to be limited when they are staffed, as too often is the case, by a barely adequate number of teachers and aides who may often be paid barely above the minimum wage (the mean income for childcare workers was $17,410 in 2003) (Lombardi, 2003). Day-care services are of necessity, after all, labor intensive, and their quality depends heavily on the number and skills of the staff members. If staff members are few and poorly paid, the excellent outcomes that have been found in model day-care centers cannot be achieved.

Another example of such diluted application is our national effort to address the problem of homelessness, a problem that continues to grow in the third millennium. One-quarter to one-third of homeless people are handicapped by such severe mental illness that they are in need of intensive services or even hospitalization (Lamb & Talbott, 1986; U.S. Conference of Mayors, 2004). Instead, they drift from shelter to shelter and sometimes cannot be persuaded to enter any at all, especially public shelters, which are commonly inadequate, sometimes unsafe, and often not even available. The severely mentally ill are prominent among the bag ladies and derelicts of our cities, and their presence on the streets is the tragic though unanticipated consequence of a social program applied too soon, without enough testing of its implementation in the real world.

This program consisted of the release from mental hospitals of seriously disturbed patients who had been rendered harmless by the antipsychotic agents that began to be widely used in the 1960s. The move was supported for humane and mental health reasons by hospital staffs, on the assumption that ample community support would be permanently provided for the released patients through community mental health centers, supervised group homes, and the like. Congress passed federal legislation in the mid-1960s to support some of these backups—but made no provision for long-term funding.

By 1980, three specialists, in a book about the deinstitutionalization experience of Worcester State Hospital, were noting bluntly: "The rapid depopulation of state hospitals was undertaken without careful planning with community agencies to develop the support services needed for the maintenance of large numbers of disabled patients outside of institutional settings" (Morrissey, Goldman, & Klerman, 1980, p. 5). There had been no prolonged trial period or follow-up study of what would happen to the released patients and in later years to other individuals with severe mental illness if federal funds for local care dried up—which was precisely what occurred after the first few years. Yet patients without family resources, who are poorly equipped to live on their own and for whom there are no adequate community facilities, continue to have to fend for themselves outside of a protected environment.

Compared to their patient loads fifty years ago, psychiatric hospitals are now almost empty, but the original idealistic plans to help patients regain their independence seem to have resulted mainly in cost saving for the states.

Patients had merely been transferred "from the back wards to the back alleys" (Borus, 1978, p. 1030). The social consequences of their deinstitutionalization had not been adequately tested in the rush to implement what had sounded like a good idea for helping patients without burdening communities.

Outside Evaluations of the Model Parent–Child Home Program

The Parent–Child Home Program's dissemination sounded like a good idea too, but its founders felt that the Program should be tested not only in its original model site but also for its practicability in real-world settings. This decision did not depend entirely on opinions of the Program by experts outside of its central office (at the time known as the Verbal Interaction Project), but their favorable judgments encouraged the effort.

Evaluation experts with a mission of finding effective programs to prevent or remediate educational disadvantage became interested in The Parent–Child Home Program within a few years after it began (see also Chapter 5 and Chapter 11). A few of these early evaluations were particularly influential:

• In 1972, the U.S. Office of Education (now the Department of Education) selected The Parent–Child Home Program as one of two preschool programs among fifteen compensatory education programs chosen as models for the country and published a booklet to describe it (U.S. Office of Education, National Center for Educational Communication, 1972).

• In 1978, the Program's research results were scrutinized by a federal panel of research experts, the Joint Dissemination Review Panel, drawn from the National Institute of Education and the U.S. Office of Education. The panel pronounced the Parent–Child Home Program "a program that works," and proceeded to disseminate information about the Program in the National Diffusion Network's yearly catalogue (The National Diffusion Network, 1979–1995).

• In 1982, the Consortium of Longitudinal Studies evaluated The Parent–Child Home Program in a study of the combined follow-up results from eleven systematically researched preschool programs. Graduates of The Parent–Child Home Program were found to be significantly superior to controls in their freedom from special class placement and in their IQs, with IQs superior to those of the controls and meeting national norms (Lazar & Darlington, 1982).

Maine to Alaska to Bermuda

While these outside evaluations were taking place, and while outcomes research was ongoing at The Parent–Child Home Program's original model site, a slow process of developing the Program's exportability was being carried on by the National Center. The big question was whether the original intervention, pioneered as part of laboratory research in low-income Long Island communities, could be duplicated in the real world. The question of practicability was paramount. The National Center was acutely aware that any effectiveness the Program had demonstrated in a protected setting would be transmitted to other locations only if its method could be replicated elsewhere.

The Parent–Child Home Program had been intended for adoption, if it worked, by schools, by public and private social agencies, by churches, by Native American groups, in short, by any organizations concerned about the future of disadvantaged children and families. After demonstration of its effectiveness in the laboratory, it was meant to be a social program with a potential for applicability in any setting of this country and perhaps other countries as well.

By the end of 1978, after twelve years of the Program's operation and outcome research involving the cooperation of 800 Program and nonprogram parent–child dyads in the model program in Freeport, Long Island, the first part of the National Center's mission was accomplished. That was the year that The Parent–Child Home Program was validated as effective, as a "program that works," by the federal Joint Dissemination Review Panel.

To carry out the rest of its mission, the National Center continued to field-test the system it was carefully developing to guide the Program's country-wide implementation at the same time as it continued to research the model program's efficacy. The system gradually became an efficient and highly successful way of exporting the Parent–Child Home Program intact, preserving its human values while furnishing the guidance and technical materials needed to reproduce it in other settings. By 1972, it was possible to report on early results of the Program's first outside adoptions (Levenstein, 1972) and by the next year to describe techniques that had been found effective in guiding a process that would produce versions of The Parent–Child Home Program so faithful to their original model as to be called replications (Levenstein, Kochman, & Roth, 1973).

Since 1969, the National Center has trained more than 200 Coordinators of Parent–Child Home Program replication sites across the United States and in three foreign countries. By 2007, Parent–Child Home Program replications were reaching more than 6,000 families yearly in a wide variety of low-income populations vulnerable to educational disadvantage.

Over the decades, local Parent–Child Home Program sites have been sponsored by schools, churches, private and public social agencies, mental health clinics, libraries, hospitals, Native American Indian tribes—by an amazing variety of auspices that provide a diverse group of primary services. Examples include:

- The Pittsfield, Massachusetts, public schools started a Parent–Child Home Program replication in September 1970 for a low-income, ethnically mixed population in a small industrial city in the Berkshire Hills. The Program was considered a bridge to school. Later a prekindergarten classroom was added to provide extra enrichment for Program graduates. *This program is still in operation and serves as a model for Massachusetts school systems.*

- The Great Neck/Manhasset public schools in Long Island, New York, have been replicating The Parent–Child Home Program since 1971, serving children from poverty areas in these otherwise affluent communities. The school districts believe the Program has served to enhance the value of schooling in the eyes of this low-income population, mainly African American, and that children in the Program are better equipped for school entry than they would otherwise be. *Still in operation.*

- The Graham Windham Parent–Child Home Program site in New York City opened in 2005 and serves families being reunited after children have been in foster care and families at risk of entering the foster-care system. The Program helps strengthen parenting skills and build parent–child bonds while also helping parents prepare their children for school. *Still in operation.*

- Westchester Jewish Community Services, initially in cooperation with the White Plains, New York, public schools and now also working in Mount Vernon in conjunction with the school district, began The Parent–Child Home Program in November 1972 in Westchester County, which has low-income housing projects and other poverty neighborhoods despite being one of the wealthiest counties in the country. The site now serves a diverse group of families, including many nonnative English speakers, in five communities across the county. It has an endowed scholarship fund for Parent–Child Home Program participants who graduate from high school, to help with college and graduate school expenses. A graduate of the Westchester site is the first Program graduate to serve on the national Board of Directors of The Parent–Child Home Program. *Still in operation.*

- The Tri-County Community Action Committee of Caldwell, Ohio, began replicating the Program in 1973 to serve Appalachian families, who were mainly white and rural, with the parents averaging a tenth grade education.

Families were scattered in a fifty-mile radius of the home office, some in isolated hollows. For many of the children and parents, The Parent–Child Home Program was one of a very limited number of contacts with the outside world. *Terminated in 1977 because federal Appalachian Commission funding stopped. The Parent–Child Home Program continues, however, to serve many isolated rural families in central and western Pennsylvania.*

• The Parent–Child Home Program site in downtown Los Angeles has been serving more than 200 families a year since 2000. The participants are African American and Latino families from the surrounding inner city neighborhoods. The site sponsor, the Eisner Family and Pediatric Medical Center, not only has identified families from its patient population but also has brought in nonpatient families through The Parent–Child Home Program who are now receiving medical care they had not previously been able to access. *Still in operation.*

• Acoma Parent–Child Development program of San Fidel, New Mexico, began a Parent–Child Home Program replication in 1975 in the Indian pueblo of Acoma, high atop a mesa, sixty-five miles southwest of Albuquerque. Three small settlements, situated at some distance from each other, housed the bulk of Acoma's population of 3,000. The program was designed to include local cultural values. *Funding stopped in 1977 in spite of petitions and protests by parents.*

• Bermuda's Department of Social Services opened a Parent–Child Home Program site in 1976 for low-income families within its commonwealth, an island better known for its attractive climate and beauty than for its educational needs. In April 1982, the Program was established as an island-wide service. *Still in operation.*

• The cluster of Seattle Parent–Child Home Program sites, the first of which opened in 2004, is funded by the Business Partnership for Early Learning and the city of Seattle's Families and Education Levy. Two-thirds of the families being served speak languages other than English, primarily Spanish, African languages, or Asian languages. *Still in operation.*

• Child and Family Services of Western Manitoba in Brandon, Manitoba, Canada, began a Parent–Child Home Program site in September 1984 to serve primarily Native Canadian Indian families receiving Income Security (welfare support). Parents are almost all single mothers with an unusually limited amount of education. The replicator offers services to families over an area covering 1,300 square miles. Brandon itself is a small city 120 miles north of Winnipeg, with agriculture as its main industry. *Still in operation.*

These examples of program replication give some hint of the diversity of sociolinguistic subcultures reached by The Parent–Child Home Program. Some of our newest sites are, in fact, explicitly focussing on aiding particular immigrant groups to acquire the skills needed to successfully navigate the education system; children from immigrant nonnative English-speaking families are among the groups particularly likely to have a school-preparedness gap. There are now sites sponsored by associations working specifically with Cambodian, Russian, African, and Hmong immigrant families. Program materials have been translated into many of the languages spoken by participant families (eighty-two languages as of 2007, from Akan to Yoruba), and bilingual home visitors are used as much as possible. At all Parent–Child Home Program sites, but particularly those that serve largely immigrant populations, a special effort is made to find books that relate to the cultures of origin of participating families, and program staff members are sensitized to such issues as the role of the extended family (Higgins Krupa, & Williams, 2006); the potential impact of hospitality customs on home visits; and the possibility that specific books or toys may be found culturally unacceptable for unanticipated reasons (Organizational Research Services, 2006).

For each cultural group, whether American born or immigrant, the Program can serve as a bridge to school readiness and educational success. At one end of the bridge—a dyad's home—the Program adapts itself in every way possible, without violating its basic principles, to the culture of that home. When feasible, books contain the text in the family's native language and English; the mother is encouraged to use her own cultural associations in conversing with her child; the Home Visitor is helped to understand (and sometimes helps her Coordinator and the National Center to understand) the customs of the culture. The other end of the bridge is fixed in the educational culture that is dominant both throughout the country and in a dyad's particular geographical locality. The Parent–Child Home Program's goals and curriculum represent this culture. The method of the Program forms a gentle link between the literacy, language, and school-readiness skills of the dominant culture and the subculture of the home.

As early as 1983, the Consortium for Longitudinal Studies praised the Program's demonstrated capability for accurate replication at secondary sites (Royce, Darlington, & Murray, 1983). The National Center has developed and continues to enhance a training system for local implementation of The Parent–Child Home Program that individualizes the guidance of each replication site and pays particular attention to the local community in which it is embedded. It may be that this humanization of the training process and a firm emphasis on Program standards are the factors that have prevented the erosion that is such a common fate of social programs when they are duplicated away from the model program's site. The more faithful the Program's copies are to the original, the better their chances for benefiting participants in the same way that has been demonstrated in research in the model program and at other sites that are well-established authentic replications. Sponsors and Coordinators of Parent–Child Home Program replications recognize this and therefore, funding permitting, commit themselves when they begin the process to becoming certified as true program replications.

Basic Program Standards: Key Elements for Establishing Program

The Program's basic standards are made explicit in the training institute, the *Handbook of Technical Materials*, the Coordinator and Home Visitor handbooks, and a forty-one-item checklist called *Key Elements for Establishing Program* (known in the Program as the KEEP):

Before replication of The Parent–Child Home Program:

1. A representative of the replicator (the "initiator") requests and receives in-depth information about The Parent–Child Home Program and its implementation.
2. The replicator, often working with the National Center, identifies funding to support the site, develops a site budget, signs a Replication Agreement (described below), and employs a site Coordinator (with at least a B.A. or equivalent). Sites serving more than fifty to sixty families must have a second Coordinator, full-time or part-time depending on the number of families being served.
3. The Coordinator is trained by the National Center at a Parent–Child Home Program training institute.

The first two years of Parent–Child Home Program replication:

4. The Coordinator has frequent e-mail/telephone contacts with the National Center.
5. After two complete years of Program implementation, the site is eligible to go through the certification process, which includes a site visit and a full review of Program files, data, and videotapes of home sessions and staff meetings.

Home Visitor qualifications and initial training:

6. Home Visitor's participation is voluntary.
7. Initial Home Visitor training consists of at least sixteen hours before starting to visit families.
8. Home Visitor has an appropriately nonjudgmental, supportive, personable attitude toward families.

Home Visitor in-service training and supervision:

9. Parents are introduced to their Home Visitor by the Coordinator.
10. Home Visitor writes a home session record after each home session.
11. Weekly Home Visitor staff conference (group supervision by Coordinator).
12. All home sessions are completed or made up by Home Visitor or substitute.
13. Home Visitor records at least two home sessions annually (the Coordinator can watch a video or can view the home visit in person by accompanying the Home Visitor).
14. Home Visitor and Coordinator have individual conferences twice a year.
15. Home Visitor prepares an end-of-year evaluation of the Parent–Child Home Program curriculum materials (toys and books).

Parents and children in The Parent–Child Home Program:

16. Parents' participation is voluntary and without fees.
17. Program is provided to target populations consisting of families with low income or low level of literacy/education or cultural/language barriers.
18. Children are approximately age two (can be as young as sixteen months) at entry and are offered the Program for at least forty-six weeks of visits over roughly two years.
19. Coordinator (occasionally, an experienced Home Visitor or a translator) conducts initial interview with parent.
20. Coordinator conducts mid-year interview with parent.
21. Parents are provided the opportunity to evaluate the Program at the end of the year, usually using an anonymous written evaluation form.
22. Training and supervision includes explicit confidentiality/intrusiveness safeguards for families.

Home sessions:

23. Two home sessions per week in both Year 1 and Year 2 of the Program.
24. At least one parent (or primary caregiver) at each home session.

25. Home session techniques: Home Visitor models interactions.
26. Home session's ultimate aim: parent leads, Home Visitor follows.

Books, toys, and curriculum:

27. A toy chest or other storage container is provided to families for the books and toys.
28. A minimum of twelve books and eleven toys are given to families each year, over a minimum of twenty-three weeks (forty-six home sessions) of services per Program year. Sites are asked to note how many, if any, are craft projects and what they are.
29. Books and toys are presented weekly in developmentally appropriate sequence.
30. For each book or toy, the Home Visitor and family receive a guide sheet which the site may develop from the National Center's model (as discussed in training) or obtain from the National Center's guide sheet library.

Coordinator's administration of The Parent–Child Home Program:

31. Follows manual and uses National Center's forms appropriately.
32. Completes annual replication record and annual KEEP and submits them to National Center in a timely fashion.
33. Files on families (electronic or paper) are well organized, up-to-date, and confidential.
34. Work flow sheets (or effective substitute) are kept current.
35. Effective system for storing and keeping track of toys and books.

Maintaining data in the Parent–Child Home Program management information system:

36. Entered and updated staff data on the management information system.
37. Entered and updated replication site data.
38. Entered and updated family information form, initial and Program child information.
39. Entered and updated family information form, parent/caregiver section.
40. Entered and updated participation form, pre- and post-year information.
41. Entered and updated family follow-up information form.

Current Replications of
The Parent–Child Home Program

As of December 2007, there were 150 replications of The Parent–Child Home Program in fourteen states and in Bermuda, Canada, and the Netherlands. Locations of all current replications, including contact information for their Coordinators, are available at www.parent-child.org. More than twenty of these sites have been in operation for more than ten years and five for more than thirty years, all still faithfully following the Program's guidelines as outlined in the *Key Elements for Establishing Program*. More than seventy-five new replications have been started since 2002. The Parent–Child Home Program partners with a number of other home visiting programs, most extensively with the Nurse-Family Partnership and Parents as Teachers, to provide a continuum of services from birth until the child enters pre-kindergarten.

The steady adherence to Parent–Child Home Program standards by replication sites over many years of operation is more familiar in fast-food franchises like McDonald's than in the adoption of social/educational programs. An *adoption* of such a program is more likely to become an *adaptation* when sponsors innocently change essential features for what seem like sensible reasons. Unfortunately, the adapters may not realize that every change may dilute and even destroy the program's original effectiveness.

The persistence of Parent–Child Home Program replications in maintaining the standards of the model program is an indication of the replicators' commitment to the welfare of their site's participants—their caring that the parents and children who are enrolled have the best chance of receiving what the Program promises. Their persistence also testifies to the efficacy of the replication techniques developed by The Parent–Child Home Program's National Center. It indicates the success of dissemination methods developed over many years and continuously reviewed for updating and refinement to ensure that replicators are equipped with the supports they need to maintain true replications of The Parent–Child Home Program.

A Statewide Dissemination Model

The Parent–Child Home Program replications in Massachusetts are coordinated through the state's new Early Education and Care Department because the state funding from the legislature flows through this agency. In Pennsylvania, the sites are coordinated through the state Department of Public Welfare, which is the funding source for twenty-eight sites across the state. In each of these states and in a number of others where the Program has clusters of sites funded with county, city, school district, and private funds, the organizational structure continues to grow as the number of sites grows. In Massachusetts, a state Advisory Council advocates on behalf of the Program and provides advice and contacts on research and funding. Advisory councils are currently being developed in Pennsylvania and New York.

Cost and Sample Budget

When the model program first began in Freeport in 1967, the average annual cost for each parent–child pair was $400. In 2007, the cost per family was approximately $2,500, varying primarily according to the number of families being served, Coordinator and Home Visitor salaries, the amount of travel involved in reaching the families, and the level of ongoing research and evaluation. Salaries make up most of the costs of the intervention. The Parent–Child Home Program curriculum materials (gifts of books and toys) are minor part of the expenses, generally adding up to no more than $250 per family per year.

Table 7.1 shows how the annual budget for a Parent–Child Home Program replication site serving fifty parent–child dyads might look.[1]

The total budget for a site naturally depends on its individual items, which may differ markedly among replications. As one example, the budget line for Home Visitor salaries may disappear completely because a replication may decide to use only volunteers as Home Visitors. However, the norm is that replication sites pay most or all of its Home Visitors, in part because it enables the site to hire bilingual Home Visitors when needed to meet the needs of the target population, and in part to hire former Program parent-participants, who can make valuable Home Visitors. If all salary items stay in the budget, differences may arise because salaries vary greatly in different parts of the country. What is far too low a salary in one place may be high in another. The sample budget shown in Table 7.1 assumes, for example, that the Coordinator is a professional, typically a social worker or certified teacher, and the Home Visitors are paraprofessionals who are home visiting part-time but may have other employment in the same school district or agency. Each replication budget is adapted to local conditions and to the particular needs of the community, but the sample budget represents a fair approximation of the average replication budget as of 2007.

The National Center's experience is that every replicator must provide minimal space and equipment to implement The Parent–Child Home Program: an office large enough to hold one or two desks, a computer with Internet access, a telephone, conference space in which the staff can meet

---

1. As in Chapter 3, material that is more supplementary or illustrative will be set in a smaller type font.

TABLE 7.1 SAMPLE BUDGET FOR A PARENT-CHILD HOME PROGRAM SITE

Personnel	Percent or no.	Cost	Total
Coordinator	100	$50,000	$50,000
Home visitors[1]	2,548 hrs.	$12 @ hr.	$30,576
Support staff	25	$20,800	$5,200
Fringe[2] @ 7.65% for Home Visitors		$2,339	$2,339
@15% for Coordinator/support staff		$8,280	$8,280

Nonpersonnel			
Curriculum materials (books/toys)		$250/family	$12,500
Travel to home visits		$2,000	$2,000
Purchase services: annual conference fee		$250/person	$250
(additional attendees are $210 each)			
Office costs, etc.[3]		$2,500	$2,500
Total			$113,645

1. Some sites use volunteer rather than, or in addition to, paid Home Visitors. Program costs are higher if paid Home Visitors are used, but most sites accept these costs to enable them to employ former parent-participants and to ensure they have Home Visitors who speak the languages of the families they serve and are available when the families are available. A Home Visitor may serve only one family or as many as sixteen. Home visits are done in one-hour blocks, a half-hour for the visit and a half-hour for travel time and completing the visit report. Home Visitors receive sixteen hours of training from the Coordinator (after the Coordinator is trained by The Parent–Child Home Program) and must attend a two-hour weekly staff development meeting.
2. Many sites have part-time Home Visitors, and fringes in the sample budget are calculated at the part-time rate. Sites hiring full-time Home Visitors must calculate fringes at the full-time rate. The sponsoring agency can donate the salary and fringe costs for support staff as an in-kind contribution.
3. The sponsoring agency can donate these as in-kind contributions. This sample budget assumes that the sponsoring agency is donating office and meeting space as an in-kind contribution.

regularly and privately, and permanent storage space for program books and toys. Anything beyond that, such as a separate office with desks and computers for Home Visitors, helps morale and adds to the quality of data input and the reports completed but is not essential for operating a high-quality replication of The Parent–Child Home Program.

Funding for Replications of The Parent–Child Home Program

All replications must be supported through a replicator's own financial resources or fundraising. Most often the replicator supports the site through grants of government aid for which The Parent–Child Home Program is an eligible service or that is being used to encourage development of Program sites. Government aid may come from school district, county, state, or federal sources, sometimes administered through the state or locality. Two important examples are:

- Title I (formerly Chapter I of the federal Educational Consolidation and Improvement Act), the federal funding stream for school districts serving economically disadvantaged children and now primarily directed towards funding the implementation of No Child Left Behind, was designed to provide support for compensatory programs that reach out to children at risk for educational disadvantage. Federal funding of this kind has been used by many school districts that replicate The Parent–Child Home Program.

- Temporary Assistance for Needy Families (TANF) funds. States have a certain amount of discretion as to how to use their excess TANF funds. These funds can be used to support parenting education and support programs such as The Parent–Child Home Program.

Other funding sources include federal Even Start funds; Early Head Start; state education funding; state public welfare funding; state and local funding for literacy, parenting education/parent involvement, and adult education; local school districts; corporations; private social service organizations; community foundations; and individual donors.

Program Evaluation in Replications

Many Parent–Child Home Program replications have conducted in-house evaluations of their local program's effect on children by assessing the children's cognitive development before and after participation. By 1974, cognitive development data from eight replications had been sent to the National Center for statistical analysis, and the average pre-post IQ gain for children in these replications proved to be about 15 IQ points (Levenstein, 1975). Encouraging as this large gain seemed to be, its importance could be questioned because of the research design: Comparison of posttest results with those obtained at pretest is considered a weak research design in preschool research because of a maturation factor, the natural improvement in small children's IQs at this age simply because they have grown older and can deal better with the test material.

More systematic evaluations of the effects of Program replications have been published in peer-reviewed journals by researchers in several states (see Chapter 5 and Chapter 11 for details). Children who had participated in the Pittsfield, Massachusetts, Parent–Child Home Program were evaluated periodically during their school years by experts from outside of the school system, who found their reading, language, and math progress and their performance on achievement tests to be superior to the progress of nonprogram Pittsfield children of similar background and equivalent or superior to national norms (DeVito & Karon, 1984). The Pittsfield site participants graduated from high school at similar rates to nondisadvantaged students (DeVito & Karon, 1990) and at higher rates than randomized controls (Levenstein, Levenstein, Shiminski, & Stolzberg, 1998). In Lake City, South Carolina, disadvantaged youngsters who had completed The Parent–Child Home Program out-performed statewide norms on first-grade readiness tests (Levenstein Levenstein, & Oliver, 2002). On Long Island, New York, disadvantaged Parent–Child Home Program graduates from several sites were found to be essentially indistinguishable from their nondisadvantaged peers when evaluated in kindergarten (Allen, Sethi, & Astuto, 2007). In short, children participating in Parent–Child Home Program replications *could no longer be considered educationally disadvantaged.*

Most Parent–Child Home Program replications regularly monitor their results by gathering preprogram and postprogram material regarding cognitive, language, or literacy capabilities; parent–child interactions (PACT), and the child's social–emotional development (CBT).[2] Some of them (such as Buffalo and other school or school district-based sites) have also followed the Pittsfield model, comparing their Parent–Child Home Program graduates with comparison groups of prekindergarten and kindergarten students from both similar and different socioeconomic groups who did not participate in the Program.

Steps to Program Replication

All replicators go through the same steps to achieve authentic replications of the Parent–Child Home Program with the help of the National Center: information-gathering, commitment, Coordinator training, closely supervised operation for two years, certification as an authentic replication, and recertification. Several of these steps were introduced as the first items of the KEEP, and we will discuss the process in more detail here.

Replicator Obtains Information

Potential replicators sometimes learn of the Program's existence by word of mouth but more commonly it is through seeing The Parent–Child Home Program mentioned in professional journal articles and newspaper articles, through Internet searches or the Program Web site (www.parent-child.org), at a conference presentation, or from directories of early childhood inter-

---

2. The PACT (Parent and Child Together) is one of the Program's assessment tools for evaluating parent–child interaction when a family enters the intervention and after they have participated in the Program; see Appendix. CBT is Child Behavior Traits, another assessment tool developed and validated by The Parent–Child Home Program; see Appendix.

ventions provided by governmental or private organizations. On request, the National Center provides a start-up packet describing the Program, its history, its research, and its replication process. Agencies interested in creating a Parent–Child Home Program site may also purchase the official *Replication Guide.*

Signed Promise to Follow Program Standards

When a replicator or local sponsoring agency has decided to implement The Parent–Child Home Program, the agency is asked to write a letter of intent, to prepare a Proposed Plan of how it will implement the Program in its community (who will be served, the initial number of families, funding sources, etc.), and to complete a Replication Agreement committing itself to follow the Program's basic standards. The Replication Agreement is a detailed document that includes the requirements for maintaining a Parent–Child Home Program and for using the Program name and copyrighted materials, as well as summarizing what the National Center provides in training and technical assistance to all sites.

The basic Parent–Child Home Program standards are described in the forty-one items of the KEEP, listed earlier in this chapter. The items were carefully selected from the Program manual to be the essential features of the model program. The KEEP delineates concretely the dimensions of a replicator's commitment to genuine duplication of the model Parent–Child Home Program.

The National Center may, in certain instances, agree to specific variations from the KEEP, so long as the variation does not violate the philosophy or basic method of the Program. An acceptable minor modification might be the addition of weekly or monthly parents' group meetings around topics of common interest or hiring a Coordinator who does not have a college degree but does have extensive experience with home visiting.

Coordinator Is Trained by the National Center

Once funding has been identified and the replicator is ready to move forward, a site Coordinator is hired by the local agency. The Coordinator participates in a training institute and receives a complete set of technical materials, everything needed to run a Program except the books and toys. The materials include manuals, practical information, and templates for all The Parent–Child Home Program forms, with permission to reproduce them for use in running the intervention. The training institute educates the Coordinator in the philosophy and background of the Program as well as in the use of the materials, the selection of the books and toys, and approaches to families, community agencies, and Home Visitors (see Table 7.2).

Coordinator training is typically accomplished through attendance at a three-day training institute held at the National Center or off site in a state or major metropolitan area that is starting a cluster of Parent–Child Home Program replications. On occasion, if a single large site is opening that would like a number of its agency staff trained, training at the replication site itself can be negotiated.

The First Program Cycle

The Parent–Child Home Program, Inc., training and site support staff keeps in close contact with new Coordinators throughout their first complete Program cycle, the first two years of the intervention, with frequent e-mails and telephone conversations and occasional in-person meetings, starting with review of the Proposed Plan containing information on the kind of population the replication plans to serve, numbers, risk factors, and other details. National Center staff provides technical assistance, budget and implementation consultations, and advice on the challenging situations that can arise. For all site Coordinators, the National Center continues to provide new technical materials, revised training materials, new sample guide sheets, fundraising information, and new book and toy suggestions as they become available. These are posted in the sites-only forum on the Program's Web site and distributed via a listserv to all Coordinators. Sites are strongly urged to send at least one representative from the site to the Annual Coordinator Conference to share experiences with staff from other sites and hear expert presentations on topics of interest.

This in-service training and technical assistance process is graphically portrayed in the real-life example, later in this chapter, of the Family Keystone Agency.

Certification of Authentic Replication

After two full years of program operation, the site goes through a site-certification process to determine whether it is eligible to be certified as an authentic Parent–Child Home Program replication. The site certification includes a site visit; submission of videotapes of home sessions and staff meetings; and review of the site's files, its documentation, and the data that have been collected on the participants. One key criterion for the site certification and the annual recertification thereafter is the submission of the KEEP, the document that outlines how the site is complying with implementing the Program's key elements.

As in the formulation of the initial Replication Agreement, some KEEP items are more essential than others are for certification and recertification, depending on the replication's setting or on other individual circumstances. For any replication site, for instance, the KEEP item, "Parents' participation is voluntary," is critical. The KEEP item stating that parents should be introduced to their Home Visitor by the site Co-ordinator may, on the contrary, not always be necessary (although the Coordinator does take care to meet all families around the time of enrollment). At some large sites, for instance, the Home Visitors are doing a great deal of recruiting, and a Home Visitor may be the appropriate person to introduce the family to its own Home Visitor, or the Home Visitor who recruited the family may end up as their visitor and not require the same introduction.

It is clear, then, that although a replication that fulfills most but not all of the KEEP items may be considered to be a true replication, this is on condition that none of the most essential of the forty-one essential items is omitted. In the last analysis, the National Center must at times make a subjective judgment about certain aspects of a replication's readiness to be certified as an authentic replication. In practice, though, a surprisingly small proportion of the decision proves to be based on subjective criteria.

The Certificate of Authentic Replication is awarded on the basis of the following criteria, most of which, as do some of the KEEP items, necessarily require judgement calls at times by the National Center:

1. Successful performance on the KEEP and submission of annual report and timely data entry
2. Satisfactory group supervision by the Coordinator (at least one Home Visitor staff meeting observed either directly or through an audiotape or videotape recording)
3. At least two satisfactory home sessions (observed through audiotape or videotape recording), including one conducted by the Coordinator
4. Program records found to meet National Center standards

The criteria for this benchmark include examination of:

- Home session reports written by a variety of Home Visitors. The reports should explain the critical components of every home visit: What did the Home Visitor do? What was the child's reaction? What did the parent do?
- One complete family folder. Do the reports show progress over two years, in a coherent fashion?
- Book and toy lists for Program I (Year One of the Program, for two year olds) and Program II (Year Two, for three year olds)
- A selection of five to six book or toy guide sheets
- Coordinator's workflow system (should include Home Visitor sign-out sheets and family sign-out sheets)

5. Insight shown by Coordinator in conversations with National Center staff about implementation of the Program and about relations with Home Visitors, families, other sponsoring agency staff, and the community. The Coordinator shows insight and understanding in her discussion of the community attitudes toward the Program and about past or anticipated problems and solutions.
6. Understanding demonstrated by the supervising administrator overseeing The Parent–Child Home Program at the local sponsoring agency about the role of the Program in the replicator agency and its future in the agency

Recertification

Sites are recertified annually by the National Center on the basis of annual data and forms documenting Program implementation. All the data points in the management information system (MIS) are included in the annual review, including the number of home sessions offered and completed, the demographics of the families served, and the completion rate for the Program year and for the entire Program. Among other requirements, a replication must complete the KEEP every year to retain its certification.

Seed to Blossom: The Replication System in Practice

In September 1984 a private social agency that we will call Family Keystone (not its real name) started a replication of The Parent–Child Home Program that was certified as an authentic replication two years later, in 1986. Although these events took place many years ago, the example remains valuable because the training and guidance of Family Keystone's replication by the National Center was unusually well documented, not only through the National Center's logs but also through detailed letters from the replicator's staff. This is because Family Keystone's location is 2,500 miles from the National Center office, and, at the time, telephone calls to and from the National Center in New York were expensive. To save on telephone expenses in those days before e-mail, much information was exchanged through letters from and to Family Keystone's staff members, often preliminary to telephone conference calls.

The result was a comprehensive documentation of replicator–National Center interaction enhanced by the detail and the clarity of Family Keystone's letters to the National Center. Therefore, the replication process at Family Keystone has been chosen as an otherwise typical example of how the National Center's replication system works in actual practice. Names and other identifying features are disguised and some terminology updated, but aside from these necessary alterations, the content of this chronological account is as it occurred.

June 1982

Family Keystone's director of preventive services sent for and received information on The Parent–Child Home Program from the National Center. Her letter was typical of such letters of inquiry:

> I have been most interested in the description of The Parent–Child Home Program in the National Institute of Mental Health Monographs.
>
> The description of your Parent–Child Home Program sounds like one from which we could gain enormous assistance in establishing our Home Management–Parent Aid program which is designed to work with our most vulnerable families. The training program used with the home visitors and the curriculum and suggestions with respect to toys and books would be most helpful.

June 1984[3]

Keystone staff members telephoned the National Center. They wished an update of information about The Parent–Child Home Program, especially new research results, since the original inquiry two years earlier. On the basis of the information they already had, Family Keystone had decided to replicate The Parent–Child Home Program with a population of primarily low-income Native American families.

After the follow-up phone call, the Family Keystone director sent a letter to the National Center, with enclosed brochures about her agency, that read in part:

> I am enclosing a copy of our 1984 Annual Report and several of the Preventive program brochures we had developed for a child welfare conference.
>
> I hope that we will develop a solid family resource bank of books, toys and teaching elements for parents as well as programs into which they can move as they are ready.
>
> As you will see from our brochures, we already have a fair degree of involvement in their homes both from our statutory programs staff, our Family Aides and also from the Preschool program.
>
> A possibility I'd like to explore is whether some of the home visitors might be drawn from our client group. Our experience with the Family Aides has been a very positive one as we have seen their growth over the last two years.

July 1984

National Center staff contacted Family Keystone about initiating a Replication Agreement and to start arrangements for an experienced National-Center-certified field consultant to train the replication staff at the agency in an on-site training

---

3. Note the passage of two years. Such a lag time from the original request for information is typical because it often takes local advocates time to sell the Program in the community or agency and then to identify funding.)

institute, a training option that Family Keystone had determined was their preference and which they had sufficient funding to pay for. The National Center provided as part of the training package videos, training manuals, information on the history and methodology, and the technical manual. Family Keystone agreed to pay the field consultant directly for her travel and other expenses, as well as pay for the fee for the training and technical assistance package.

Family Keystone then sent the National Center a letter of intent to replicate The Parent–Child Home Program and two signed Replication Agreements.

August 1984

The Parent–Child Home Program training institute took place August 21–23 at Family Keystone's offices. It was attended by several agency staff members, in addition to the new Coordinator and her supervisor, to prepare the agency for its coming implementation of the Program. In their posttraining evaluation, all commented on the value and completeness of the training. The new Coordinator's reaction was typical: "I felt the training institute was comprehensive in covering the many aspects of the Program that will be needed to implement it. I thought it was great."

December 1984

Letter from the Coordinator of Family Keystone's Parent–Child Home Program to the National Center, in preparation for a telephone conference in January 1985:

We are now into our tenth week of The Parent–Child Home Program and feel that it is going well so far. We have a few questions to ask and will telephone you on Wednesday, January 9, at 8:30 A.M. our time to discuss the following:
1. In completing PACT Item 1: Parent tries to enforce directive, how is it rated when the parent enforces the directive in a very negative manner, such as yelling or becoming very angry with the child? The same could apply to #13, when parent persists in enforcing directives by yelling or threatening child.

2. In PACT Item 5, how does one rate the family when the scolding is done in a nonverbal manner?

3. How does one rate a family when there is great fluctuation in behavior?

4. When the children were pretested at age two, were they testing within normal limits?

5. How did you find the Program worked with extremely disorganized, chaotic households? We have one family in particular. We are wondering if there is enough happening in the parent–child interaction to keep involved with the family.

We have twelve families and eight home visitors participating. We had our first family withdraw when the mother, with her four children, left her husband and moved away.

We are excited about the Program thus far, feel that it has great potential in both learning and relationship areas and look forward to talking with you.

TABLE 7.2 SAMPLE AGENDA FOR A PARENT–CHILD HOME PROGRAM TRAINING INSTITUTE

DAY ONE

9 A.M.–noon

I. Introductions
II. What is The Parent–Child Home Program (PCHP)? Who does it serve?
    A. History of the Program
    B. Purpose of the Program
    C. Goals of the Program
        1. Why we focus on parent–child verbal interaction?
        2. Why we serve children who are sixteen months to three years old?
        3. Empowering the parent
    D. Who runs individual programs/how many/where?
    E. Video: *Soaring to Success Through Books and Play*
III. What are the components of early literacy?
    A. Verbal interaction
    B. Socioeconomic class
    C. What the research tells us
IV. Nuts and bolts: The PCHP's home visiting curriculum
    A. What is a home visit?
    B. How is a home visit conducted? Introduction visit and review visit
    C. The role of the Home Visitor
        1. Setting boundaries
    D. The role of the Coordinator
    E. Program families
        1. Coordinator contact with families
        2. The family interview
        3. Mid-year/end-of-year evaluations
        4. Making referrals
    F. The affective and cognitive curriculums
    G. How to model verbal interaction
        1. During reading—Video: *Home Visits* (Lucila)
        2. During play—Video: *Home Visits* (Michael)
        3. Video: *Home Visits* (Christopher, Tramont)

(continued)

TABLE 7.2 (*Continued*)

noon–1 P.M.: LUNCH

1–4 P.M.

V. Continuation of discussion about Home Visit videos
   A. Keeping the parent involved
   B. The bilingual home visit
VI. Families at risk
   A. Brainstorming risk factors
   B. Weighing the risk factors: Using a needs index
   C. Dealing with language and cultural barriers
   D. Impact of welfare reform
   E. When both parents work
   F. Transient-homeless families
   G. Maternal depression
   H. Substance abuse
   I. Child abuse and neglect
   J. The teen parent
   K. Red-flag behaviors in young children: The need for further evaluation
VII. Challenges associated with home visiting
   A. Discipline issues
   B. The impact of culture
   C. Dealing with siblings
   D. The overcrowded household
   E. Working with fathers
   F. Home Visitor safety
   G. The TV, Nintendo, Play Station, cell phone, radio, barking dogs, cockroaches, hungry child, crying baby, and other distractions
   H. Using a participation agreement
VIII. VISM (Verbal Interaction Stimulus Materials), books and toys
   A. Selection criteria
   B. Importance of toys
   C. Putting together a schedule
   D. Vendors
   E. Guide sheets

DAY TWO

9 A.M.–noon

I. Data collection
   A. Management information system
   B. Assessments overview

noon–1 P.M.: LUNCH

1–2 P.M.

II. Administration
   A. Setting up a schedule
   B. Maintaining family files: Information that should be kept
   C. Time sheets
   D. Flow sheets
   E. Ordering and inventory
   F. Forms required by the National Center
      1. Proposed Plan to replicate PCHP
      2. KEEP (Key Elements for Establishing Program)
      3. PCHP replication record
   G. Other forms provided by the National Center
   H. Evaluation and assessment tools
   I. Suggested supplies, equipment, facilities
   J. Resource materials
   K. Budgeting, marketing, fundraising

2–4 P.M.

III. Child Behavior Traits (CBT) and Parent and Child Together (PACT)
   A. Group practice
   B. Issues of inter-rater reliability and objectivity

DAY THREE

9 A.M.–noon

I. The heart of the Program: Hiring, training, and supervision of Home Visitors
   A. Putting together the job description
      1. Duties
      2. Salary
      3. Hours
   B. Finding the right candidates
      1. Getting the word out
      2. Application
      3. Interview
   C. Putting together the initial training
      1. Training for paraprofessionals
      2. What should be on the agenda
      3. Training techniques
      4. Emphasizing confidentiality, ethics, and respect for families
   D. Ongoing training and supervision
      1. Home visit reports: The basics
      2. Weekly staff meeting
      a. The Coordinator's role
      b. Group dynamics
      c. VISM exploration
      d. Dealing with family issues: The importance of confidentiality
      e. Video: *Weekly Staff Meetings*

(continued)

TABLE 7.2 (*Continued*)

    3. Coordinator–Home Visitor relationship

    4. Tapings and observations: Giving feedback

II. Another look at home visits

  A. Ending a home visit

  B. Why not to have a lesson plan

  C. Video: *Home Visits* (Cecilia, Amy)

  D. Video: *Home Visits* (Ashley)

noon–1 P.M.: LUNCH

1–2 P.M.

III. Coordinator relationship to National Center

  A. Coordinator certification

  B. Program certification

  C. Maintenance of records/forms: What data to keep

  D. Ongoing technical assistance

IV. The Community

  A. How to do effective outreach

    1. Tools: Brochures, meetings, posters, newsletters, etc.—getting the word out

  B. Health/safety of Home Visitors

  C. Issues specific to the community

    1. Neighborhoods/apartment buildings/projects

    2. Community demographics: Who are the young families?

    3. Legal resident status/immigration

    4. Language issues

    5. Racial issues

  D. Building a network

    1. School–community partnership

    2. Support services for families

    3. Sources of referrals

    4. Referring to other services

    5. Support services for staff

    6. Doing presentations

  E. Related activities

    1. Parent groups

    2. Field trips

    3. Play groups

2–3 P.M.

V. Introduction to evaluations of Program implementation and family outcomes

  A. Why evaluate

  B. Types of evaluations

The National Center's director confirmed the telephone appointment and requested that certain information be available for the conference call: "Could you please try to fill out the Proposed Plan so that we can talk about it a bit in our telephone conference? It is in your training materials and was also sent as part of the Replication Agreement."

January 1985

The conference call between Family Keystone and National Center covered all the issues noted by the Coordinator plus others, including topics of special relevance to cultural customs and language, and lasted an hour. Three key Family Keystone staff members participated in the conference: the Parent–Child Home Program Coordinator, the director of preventive services, and the director of Family Keystone, Inc.

March 1985

The Family Keystone Parent–Child Home Program Coordinator sent the completed copies of the Proposed Plan to the National Center and scheduled another conference call:

> The home visitors have three weeks of visiting left. Then I will visit each of the families again and the children will be assessed with the Psycho–Cattell and Peabody Picture Vocabulary Tests. I don't know what results of these tests will be, but the results we have seen have been very rewarding and exciting.
>
> Mothers who have not kept appointments and have not spent time playing with their children are now there for home sessions and interacting with their children.
>
> Do you have information on the validity and reliability of the PACT?
>
> In the second year of the Program, do the Home Visitors continue to meet weekly for supervision? Is the visiting with the families carried out in the same manner?

April 1985

A letter from the National Center confirmed the conference call and enclosed the requested research data: "Enclosed is a copy of a presentation on which a chapter in *Parent–Child Interaction* is based. The tables in it give the correlations of PACT verbal interaction items with children's school competencies, as well as concurrent correlations. The high coefficients are evidence of the validity of linking the competence of children to their early verbal interaction with their parents."

The next telephone conference between the National Center and Family Keystone staff included discussions of measures to evaluate the Program's effects on parents and children. The Coordinator also asked whether the National Center staff could review some of the Program materials she was using, which she would send along with an expanded description of the community and families reached by Family Keystone's Parent–Child Home Program.

May 1985

The Parent–Child Home Program Coordinator sent the National Center for review her list of books and toys, several guide sheets, and a table of the Program dyads' demographic characteristics. Her letter described in some detail the community and population served by Family Keystone's Parent–Child Home Program site and set up another conference call:

Please find enclosed a list of the toys and books that we used this year and the guide sheets for the three substitutions. The substitutions *All Fall Down* and *Pat the Cat* were made when the books we ordered from the suggested list did not come in. The puppet had Goldilocks at one end and a bear at the other, with a skirt that could be flipped either way. It was popular with the older children. There was a colorful inexpensive book telling the story to accompany it.

Here is more information on the type of people we are serving. The agency serves a 1,300 square mile largely rural area with increasingly large farm operations requiring limited labor and dying villages as a result of the migration of the young people to the larger urban centers.

There is one city of around 40,000. There is a sizable degree of movement because of the number of transfers of junior people in national companies. It is also first stop for many of the Natives from six small [Native American] reservations in the area. They are very transient, moving back and forth from the Reserve, with consequent problems in finding adequate housing and employment. Their children move schools frequently during the year.

Our family service caseloads are highest in the city. About 50 percent are concerns about adolescents. The other fifty percent are families with infants, toddlers, and school-aged children. A high proportion of the families are abusing alcohol but not ready to seek or accept help.

The population involved in the Parent–Child Home Program this year were thirteen families, all were referred by social workers of Children's Aid Society. This meant there was concern related to the care of the children. This could range from a parent's request for information about the care of their children to parents who are neglecting and abusing their children. All were of low income and all mothers' education was below the Grade 12 level.

Please find enclosed a chart listing the characteristics of the families involved in the program. The visiting and the assessment of the children are now completed. The data are not yet all in. We will telephone you on June 19, 1985, at 10:00 A.M. your time to talk further.

In order to make sure the replication is satisfactory, I am wondering in what areas we need to make changes next year.

June 1985

As had become usual, the National Center staff met by telephone for about an hour with three Family Keystone staff members. Most of the meeting was devoted to the National Center's review and critique of the Coordinator's well-chosen list of books and toys and her guide sheets, as well as comments on the demographic and cultural characteristics of the families being served in relation to their special needs from the Program.

November 1985

The Coordinator sent a progress report and requested a telephone conference:

> We are just beginning our second year of the Parent–Child Home Program, with eleven families returning for Program II and four new families beginning the first year. Of our original thirteen families in the first year, one family moved away shortly after the Program began, and the second family moved out of town this summer after completing the first year. We are fortunate in having the other eleven return. We began with four new families for Program I instead of the expected five because one mother entered an alcoholic rehabilitation program; we hope to include her later.
>
> All of the Home Visitors returned except one who obtained full-time employment. We have five new Home Visitors.
>
> Last year's experience was a very positive and rewarding one for all of us, and we look forward to this year. As I indicated in our last telephone call, there was not a statistically significant increase in the children's cognitive development in year one. However, all the children remained at the same level of development or showed an increase, and we regarded this as positive, as often children from [this local sociological] background show a decline from age two on.
>
> There was a statistically significant increase in the mothers' interactive behavior with their children as rated in the PACT, and in the children's social–emotional development as rated on the CBT. The relationship between CBT and PACT scores was also statistically significant.
>
> The individual gains in the families reported by the parents and the Home Visitors added to our feelings that the Program was a worthwhile and exciting one. I hope the second year goes as well.

December 1985

A member of the National Center staff spoke with the Coordinator of Family Keystone's Parent–Child Home Program and responded to her specific questions about the supervision of her Home Visitors (she now had a large number, some experienced and some not) and about the use of videotapes to measure changes in mothers' interactive behavior with their children.

January through April 1986

The Coordinator called to ask about the cultural advisability of various end-of-program activities, including presentation of certificates to the mothers and having a party at the end of Program II or for all families at the end of the Program year.

June 1986

The National Center director wrote to the Coordinator about the site's completion of the second year of the Program and the next steps towards site certification:

> I've enclosed a copy of our criteria for certification and of the KEEP, so that you can review the standards and gather together the necessary materials to complete the certification process. As you can see, you will need to provide the National Center with videos of two home sessions (including one of you yourself doing a home visit) and of a Home Visitor staff meeting, as well as the following documents: a completed KEEP; six Home Session Reports; one complete two-year family file; your current list of books and toys and the guide sheets that go with them; and your work flow sheet, or its equivalent, for both Program years.
>
> I'm pretty sure you will find the certification evaluation an interesting and nonthreatening experience, like a continuation of your training.

June and July 1986

The Coordinator attended The Parent–Child Home Program Annual Conference at the end of June and went through the certification process for her site, which became certified as an authentic replication of The Parent–Child Home Program.

June 2007

The Parent–Child Home Program replication operated by the agency we have been calling Family Keystone has now been functioning continuously for twenty-three years.

8.

Preventing a Dream from Becoming a Nightmare

The Ethics of Home Visiting Programs

The first institution to conduct a home-based program for families was the family itself. Whether nuclear or extended, matrilineal or patrilineal, poor or rich, families acted for most of human existence as mini-Departments of Health, Education, and Welfare providing medical and nursing care, the cognitive socialization of the young considered necessary for survival, and as much social service as they could manage.

Outside institutions gradually took over a large part of these family functions until, by the middle of the last century, it began to appear to many that the family had only three residual jobs: nurture and socialization of infants, replacement of societal members lost through death, and provision of an emotional haven from the pressures of the outside world. By the 1970s, even these functions seemed no longer to be the exclusive province of the family, suggesting to some that the family as an institution might soon be visible only in museum archives and photographs.

Many people from institutions concerned with education, health, and social supports insist, on the contrary, that the family is irreplaceable and that its very strengths should be used in the service of its components by supporting family members, when support is necessary, as much as possible within the home and in the family context. This is not a new concept: School systems long ago established home-tutoring programs for children with special needs; the visiting nurse associations began operating before

1900; and for hundreds of years, churches have been administering to the sick and helpless in their homes.

Yet the very advantages that can make a home-based, parent-involving early education program particularly effective when the child is very young are features that make such a program especially vulnerable to ethical problems. These advantages include the convenience to parents, especially low-income parents who are often harried and depressed; the familiarity of the home setting for the child; the home visitor's one-to-one relationship with child and parent; and, most of all, the use of the close, enduring parent–child relationship for the social–emotional and cognitive development of the child. By going into the home and dealing directly with the parent–child relationship, the home visitor comes close to the very heart of what makes humans human. It is a place where one should walk very carefully.

Such a sensitive setting demands more than ordinary vigilance to safeguard the rights of the individuals and families reached by the program, including the right to privacy, the right to retreat to one's home without intrusion by an outsider, and the right to choose between—or refuse—intervention programs that are not legally compulsory.

A few years after the Verbal Interaction Project (now the National Center of The Parent–Child Home Program) launched the development of the Mother–Child Home Program (now The Parent–Child Home Program), a professor speaking at a national conference called it "the nightmare of the future." His concern was that the Program, because it was home-based, had a serious potential for infringement on the privacy and rights of families.

This aroused some indignation within the Verbal Interaction Project, where it was felt that safeguards against such risks had been built in to both the research procedures and the Program. In addition, the research of the Program already indicated that it might be a dream of effectiveness and social feasibility.

Nevertheless, the echo persisted of what we gradually came to recognize as a socially responsible warning against the possibility that our program could indeed become a nightmare of coerciveness and intrusiveness to families like the Willards and the Carters, in spite of our good intentions. A prime obligation of any social intervention program within a democratic society is to ensure that the program and its evaluation research are consistent with democratic values. This is especially true of home-based intervention programs.

An ethical consideration is present even when the family is first invited to join the program. While saying that participation is strictly voluntary, program staff members in their eagerness to help the family may pressure a parent subtly or overtly to accept that invitation—a violation of individual rights that in any case is likely to achieve only a pseudo-victory in the form of half-hearted cooperation from inwardly reluctant parents.

Once they have made their initial commitment, if they then change their mind and decide to separate themselves from a home-based program, parents must evict it. This is hard to do. People are more often polite than not and do not feel it is courteous to withdraw hospitality once it has been extended. The humane and caring qualities of the staff people who work in home-based programs may paradoxically increase a parent's reluctance to struggle against infringements of his or her own rights. In center-based preschool programs, which are located in a classroom, the parent and child can escape the program by simply remaining at home. The recipients of home-based programs, the Willards and the Carters, are already at home; they have no place to retreat to.

Another issue of crucial importance is that of confidentiality. In their contacts with family members, home visitors inevitably pick up details about a family that should be kept confidential in the interests of family privacy. Divulging such information, whether by telling a friend the juicy details of a parent's sex life or in the more subtle form of disclosing to a colleague, without specific permission, the participation of a specific mother in the program, is an indefensible breach of trust.

Furthermore, home visitors can be tempted to be intrusive, to give uninformed advice and opinions, to insist that families conform to a particular visitor's version of mainstream language and culture, even to gossip about other families in the program. There is a real danger that a home-based program can become a busybody nightmare. That the intrusiveness in home-based programs is likely to be subtle and unintended only increases the family's vulnerability to it. Subtle intrusions can be as seemingly innocuous as a home visitor commenting uninvited on a family photo—"My, doesn't he look sad!"—or walking over to the television set and turning it off. It is necessary first to identify the intrusive behavior, to become aware of its existence in one's own program before one can take steps to eliminate it as much as possible.

What may be termed service overload, overstretching the skills of the home visitor and the aims of the program, can create yet other ethical problems. Once the program has been accepted by the parent, the administrators and the home visitors themselves may be tempted to supply a whole range of services just because they have their foot in the door: child rearing, nutrition, health, dental care, and food preparation are just some of the fields where home visitors could find themselves offering advice. Few home visitors can be experts in all of these areas, so some of their well-meant suggestions could be of questionable quality. An even more important doubt is whether families truly desire intervention in all of these areas or whether they accept them out of politeness or out of deference to authority. Insensitivity to the parents' real wishes, which they may be unable to express out of courtesy to a guest in their home, can lead to a home program, or some of its components, being delivered long after it has outstayed its original welcome.

A final ethical issue relates to the responsibility of administrators to show that resources such as money and the time and effort of both staff and recipient families are indeed doing somebody some good. This social accountability requires a practical translation of the program's broad abstract aims into tangible and measurable goals, as well as a clear definition of the program's method. Program directors risk making claims for their program's model without closely monitoring the amount and quality of the program as it is actually being delivered, especially with home-based programs where the story of what happens in a family's home can easily slip into being allowed to depend completely on the home visitor's self-report. Since home-based programs are not readily accessible to public scrutiny, abuses in this category can range from human error (e.g., home visitors reporting misinformation to their supervisors, perhaps exaggerating the number or content of home sessions to put themselves in a better light) to the near criminal (e.g., the promised program not delivered at all or delivered in a grossly inadequate manner).

Claims for the program's effectiveness may also be made without adequate and systematically collected evaluative data—enthusiasm is no substitute for research. It is ethically imperative that we understand the distinction between the dream and the reality of an intervention program.

The nightmare potential of home visiting can be illustrated by the experience of one psychological intervention in the homes of distressed heart disease patients where visits with loosely defined structure and content by nurses whose abilities may have been taken too much for granted actually had a deleterious effect on patient survival (Frasure-Smith et al., 1997). Well-meaning home visitors and the programs they represent are unlikely to knowingly violate their responsibility to their clients or to the larger social good, but it is easy to do both in a home-based program, in large part because staff members may not be aware of the risks.

As with every home-intervention program, implementation of The Parent–Child Home Program entailed numerous ethical issues. It chose to face these issues head on and worked hard to resolve them, often with difficulty and sometimes with pain, recognizing that if socioethical problems have not been solved in a model program, they will plague it when it is being replicated in the field. The preventive and corrective strategies developed by The Parent–Child Home Program, and emphasized in the training of Coordinators and Home Visitors, are based on several fundamental beliefs:

• People using home-based programs have the same rights as people who use center-based programs, or indeed people in general, to quality services, to the freedom of choosing or not choosing to use those services, and to freedom from overt or subtle coerciveness and from invasions of their privacy.

• People in their own homes are particularly vulnerable to violations of those rights.

• Once a do-gooder has entered a home, it may take too much courage and initiative on the part of a host to terminate the relationship and ask that person to leave.

These beliefs entered into the evolution of every aspect of The Parent–Child Home Program, molding the special care built into the Program's model to protect the rights of families by explicit safeguards (Levenstein, 1981):

• Every detail of The Parent–Child Home Program was created and is monitored to be of the highest quality, whether it be tangible such as books and toys or intangible such as home-session procedures.

• Home Visitors and other staff members are trained to preserve confidentiality about every family detail, including a ban on using participants' last names even in the Home Visitor staff meetings. Records of family contacts are kept in locked files (and now in double-password-protected computer files).

• The Program is delivered to a parent only if he or she clearly states the wish for it and displays no behavioral or nonverbal signals to the contrary.

• A Home Visitor may enter a dyad's home only when admitted by an adult (a two year old's enthusiastic welcome is not enough).

• A Home Visitor remains silent or departs when family events occur that are obviously not meant for strangers' eyes or ears.

• Any kind of intrusiveness is avoided. The parent is not even helped to find apparently needed community services such as medical assistance unless he or she asks for aid in accessing them. The Home Visitor is trained to fit into the family's subculture as far as possible, whether it is unique to a particular family or part of a larger cultural/ethnolinguistic group within mainstream society. Neither Home Visitor nor Coordinator takes over in any way.

- Home Visitors provide only the home-session services in which they were trained, in particular offering no counseling of any kind, whether psychological, nutritional, educational, medical, or otherwise.

- To avoid competing with the parent for the child's affections or creating in the parent feelings of dependency or of obligation to Program staff, the Home Visitor is taught to be friendly but not to become a friend to either parent or child.

- The Program does not interfere with a family's way of life but tries, wherever possible, to provide toys, books, and verbal interaction designed to enhance the child's pride in his or her own subculture. Even when parents insist, as they often do, that the sessions be conducted in English, the Home Visitor is alert to opportunities for relating the conversation to the family's culture. However, nothing is forced. Respect is conveyed as a natural part of the home session. Even the Home Visitor's growth-enhancing modeling is on a "take it or leave it" basis.

- Program participants are treated with courtesy and respect by all staff members, regardless of the position the staff member holds in the Program.

- The Home Visitor is trained to be responsive to nonverbal messages from the parent that the service is or has become unwelcome: He or she may fail appointments or during home sessions retreat to cooking dinner or talking on the telephone. If such signals are picked up, the Home Visitor's supervisor may consider having a talk with the parent to see which way the wind blows; there may be dissatisfaction with the individual Home Visitor, perhaps because of misunderstandings that can be cleared up, or there may be real dissatisfaction with the Program—in which case the service should be withdrawn without argument.

Finally, several key aspects of the broader Parent–Child Home Program method have a central importance in preserving ethical standards:

- Great care is taken to maintain quality control in replications, from initial training through recertification through procedures for considering proposed local variations, as described in Chapter 7.

- The content and the structure of home visits are defined explicitly, and Home Visitors' training emphasizes their limited role, allowing relatively little scope for improvisation.

• The Program's nondidactic approach reinforces respect for parents and for their role.

• The site's Coordinator personally meets each parent at the start of the Program, facilitating the handling of any problems that might arise with a particular Home Visitor.

• Documentation of the Program's process and its outcomes at replication sites is encouraged by the Program's central office, both in the context of formal research and for purposes of internal monitoring.

Many home-based intervention programs with a variety of purposes have sprung up in recent decades. They are usually staffed by people whose enthusiasm for their program and genuine caring for the families served by the program are evident to any observer. Yet at times, a staff's compassion may be greater than its awareness that good intentions are not enough when delivering programs to the homes of families, especially low-income families. Such families are often all too accustomed to accepting without protest well-intentioned but unrequested aid of one kind or another, whatever the families may feel privately about the unwanted help. This time-honored defense (apparent docile compliance) against the intrusive "helping hand" can be reinforced by the passivity and depression endemic among low-income single mothers. The result for a program is often covert resistance and quiet sabotage by its intended recipients, resulting for them not only in the loss of a program's possible benefits but also in a reinforcement of their feelings of helplessness and low self-worth.

Home-based programs have an enormous potential for reinforcing the great strengths their participants already possess, but they must be applied sparingly and carefully, always treading lightly—as the Bauhaus architects said, "less is more." The Parent–Child Home Program's socioethical safeguards can free both staff and parents to concentrate on the joys and responsibilities of the Program. Humanistic values, related in part to the Program's close relationship with social service agencies in its early years, have played a major role in its maintenance of ethical standards, just as the scholarly scientific values of the academic community have permeated its methods. Perhaps the safeguards developed by The Parent–Child Home Program may help serve as a model for the delivery of other home-based programs, to ensure that none of them will become a nightmare of the future.

9.

Ludic Literacy

Prelude to Instrumental Literacy

The rate of illiteracy in the United States is alarming. In 2003, 30 million, or 14 percent, of adults had virtually no literacy skills (*Below Basic*), and another 63 million could read only at a basic level barely adequate for the simplest everyday tasks (National Center for Education Statistics, 2005). In response to our society's concern, a drive has been intensifying over several decades to offer, coax, or even bribe the nonreading adult public into literacy classes. It is a well-intentioned effort aimed at equipping people with reading skills needed—for instance—to fill out applications for jobs and driving licenses, to read signs, and to fit in generally with a literate and often technological environment. However, many planners of literacy programs have lost sight of a crucial factor. If reading is to become easily functional and thus instrumental for practical reasons in people's everyday lives, it should be intrinsically motivating, pleasant for its own sake, or *ludic*. Ludic is shorthand for the cluster of pleasant, playful sensations implied by the Latin verb *ludere*, "to play" (Nell, 1988).

Paradoxically, whereas a considerable portion of the American population has resisted learning in general, and reading in particular, interest in adult education for people who are already literate has greatly expanded in this country. It seems to fill such an important need that many highly literate adults are willing to go back to teacher-dominated classrooms to gain the further education they want. For example, Elderhostel programs of adult education for people long out of college have proliferated and spread at a dizzying rate.

Literacy specialists often assume that this hunger for learning will hold true for attendance in literacy classrooms too, that low-literate people are also eager to return to a school classroom to learn to read well. Most policy makers agree that *instrumental* literacy, literacy acquired for a practical reason, is necessary for people to function competently in the many technological aspects of our society. However, formal classroom teaching is a less than compelling choice for many, perhaps most, low-literate persons. No matter what the tangible external rewards of instrumental literacy, a classroom is not likely to attract depressed, single-parent mothers who have dropped out of high school (to take one segment of the low-literate population) unless they have first been intrinsically motivated by starting with ludic reading, have discovered the *enjoyment* to be found in reading. Through increasing their literacy by reading for pleasure, they are then ready to read for utilitarian reasons. This chapter will argue that ludic literacy thus can be, for otherwise unmotivated adults, the threshold to instrumental literacy.

According to the National Coalition for Literacy, literacy programs are reaching only 3 million people, a mere 10 percent of the adults with grossly inadequate reading skills (Lipschultz, 2006). Even more dismaying to those who wish to combat illiteracy in this country through literacy classrooms, one third of those who start literacy courses (usually one semester long) drop out before completing them (Hunter & Harman, 1979) and only one in three enrollees succeeds in advancing one educational level (Goetz, 2005).

More Americans are low literate in 2003 than in 1992 (National Center for Education Statistics, 2005), so that the trend noted by Cross more than twenty-five years ago toward an ever-increasing gap between the well educated and the poorly educated seems disturbingly prophetic (Cross, 1981).

The small proportion of adults actually reached by group or individual literacy classes throughout the United States (e.g., government funded Adult Basic Education and Right to Read; the privately supported Literacy Volunteers of America; and the famous Laubach "each one teach one" program (Laubach & Laubach, 1960)) are usually well-motivated people. They tend not to be poor; their cultural milieus value education; and they often have immediate practical reasons for acquiring literacy, even if it means only to be able to read and write in English as a second language.

In spite of the accumulation of an enormous literature on literacy programs, there are few data about their effectiveness and almost none about the reactions of the intended or actual recipients of the programs. An exception is one small study of literacy class enrollees (Taylor, Wade, Blum, Gould, & Jackson, 1980). The study tended to confirm that illiterate people are seldom intrinsically motivated to seek literacy programs. In fact, interviews with the study's subjects (literacy students who were in the class for specific practical reasons such as being able to qualify for a driving license) revealed that students' background subculture was permeated with a kind of amused contempt for people who required literacy in their everyday living rather than using more primitive but time-hallowed nonwritten means of social communication.

Yet it can be only a question of time before the demands of our increasingly technological and service-oriented society will reduce such contentedly illiterate subcultures to a very small number. The 1975 report on Texas University's federally sponsored Adult Performance Level Project indicated that 23 million adults lacked minimal functional competencies vital to success in such a society (Adult Performance Level Project, 1975). Despite some controversy over its approach, this report has brought a shift toward assessing the effectiveness of literacy programs through students' attainment of the kind of life-related performance tasks identified by the Adult Performance Level survey as functional competencies important to surviving in American society. A competency-based learner assessment system, the Comprehensive Adult Student Assessment System, is now frequently used to satisfy funders' requirements for adult literacy program evaluation.

The limited effectiveness of the strategy of literacy classes suggests that the learning of attitudes toward literacy and the acquisition of literacy, at least by low-literate parents and their children, might do well to avoid the classroom altogether. The classroom has not been a conspicuously successful setting for adult or even child literacy programs. Indeed, the family is the basic educational unit for the preschool child's initial socialization, with a parent being a child's first teacher for all of his or her learning, including the child's attitudes and readiness for literacy, as well as for functional psychosocial skills. In the United States, this parent is more likely to be a child's mother than his or her father. The responsibility for a child's early psychosocial and cognitive growth is thus either primarily or completely in the hands of the parents and especially of the mother, who is much more likely to be a child's sole parent; the parents, in effect, become society's representatives in the cognitive and social–emotional education of the preschool child.

If the child's parents are literate, the tasks of leading the child to literacy are usually a natural part of interaction with the child. But if the parents are not, what then?

To help their child, and themselves too, the parents should become literate enough to read to a toddler too young to learn to read alone. They should be literate enough to enjoy reading for themselves so that they are able to convey to their child that reading itself is intrinsically motivating or ludic. If reading becomes enjoyable enough, a parent may eventually be externally motivated—by goals of being able to fill out a job application or to be able to help an older child with homework—to enter or continue his or her own classroom education, including classes that teach instrumental literacy.

Television programs reach into almost every home in the country, no matter how impoverished, urgently conveying messages to mothers and fathers about the importance of education for opening job and other social opportunities for their children. Data from early intervention follow-up studies have indicated the importance of expanding parents' own roles in supporting their children's education (e.g., Consortium for Longitudinal Studies, 1983; Levenstein, Levenstein, Shiminski, & Stolzberg, 1998). The yearning of even the most illiterate parents for the school success of their children can be crystallized into enrollment in literacy programs for themselves and their preschool children, on condition that the programs are inviting enough to motivate the most disadvantaged of parents, those most in need of such programs. This observation has led to the current concept of two-generation family literacy programs, often funded under the umbrella of Even Start. It is clear from the extremely low enrollment of such persons in classroom literacy programs that new approaches must be used to meet their need for basic reading literacy and subsequent ability to master what Cross (1981) refers to as "adult functional competencies." Those new methods must be intrinsically motivating and, in fact, enjoyable if they are to capture the enrollment and continuing cooperation of that target population. In short, *ludic* reading should precede reading for practical, instrumental competence.

What are the characteristics of ludic, or pleasurable, reading? A leading educator, Lauren Resnick, named one that seemed to her indispensable: "Engagement with the text is the primary requisite for pleasurable literacy, and many kinds of texts—from pulp crime stories and Gothic romances to high literature—are capable of providing that engagement." Resnick (1990, p. 180) went on to note: "Psychologists and literary scholars seem to agree that readers of popular stories—mysteries, romances, and the like—focus all energies on understanding the situation described and perhaps on imagining themselves in that situation."

Similarly, Csikszentmihalyi (1990) has commented, in relation to school experience, that "lamentably few students recognize the idea that learning can be enjoyable," and that "the obstacles that stand in the way of learning are primarily motivational" (pp. 116, 118–119). He reminds us that although reading, writing, and computation developed out of ancient rulers' economic needs, each kind of learning eventually became enjoyable—ludic—for its own sake: "The writer who discovers the possibility of creating a fictional world more intriguing than the world of actual experience, and the reader who discovers that world, will seek out literacy for its own sake, whether it provides them with jobs in the long run or not" (p. 125). Further: "The phenomenology of enjoyment seems to be a panhuman constant" (p. 127). Csikszentmihalyi declared: "The theoretical model that describes intrinsically rewarding experiences is *the flow model.* . . . When a person feels that skills are fully engaged by challenges, one enters the state of flow" (pp. 127–128).

Individuals are frequently in the position of deciding whether a specific stimulus is interpreted as a challenge or an obstacle. Flow experiences are characterized by challenges matched by a person's skills, by clear goals and immediate feedback about meeting the goals, by concentration, and by transcendence of the self. Thus, the experience becomes rewarding in itself, or *autotelic.*

Arguably, guiding parents to literacy should be aimed at helping them to read autotelically, for literacy's intrinsic rewards, before they can use literacy effectively for extrinsic rewards. As Amabile (1983) has found in regard to preserving children's spontaneous interest in reading, this guidance should avoid imposition of strict controls, emphasis on evaluation and competition, or making the new reader feel self-conscious. Thus, it will help parents' attitudes toward reading if the person directly attempting to influence them can convey how much *fun* literacy can be. The 1994 National Assessment of Educational Progress study of national reading achievement found that the contextual element of fun characterizes the experience of expert readers at every grade level tested (Campbell, Donahue, Reese, & Phillips, 1996).

New methods that include ludic reading may involve unaccustomed locations as well as a different pedagogy. Unconscious resistance to novel approaches is described by Szwed (1981), who ended his questioning of literacy orthodoxies and his plea for examining the actual uses of literacy with the recommendation that focus be on the school's relation to the community, its knowledge of the community's needs and wishes, and the community's actual resources.

In writing about an important side issue, the Nigerian American scholar John Ogbu postulated the influence on school learning of differences between *voluntary* and *involuntary* immigration to this country, a country made up as it is in large part of immigrant ethnic groups. African Americans who descend from slaves are *involuntary* immigrants and, in Ogbu's view, as such resist the literacy values of larger society. "Some black youths obviously become more or less imprisoned in peer orientation and activity that are hostile to academic striving. . . . They refuse to learn, to conform to school rules of behavior and standard practices; these are defined as being within the white American cultural frame of reference" (Ogbu, 1990, p. 163). Those who hope to guide African American parents toward literacy should be aware that similar obstacles may exist for them. Arguably, such guidance is more likely to succeed if parents are aided individually, in the privacy of their own homes, away from peer pressures against literacy success as well as from the threat of public humiliation.

Although agreeing that interest probably has a role as a motivating factor in learning in general (including literacy learning), Suzanne Hidi saw a need for more empirical evidence. Hidi (1990) wrote of the *interestingness* of situations, both individual and situational. She had tried to track down data supporting the functional role of interest in facilitation of cognitive processes, specifically of learning in the classroom. She felt this functional relationship had yet to be sufficiently demonstrated, despite many studies pointing in the same direction. Despite these cautions, she went so far as to assert: "I wish to argue that one energetic feature of the organism—interest—is central in determining how we select and persist in processing certain types of information in preference to others," though she had begun her review by noting that "very little progress has been made toward integrating cognitive factors with motivational and affective aspects of thinking" (Hidi, 1990, p. 549). She cited studies demonstrating that individuals ranging in age from three years to college age pay more attention, persist for longer periods, and acquire more and qualitatively different knowledge if they are interested in a task or activity than are individuals without such interest.

Hidi's focus seemed wholly instrumental—the influence of interest on amount and rate of learning rather than on the joy of learning—but she too was intrigued by the positive affective elements of cognitive activity, whatever these may be called. She ended her article by affirming (pp. 565–566): "If the arguments presented in this paper gain further empirical support, they should lead to a wider recognition of the unique role interest plays in determining the course and outcome of our mental activities. Then perhaps the potential impact of interest as a motivating force and as a mental resource can be fully realized, rather than assumed, by both researchers and practitioners."

Compared to Hidi's rigorous standards for what is acceptable as evidence for the relation between motivation and learning, most writing about literacy is anecdotal or speculative. Fader's *The New Hooked on Books* falls into the former category yet is very persuasive about the new reading enthusiasm that can be provoked in reading-resistant adolescents by making a large quantity of interesting books easily available to them (the Saturation-Diffusion method): "Saturation refers to the materials used in every classroom to induce the child to enter the doorway of literacy" (Fader, 1976, p. 83).

The Parent–Child Home Program has been promoting child and parent literacy for forty years through saturating families with children's books that are developmentally suited to toddlers, are attractively illustrated, and meet high literary standards. The Program was specifically designed to be nondidactic and is permeated with a ludic spirit intended to make learning and the road to literacy intrinsically motivating for both child and parent. Its Home Visitors model ways of reading together and playing together that are explicitly intended to be fun. Program data relating parent–toddler interactions with later academic outcomes indicate that enjoying those interactions is not just a side benefit but essential to success (Levenstein, 1986), and the Program's ludic aspect likely contributes to its achieving the enrollment and continuing cooperation of even the most disadvantaged, low-coping, and depressed parents (Levenstein & O'Hara, 1993).

The Parent–Child Home Program experience is echoed in Scarborough and Dobrich's (1994) warning, in their review of more than thirty outcome studies of parents reading to their preschoolers, that reading to toddlers is capable of having a negative rather than a positive impact. The authors' explanation for these paradoxical data is what they term the *broccoli effect*: If the reading has not been enjoyable, the youngsters may develop an aversion to literacy just as they may grow up disliking broccoli if that vegetable was forced upon them in early years. Some parents, in their zeal to help their children, may force formal and joyless reading aloud as a duty for both child and parent, rather than as the pleasurable activity modeled by Parent–Child Home Program Home Visitors.

We have reviewed scholarly support for the importance, even indispensability, of the role of interest in people's willingness to acquire basic or functional literacy. Hidi attempted to identify the dimensions of interestingness; Amabile listed the elements that militate against children's interest in learning; Csikszentmihalyi gave a moving account of the flow experience; Resnick sensibly conjectured that engagement in the reading content must be present for reading enjoyment; and Fader offered his observation that saturating the environment with interesting books can stimulate even poor readers into reading for enjoyment. Low-literate parents' interest in the educational goals, materials, and method of The Parent–Child Home Program sparks and maintains their commitment to what is essentially a literacy program for both parent and child.

It remained for Robert White to marshal what appears to be incontrovertible evidence from empirical studies of animals and humans for the existence of an interest-aroused instinct—as strong as those for sex or hunger—for the individual to master the environment (White, 1959; 1963); where reading is concerned, this concept is closely related to Csikszentmihalyi's concept of flow. The drive toward mastery can result in an urge to read not only in a child but also in an adult, as the results of The Parent–Child Home Program show. In the Program, for both parent and child, feelings of competency are built on their actual competence, and the self-respect and interest in literacy activities of each increase in turn because of those feelings, creating a positive self-fulfilling prophecy.

The Parent–Child Home Program has tried incorporating these concepts to address adult literacy explicitly, beyond the literacy enhancement implicit in the Program's usual method. In 1989, a replication of the Program in a small South Carolina school system, with funding from the federal Even Start family literacy program, undertook overtly to promote parents' ludic reading and thus, it is hoped, their lifelong interest in reading as a source of pleasure and practical knowledge by installing a further literacy component for the participant-parents. In addition to the basic Parent–Child Home Program, these parents (all women, mainly African American, with an average education of fifth grade) received interesting storybooks for themselves at the same time that their children received their weekly books. Almost all of the books given to the mothers were fiction and were either chosen to fit the mothers' interests and reading ability, which ranged from total illiteracy to seventh grade reading ability, or were simplified well-known classics such as *David Copperfield*. A mother's Home Visitor usually read the book herself, thus adding to her own reading skills, so that she could take a few minutes to exchange opinions of it informally with the mother during the following week's home session. The children, all at risk, showed excellent cognitive progress by the Program's end, more than half of them no longer judged in need of Chapter I school academic aid (Springs, 1990). Anecdotal evidence from Home Visitors and the Parent–Child Home Program site director indicated that almost all of the mothers were eager to receive the books and showed by their conversations that they both read and enjoyed them.

With approaches such as this Parent–Child Home Program experiment, the experience of efficacy or flow can, it would seem, be put to the service of low-literate persons who wish to acquire instrumental reading competencies. But to accomplish this, the efficacy or flow experience itself must first have been stimulated through people having internalized the joy of reading—through ludic literacy.

10.

Messages from Home

Meditations and Conclusions

"What I have taught my two year old, he remembers very well!"
—Written comment of a Parent–Child Home Program mother

orty years have gone into developing The Parent–Child Home
Program, building a reliable replication method so that the Program
could be exported outside its original research setting, documenting
its beneficial effects, and disseminating its model ever more widely. The
Program has helped children in myriad settings—inner city, rural, suburban; European American, African American, Native American, Asian
American; Alaskan Eskimo villages, New Mexican Indian reservations,
northern Canada, the Commonwealth of Bermuda, Turkish immigrant and
Gypsy communities in the Netherlands; immigrants to the United States
from dozens of countries—under the auspices of every sort of nonprofit organization.

Wherever the Program has been adopted, every attempt has been made
to keep it an exact copy of the original to give participants the full benefit of
the intervention's effects. This also means that the National Center has had
feedback from each replication's experience with what is in effect the original Program.

By now, the experience of the model Parent–Child Home Program and
of its hundreds of replications over the years have produced some compelling messages. They come, literally, from the homes of participating low-
income parents and their children.

Message One: Hope

Periodically in this country the pendulum of public interest in education swings to disquiet about the problems of high school students, particularly those who come from low-income families and who are not planning to go to college. Generally, a major concern is with the poor academic achievement of many such students. Their preparation for any but entry-level jobs is even more inadequate if a student does not remain in school long enough to receive a high school diploma.

In the last decades, while the mere holding of a high school diploma has become less and less of a qualification, disturbingly little headway has been made in improving graduation rates. The first edition of this book cited a 1985 *New York Times* story headlined: "Study Finds City Schools Made no Progress in Reducing Dropouts" (Rohter, 1985), which reported that 11.4 percent of the students in public New York City high schools dropped out during the 1983–1984 school year study and that 38.4 per cent of all entering freshmen would leave school before they graduated. More recent reports show that 42 percent of New York City freshmen and 32 percent of high school freshman *nationwide* fail to graduate on time (The New York City Department of Education, 2006; United Health Foundation, 2005).

High school is boring and embarrassing for students who are unable to cope with it. Dropping out may seem a logical solution to them. This is obvious to most observers, but few see a connection between the weaknesses in young people's academic performance in high school and the academic problems of first graders.

In fact, however, these failures are intimately related. Children's disadvantage in acquiring skills as early as first grade, stemming from insufficient preparation before entering school, continues and compounds throughout their school careers. As long ago as 1966 the sociologist James Coleman, in his famous report, *Equality of Educational Opportunity,* made the remarkably contemporary observation that the educational disadvantage with which a group begins school remains the disadvantage with which it finishes (Coleman & Campbell, 1966).

Children from Hesitater families in what was once called the underclass compose one of the largest groups to begin school with an educational disadvantage. They often start kindergarten after having had inadequate access to the *hidden family curriculum* in their preschool years. The gap between these children and those who have had in their own homes this casual, informal preparation for school becomes all too evident in first grade. Such highly disadvantaged pupils tend to lag in acquiring the reading and math skills that are the foundation for most of their learning in higher grades. The closer they get to high school, the wider the gap grows.

The first message from home is a message of hope for such families and for society. The Parent–Child Home Program provides a feasible option to prevent the early elementary school disadvantage that is the precursor of high school failure. It fosters the development in low-income children's homes of the hidden curriculum latent in all families.

In children's very early years, before they reach center-based preschools and long before they reach elementary school, much of their academic disadvantage at the high school level can be headed off—and so can some of the cost to society and the taxpayer of expenditures for special education, welfare support, and criminal-justice proceedings. A Michigan research group headed by educator David Weikart published a study in 1984 that concretely documented the economic profit to society of effective preschool education (Berrueta-Clement, Schweinhart, Barnett, Epstein, & Weikart, 1984), echoed recently by the comptroller of the City of New York in his calculations from Parent–Child Home Program data (Hevesi, 2001) as well as by cost-benefit analyses by other groups.

The hope embodied in the first message from home is grounded in objective evidence: the short-term and long-term data from forty years of investigating the effects of The Parent–Child Home Program on pre-preschool children and parents. Though the research is not entirely free of methodological limitations, studies by both in-house and outside evaluators have found that both the model program and its replications aid low-income children's intellectual growth and later school performance. Program children's school readiness scores (Levenstein, Levenstein, & Oliver, 2002; Shiminski, 2005a); their third grade and fifth grade reading, math, and cognitive scores (Bradshaw-McNulty & Delaney, 1979; Lazar & Darlington, 1982; Levenstein, O'Hara, & Madden, 1983); their performance in middle school (DeVito & Karon, 1984, 1990); and their high school graduation rates (Levenstein, Levenstein, Shiminski, & Stolzberg, 1998) not only significantly surpass those of nonprogram children of similar background but achieve the levels of national norms for middle-class youngsters. There is thus good reason to think that the Program as implemented in sites across the country helps to provide low-income children with the home enrichment they need to achieve success in higher grades by enabling them to achieve academically in the early grades.

Message Two:
The Parent–Child Network

The second message from home is that a supportive parent–child network, which could only be surmised when The Parent–Child Home Program began, actually does exist. Studies have shown that the Program evokes from parent-participants the kinds of interaction with their preschool children that foster children's ability to cope with the challenges of elementary school. Parent and child together—responding positively to each other in play and conversation—weave a strong mutually supportive network from their interaction, linked to their emotional relationship. Like many invisible supports between parents and children, it is hard to tell which strands come from the parent and which from the child.

Parent–Child Home Program researchers have shown that when parents use certain positive verbal and nonverbal interactive behaviors with their children during the children's preschool years at home, the children turn out to display specific competencies in first and second grade (Levenstein, 1986). If the parents actively converse with their preschool children while showing warmth and affection, the children are likely in elementary school to be self-confident, task oriented, intellectually competent, and creative, and to have good reading and math skills. At the same time, the data indicate the importance of keeping that parent–child interaction casual and nonpressuring. Laughter and joy seem to play important roles in weaving the network, whereas a didactic approach on the part of the parent has, paradoxically, a negative effect on children's school-age learning.

The development of a network out of reciprocal parent–child responsiveness explains the power of Dr. Bettye Caldwell's Home Observation for Measurement of the Environment (HOME) instrument (Bradley, Caldwell, & Rock, 1988) for predicting children's cognitive development from their home environments and their parents' activity in infancy. In Parent–Child Home Program research, the parent usually has been observed to be the one to start the conversational ball rolling between herself and her young child and to bestow occasional hugs or their equivalents. But it is the child's responses that keep the ball in motion. It is apparent over and over in home sessions and in videotaped parent–child play that when a child smiles or replies or points to the right book illustration or puts a puzzle piece in the right place, the parent is delighted. With such positive feedback, the parent is encouraged to continue the interaction. Together they weave a network that supports the child's school-age competencies, the parent's self-esteem, and the sense of well-being in both of them that can be called mental health.

The parent-child bond is the secret edge The Parent–Child Home Program offers over school-based or center-based programs. Preschools provide social experiences and large muscle playground and classroom equipment most parents can't give, even those well above the poverty level. However only families can provide the early combination of emotional and cognitive growth that creates the supportive basis for children's later school success—and all parental figures, no matter how low their educational or social level, can be guided to accomplish this.

Message Three: Strivers and Hesitaters

One of the persistent American social myths, which fuelled welfare reform in the 1990s, says that single parents receiving public assistance are uniformly apathetic, incompetent mothers who would stay contentedly supported by welfare checks all their lives if they could.

Most social agency staff members who work among the poor have seen flaws in this vision but have had few systematically gathered facts to substantiate their perceptions. Concrete evidence to confute this distorted view of the disadvantaged is the third message that emerges from The Parent–Child Home Program: Home Visitors' recorded ratings of parents' interactive behavior in home sessions with their children provide empirical data to explode the myth of the monolithic welfare class.

During the first years of the Program, we observed that many participant-mothers, at the time they first enrolled, were indeed apathetic and unable to deal with everyday crises. We came to call these women *Hesitaters* for their great difficulty in moving forward with their lives, immobilized as they were by depression and hopelessness. Their inertia was manifested in their lack of interaction with their children in their early Parent–Child Home Program home sessions and sometimes throughout the first year of the two-year program. Superficially, they presented a picture close to the stereotype of the welfare poor. But most of the Hesitaters slowly changed—toward more interaction with their children, toward increased initiative in dealing with daily problems, toward self-respect. Because of their capacity to change, most Hesitaters in The Parent–Child Home Program, once the Program offered them the hope of something better for themselves and their children, eventually revealed themselves to have it in them to become more like what the Program called *Strivers*.

Though Hesitaters are the core of The Parent–Child Home Program's target population, we observed early on that some Program parents did not have Hesitater characteristics. These Striver parents entered the Program with the same low income as the Hesitaters and were similarly receiving public assistance, but they stood out in the eyes of Home Visitors by becoming active in home sessions almost at once, in Session 1 or 2. They grasped the Program's interaction techniques intuitively, or learned them immediately from the Home Visitors, and caught on promptly to applying them in their everyday lives. It was quickly apparent from the home session activity of these mothers that their basic difference from the Hesitaters was in *motivation* beyond the universal of parental love, which had drawn them to participate in the first place. They seemed determined to take charge of their lives, to be free of the demeaning morass of public assistance, to escape from the world of the disadvantaged. They needed little help from the Program except for the gifts of books and toys plus a little home-visitor modeling to encourage them to do what they knew instinctively and to guide them away from pushing their children too hard.

A higher rate of high school graduation (in one set of families, 78 percent vs. 29 percent) (Levenstein, 1988, pp. 144–145) was the one obvious background feature that distinguished Striver from Hesitater parents before they entered the model Parent–Child Home Program. The high school diploma may well indicate a trait of persistence—the ability to "hang in there"—that is of greater importance than the additional educational content. All of the parents met the Program's entry requirements of having no more than a high school education, but the Strivers' higher rate of actual twelfth grade *completion* was consistent with staff observations of Strivers being more psychologically intact.

Many observations suggested, however, that Strivers too had to deal with problems such as depression and low self-esteem although not to the degree that these problems impeded the Hesitaters. Hesitaters were felt by staff members to improve in their self-confidence and self-competence more dramatically than Strivers did as they perceived their own progress in the Program, but the mental health of many Strivers likewise seemed to display improvement as their time in the intervention went forward.

The Program's discovery that there were both Hesitaters and Strivers within its own research samples greatly alters the lazy welfare mother stereotype. It leads to the recognition that many parents on public assistance are so strongly motivated to improve their own and their children's lives that they are quickly able to make their own a valuable method to give their children a better chance of climbing out of poverty. Program research also demonstrates that with the intensive Parent–Child Home Program, Hesitaters can become Strivers, with the same ultimate goal of achieving decent jobs and an education for themselves and their children.

Message Four: Social Feasibility of the Program

Over the years of developing and studying The Parent–Child Home Program, its practicability for nationwide use has been explored and refined. The fourth message from home is that the method is feasible as a social program almost anywhere in this country and in many other parts of the world. It is exportable, inexpensive, popular at all levels from Program participants to Home Visitors to agency executives, and can generate entry level jobs through the role of the Home Visitor.

Exportability

One crucial question for any potential social program is whether the model program will be reproducible and therefore effective outside of its original laboratory setting. Many years went into developing the exportability of The Parent–Child Home Program, with generation of standardized procedures for disseminating information about the Program and for assisting adopter organizations to implement accurate replications of the original model program. The user friendliness and efficiency of these procedures is confirmed concretely by the continued existence in 2007 of fifteen very early program replications whose operations have been ongoing, with their key elements intact, since before 1980 (see www.parent-child.org).

It seems clear that the Parent–Child Home Program is exportable with its crucial characteristics in place. Thus, it can be expected to have much the same benefits for low-income families wherever it is replicated.

Cost

The annual cost of the Program in 2007 was roughly $2,500 for each parent–child pair—less than that if volunteers are used rather than paid Home Visitors. Program budgets are largely determined not by the cost of the books and toys but by the amount required for salaries, which necessarily vary in accordance with local standards. These costs compare favorably with other early intervention programs.

Popularity

Many observers are won over by The Parent–Child Home Program, possibly because, aside from its arguable charm, it has a certain face validity ("Of course—that's it! Give them what I had [or: what I missed] when I was a kid!"). Also, because of its light touch and explicit ethical safeguards, it keeps the Hippocratic oath to "abstain from all intentional wrongdoing and harm . . . and whatsoever I shall see or hear . . . I will never divulge."

Such preservation of family privacy is of crucial importance, as is the Program's respect for a family's way of life. The program tries to incorporate wherever possible the family's cultural/sociolinguistic differences from mainstream culture while at the same time offering links to that mainstream culture in the form of the curriculum and some of the books and toys.

Most of the disadvantaged parents and children who are approached are quickly drawn to The Parent–Child Home Program and remain committed to it as participants. Home Visitors like the Program because it is enjoyable to learn and deliver; because they appreciate being trusted to do a meaningful job whose effects are clearly and quickly visible; and because they are pleased by their semiautonomy within a firm supervisory structure. Coordinators and replicator executives become committed to the Program because it makes sense (*face validity*) and because it aids low-income groups with a minimum outlay of resources and maximum approval by the community.

Entry-Level Jobs in the Program

Program parents learn The Parent–Child Home Program well from their own experience. When they "graduate," many are ready to be trained by the Program to become paid Home Visitors themselves, if they so desire.

Home Visitors do not have to be former parent-participants; they may have any education or work experience. A Ph.D. psychologist could function as well in the role as a high school- educated welfare recipient could— but the salary she would command would be much higher than any budget could afford. So far, all replications have hired as their paid Home Visitors (sometimes alongside better-educated volunteers) individuals with limited educational and work experience. They are often the most effective Home Visitors, enabling the site to reach out to families who might not respond to a knock on a door from a professional and providing wonderful role models for the new Program parents.

That experience incidentally offers to those parents who need it the opportunity to learn the basic skills necessary for any job: Home Visitors must keep home session appointments punctually and consistently, write legible home session records and keep them up to date, and show up promptly for weekly staff conferences (group supervision).

Message Five: They Aren't Laboratory Rats

A basic problem for those who conduct research with young children is that preschoolers, unlike laboratory rats, cannot be commandeered. Nor can they volunteer themselves to be research subjects. In our society, even when an intervention program for young children does not involve research, it requires at least the parents' consent and usually their cooperation.

A two year old can't join even a nursery school on his own, let alone The Parent–Child Home Program. Certainly a two-year-old child could not agree to be in a pool of potential research subjects and await later randomization into a program or a nonprogram group, as a preliminary to a subject-randomized research study.

Parents who don't cooperate on their children's behalf with an early childhood program, or with studies of it, have selected themselves and their children out. Parents who give their cooperation have selected themselves and their children in. They and their children are volunteers for the program or for the research.

Why does this create a problem for research? A parent's failure to take advantage of a program beneficial to child and parent can be considered distressing. But why is this uncooperativeness a problem for research?

The problem, as became clear in the subject-randomized research of The Parent–Child Home Program's effects on IQ test performance, lies in the sample bias that can be created by selection of subjects by the researchers or by self-selection of the subjects themselves. In evaluation research involving consensual subject-by-subject randomization, self-selection tends to exclude the most disadvantaged and therefore risks resulting in a subject pool that is not truly representative of the population a program is meant to reach.

As discussed in Chapter 6, a high degree of self-selection by subjects to be evaluated for measuring the effectiveness of a potential intervention program becomes a social problem when the program to be evaluated is a potential social remedy. If the children and parents are recruited to enter an intervention program intended to prevent school problems, and there turns out to be no difference in child outcomes between program and nonprogram groups because most of the parents are ambitious Strivers with well-functioning children, observers may be led to reject the program on the basis of flawed experimental evaluation research—potentially a serious loss to society.

As long as preschool children are dependent on their mothers and fathers for cooperation with programs aimed at them, the true effects of the programs may often be best measured by using experimental research designs that enroll subjects who have been previously randomized by location or group, to minimize the problem of self-selection. Even then, the parents' initial willingness to come into a program and their continuing cooperation should be carefully estimated and taken into account in evaluating the results. The ideal subject-randomized experiment is difficult to attain with very young children under ordinary conditions, which require parents' informed consent, especially when the target population is historically disadvantaged groups who may be even less eager to cooperate with research projects.

Message Six: Closing the Gap

*"The historic goal of preschool and remedial programs for
students from low-income families has been to close the
achievement gap separating them from children of higher
income families."*

—G. I. MAEROFF

This was how Maeroff began an article in the *New York Times* in 1985,
voicing succinctly the goal of the Parent–Child Home Program. His
headline was: "Despite Head Start, 'Achievement Gap' Persists for the
Poor" (Maeroff, 1985). He went on to report a study in one very large
school system that found that although the school performance of students who had graduated from Head Start was "better than they would
have done without it," the academic achievement of most lagged behind
national norms and behind that of the non–Head Start-eligible school
population (Hebbeler, 1985). Many years and many studies later, the
evidence that Head Start has a substantial impact on its participants'
achievement gap later in their schooling is still not as strong as had been
hoped (Garces, Thomas, & Currie, 2002), partly because, as both
Edward Zigler and Jeanne Brooks-Gunn have pointed out, some of those
hopes were so overblown (Brooks-Gunn, 2003; Zigler, Haskins, &
Lyon, 2004).

The most thorough studies of the long-term effect on the achievement
gap of The Parent–Child Home Program over many years have been in the
Pittsfield public schools. Socioeconomically disadvantaged program graduates not only met national academic norms in middle school and high
school (DeVito & Karon, 1984, 1990), but matched the rates of graduation
from high school of middle-class children—they dropped out of school at
half the rate of non–program-randomized controls and of other low-income
students in the district (Levenstein, Levenstein, Shiminski, & Stolzberg,
1998; see also Chapter 5).

The sixth message from home is succinct: for graduates of The Parent–Child Home Program, the achievement gap seems to have been closed.

Message Seven: Print Literacy in
the Electronic Age

We have entered the Electronic Age of Learning. Exciting video and computer possibilities have opened new ways of extending children's cognitive
and creative abilities. Just as Gutenberg's fifteenth-century invention of
movable type and the printing press opened the way to literacy for ordinary

people, the learning possibilities of the Electronic Age seem to represent another giant step forward.

Yet like other gifts from the gods—like fire, which makes a good servant when properly controlled but a bad master when it is not; like nuclear power, which still hovers between serving and destroying the human race—computers pose potential problems.

One such problem is the kind of dependency forecast a century ago by E. M. Forster's fable "The Machine Stops." This story envisaged, with eerie technological accuracy, the support of a rather dreary civilization by a vast worldwide Machine. The Machine served people's every need as they lived their underground lives in cell-like apartments and conducted their contacts with each other by videophone—a depressing fantasy of social isolation that threatens to be matched, in only slightly less intense form, by the realities of the computer age. In Forster's story, the Machine faltered, the lights dimmed, and the air became foul. At last, the Machine stopped, and civilized humanity died out (Forster, 1909). Forster's cautionary tale is frighteningly contemporary now that American children spend an average of five hours a day in front of one screen or another—and 12 percent of marriages start online.

Another problem related to the Electronic Age of Learning is the yawning gap between Web-savvy youngsters empowered to tap worldwide electronic resources and the sons and daughters of the poor who, lacking computers at home and knowledgeable parents, are left ever more behind. This *digital divide* may appear to be narrowing, with less advantaged children beginning to pick up computer skills, but some of the leveling of the playing field can be illusory since the concrete purposes for which young people use computers vary wildly from chatting with new acquaintances to playing shoot-'em-up games to downloading music to shopping to viewing pornography—exploring intellectual interests is not at the top of everyone's list.

A final problem centers around the threat to what some call *print literacy*, in contrast to *electronic literacy*. Although the postliterate society will never literally come to pass—computer use does require reading skills, and writing remains essential if only for composing instant messages—book reading risks dying off. It is true that reading a book takes more sustained effort than watching a video or clicking through a Web site, but a well-written book can stretch the reader's mind, imagination, and empathy. The very ambiguity of a book calls forth thinking and feeling beyond what the screen can evoke; subjects can be explored in depth rather than skimmed along the surface, and people's capacity to identify with and feel for others can grow through acquaintance with books.

Print literacy is necessary to enter the world of books. It is possible that this realm of imagination may soon be closed to all but an elite, those for whom electronic literacy is a practical means to an end but not a unique source of information and pleasure. Others may acquire just enough print literacy to study and carry around the manuals for learning a trade. The rest may swell the numbers of the disadvantaged classes at the bottom of the social pyramid, classes even more illiterate and emotionally alienated than they are today. Without print literacy, the dream of escape from poverty can be hopeless.

The seventh message from home is that The Parent–Child Home Program lays the groundwork for print literacy and love of books very early in children's experience. Its method for doing so increases children's accessibility to feelings, their own and those of others. The increased bonding between parents and children and the deepened social–emotional development of children are what make possible the growth of human empathy and of humanness itself. The Program has the power to offset some of the nonhuman, even antihuman, aspects of the Electronic Age.

Message Eight: Actualization of Cognitive Theory

The main conceptual message of the second edition of *Messages from Home* is that the successful early education intervention it describes is the ultimate illustration of the validity of the cognitive development theories of Jerome Bruner and Lev Vygotsky. The Parent–Child Home Program puts their ideas into operation in a practical and long-lasting way that expands on Vygotsky's laboratory experiments and Bruner's vivid examples.

In developing The Parent–Child Home Program, its founder brought two additions to the crucial feature of concept-building verbal interaction between toddler and parent:

1. The element of motivation for the dyad's participation in the Program: Motivation is provided by gifts of attractive, educationally valuable objects (interactive toys and illustrated books) to be the subject of dyad conversations; by absence of overt teaching (limiting Home Visitor to *demonstrations* of verbal interaction); by program acceptance of cultural variations (e.g., languages other than English); and by respect for the dignity of parents (home visits scheduled at parents' convenience; no advice or intrusive comments or attempts at close friendship by Home Visitors).
2. The use of parents as the adult half of constructive dyadic interactions not only because of their proximity, but also to take advantage of the already existing emotional bond between parent and toddler.

It is not common for an early childhood intervention thus to overtly operationalize the theories on which it may be based. A cognitive theorist may be mentioned as influential (e.g., Piaget in the Perry Preschool Project), but there is often little attempt to pinpoint how the theories are borne out by an intervention's specific features. Even the first edition of *Messages from Home* did not emphasize the implications for developmental cognitive theory of the Program's success. The Parent–Child Home Program is, of course, intended to be, and has succeeded in being, socially valuable, but a parallel importance lies in the practical validation by that success of the ideas in which it was grounded.

As an educational tool, this second edition of *Messages from Home* has an overt subject—a detailed description of The Parent–Child Home Program—that is intrinsically interesting and timely for educators, giving them the chance to become familiar with an effective early intervention as have their colleagues in the 150 currently active replication sites. In the context of the Program itself, this book is intended to have sufficient instructional value to serve as an intriguing and important element in the training of replicators. But for college students of developmental psychology, early education, sociology, and social–educational policy, the book may have scholarly interest above and beyond its social value as an exploration of some practical implications of the developmental cognitive theories of two eminent psychologists.

Message Nine: A Gift from the Poor?

The ninth and last message from home begins with a question: What will be the future application of The Parent–Child Home Program? Will it be used more and more as a resource for the socioeconomically disadvantaged, as was intended at its creation? Or will it largely add to the resources of middle-income parents and children? Might it eventually become a gift to the middle class from the disadvantaged parents who helped in its development?

The Parent–Child Home Program is only one of a number of well-researched exemplary preschool and elementary school educational programs developed in the 1960s and 1970s using government or private foundation funding, with the mission of serving disadvantaged children. Program development and validation was funded, but as soon as the initial efficacy research was completed (and sometimes even before), much of the financial support stopped. Few of those programs still survive among the many that demonstrated their effectiveness by careful evaluation research. Notable victims of the funding crunch were the original Perry Preschool (Schweinhart et al., 2004) and the Abecedarian Project (Campbell, Ramey, Pungello, Sparling, & Miller-Johnson, 2002), two programs lauded frequently today for their long-term benefits.

After a sixteen-year, $3 million dollar investment in researching and developing the Parent–Child Home Program by running a model program, the National Center moved on to training sponsoring organizations elsewhere to implement its method with various groups of disadvantaged families. Funding of the model program site on Long Island, which had always been earmarked for supporting development and research, ended long ago. During the 1980s and 1990s, before it secured relatively stable funding as a dissemination and certification point, the National Center was able to maintain its guidance of new replication sites largely because of the continuing activity of some staff members on a volunteer basis and because of in-kind contributions of space, telephone, and secretarial service.

The ability of The Parent–Child Home Program to survive its lean period was a rare exception in the field of early interventions aimed at the disadvantaged. Most programs, to continue and spread their good word, require the nourishment of financial support to prevent their death by malnutrition.

Apart from the Program's readiness to be used for help *to* low income parents, it can also be seen as a gift *from* the disadvantaged to any parents who wish to use it, whatever their socioeconomic status. Thousands of poor families have helped to refine a program that can be used to aid young children of any income level in any part of the English-speaking world—and, as shown by its use in non–English-speaking populations in the United States and in the Netherlands, elsewhere too. All parents are thus indebted to the disadvantaged parents and children who pioneered this effective and joyous method of enhancing the skills of young children while adding to the strengths of their parents.

The low-income parents for whom The Parent–Child Home Program was intended do not have the resources to make use of it on their own. They must have the assistance of replicator organizations such as schools and social agencies. After many years in the shadows, home visiting programs and early childhood interventions for disadvantaged families have now regained some space in the limelight with the considerable long-term successes reported by several such programs, including The Parent–Child Home Program itself. And yet the funding that makes it possible for organizations to implement such programs remains fragile and often elusive.

So the last message from home is a question, and a bittersweet one at that: Will The Parent–Child Home Program continue to thrive in its service to the disadvantaged, or will it evolve into a method for merely further enriching the hidden curriculum of the middle-class family?

The answer cannot be found in this book. It lies in the hands of policymakers, legislators, executives, and purse-string holders at all levels. Only they can decide whether The Parent–Child Home Program will remain a gift *to* the disadvantaged as well as *from* them.

11.

The Parent–Child Home
Program in Writing

Publications by and about the Program,
1968–2007

The Parent–Child Home Program has closely scrutinized its method and its outcomes every step of the way. The result has been a large body of scientific literature, flanked by numerous reports in newspapers and other media. This chapter tells the tale of the Program from its beginnings in the words that have been written about it. A first section presents in chronological order the articles, reports, and book chapters produced for a professional audience over forty years. A second nonprofessional section includes government reports and a sampling of journalistic pieces aimed at the general public. A complete citation is provided for each item, followed by a summary, a comment, or an extract. Some readers will be fascinated to read this account of The Parent–Child Home Program story from beginning to end, whereas for others this listing may serve more as a source of reference information to be dipped into as needed. Of necessity, this chapter includes some technical material.

It should be recalled that the original name of The Parent–Child Home Program was the Mother-Child Home Program; its original central office was called the Verbal Interaction Project; and its home visitors were called Toy Demonstrators. Since these names were changed only in 1997 to The Parent–Child Home Program and, simply, Home Visitors, some older writings use the earlier designations.

Publications about The Parent–Child Home Program

For a Professional Audience

Most of these writings are research studies that examine the Program's effects on child-participants' cognitive development, its effects on low-income children's school performance at follow-up evaluation, its impact on parents or on parent–child verbal and bonding interaction, or issues related to the evolution and replication of The Parent–Child Home Program's model. Several others are articles and book chapters that focus on the theoretical basis of the Program or the broader implications of its experience. All published writings specifically concentrating on The Parent–Child Home Program are listed here in order of publication; a few conference presentations or unpublished reports to granting agencies are included because they include research results of interest not published in other form. Also included are published opinions about The Parent–Child Home Program from child development, education, and public policy experts, and reviews or meta-analyses that include this program along with others as part of evaluations of home visiting or of early-childhood intervention in general. **The listings of writings that include novel Parent–Child Home Program research data are set off by a bold type font.**

As a whole, this body of data provides evidence for the validity of the theoretical concepts of the thinkers described in Chapter 4 and fleshes out the summary of research findings in Chapter 5.

Levenstein, P., & Sunley, R. (1968). Stimulation of verbal interaction between disadvantaged mothers and children. *American Journal of Orthopsychiatry*, 38, 116–121.

A report of the effects achieved by a small pilot project that preceded The Parent–Child Home Program. The verbal IQs of two matched groups of disadvantaged preschoolers were compared at baseline and after the experimental group had been exposed for four months to stimulation of verbal interaction with their mothers through home visits and play materials. There was a statistically significant rise in the verbal IQ of the six children in the experimental group on the Peabody Picture Vocabulary Test, from 75.8 to 89.5 ($p < .05$), contrasting with stable scores for the six in the control group (from 80.8 to 80.4).

Levenstein, P. (1969, December). *Individual variation among preschoolers in a cognitive intervention program in low-income families.* Paper presented at the Council for Exceptional Children Conference on Early Childhood Education, New Orleans, LA.

At the end of one year of the model Parent–Child Home Program in Freeport, Long Island, thirty-three low-income preschoolers had made an average IQ gain of 17 points. Within the group, however, individual children ranged from a gain of 33 points to a loss of 7 points. This diversity in cognitive outcomes brought intragroup variability into relief: Target populations are made up of individuals who may not respond uniformly to the same intervention.

Levenstein, P. (1970). **Cognitive growth in preschoolers through verbal interaction with mothers.** *American Journal of Orthopsychiatry, 40,* 426–432.

A report of the IQ outcomes of child-participants enrolled in the model Parent–Child Home Program for seven months during the 1968–1969 school year. Three federally supported housing projects for low-income families, in three different Long Island communities eighteen miles apart, had been randomly assigned to three experimental conditions. Families with two year olds or three year olds in one project received one year of The Parent–Child Home Program, and those in the other two projects became control groups, one receiving only yearly cognitive evaluations and the other receiving, in addition, nonverbally stimulating gifts (scarves, step stools, flashlights, etc.). The Parent–Child Home Program group gained 17 points on the Stanford-Binet Intelligence Test after the Program, going from 84.9 to 101.9, whereas the combined control groups' IQ remained stable (89.9 to 90.4). Peabody Picture Vocabulary Test scores rose from 76.8 to 89.0 in experimental children and from 83.4 to 84.0 in the controls. The advantage of experimental children was statistically significant for both tests ($p < .001$ and $p < .05$, respectively).

Levenstein, P. (1971). **Learning through (and from) mothers.** *Childhood Education,* 130–134.

This study examined the behavior and attitudes of participating mothers during their first Parent–Child Home Program year in 1970–1971. When they began the Program, two-thirds of mothers were rated as participating only minimally in home sessions; by the end of the year, the proportion with minimal participation had dropped to one-third. Conversely, the number who were highly active rose from 25 percent to 51 percent. In end-of-year interviews, 60 percent of mothers said they wanted their children to go to college, hoping they would become teachers (26 percent), doctors (26 percent), or other professionals. Home Visitor behaviors felt to contribute to these results included "a policy of preventing intense relationships from growing between Toy Demonstrators and child," and nondidacticism exemplified by Home Visitors' refraining from correcting mothers' grammatical errors.

Wargo, M. J., Campeau, P. L., & Tallmadge, G. K. (1971). *Further Examination of Exemplary Programs for Educating Disadvantaged Children, Final Report.* Palo Alto, CA: American Institutes for Research in the Behavioral Sciences.

"This study was the third in a series conducted by AIR for the U.S. Office of Education which had as its primary objective the identification and description of successful compensatory education programs for disadvantaged children. . . . Programs were considered successful if they demonstrated cognitive benefits that were statistically and educationally significant. . . . Well over 1,200 evaluation reports were reviewed to identify candidate successful programs. . . . In-depth analysis of all available data resulted in the identification of 10 programs that met the majority of the project's established criteria for success. . . . The four primary reasons for rejection were (1) inadequate sample selection, (2) failure to employ reliable and valid instruments, and (3) failure to demonstrate statistically, and (4) educationally significant cognitive benefits." The Parent–Child Home Program was one of those ten selected programs, one of only two preschool programs in the United States that were considered successful compensatory programs for disadvantaged children. The other program, conducted in a school, was operational for only one year.

Levenstein, P., & Levenstein, S. (1971). Fostering learning potential in preschoolers. *Social Casework, 52*(February), 74–78.

Any family agency wishing to help prevent school failure should "(1) place primary value on the family as an institution and on respect for the needs of individuals, whether staff or client; (2) be structured with a minimum of bureaucratization; (3) have a variety of personnel available to it; and (4) be ready to respond with its own resources or referral to community resources to the requests of mothers for help in any area of their lives."

Levenstein, P. (1972). But does it work in homes away from home? *Theory Into Practice, 11,* **157–162.**

The first four replications of The Parent–Child Home Program in educationally disadvantaged populations operated under the auspices of a school system in Massachusetts, a childcare agency in New York City, and family service agencies in New Jersey and in Massachusetts. Children's IQ gains after one year paralleled those in the original model program on Long Island: preprogram Cattell = 90 and Peabody Picture Vocabulary Test = 80; postprogram Stanford-Binet = 106 and Peabody Picture Vocabulary Test = 90 (significant, $p < .001$, in both cases).

Levenstein, P., Kochman, A., & Roth, H. (1973). From laboratory to real world: Service delivery of the Mother-Child Home Program. *American Journal of Orthopsychiatry, 43,* **72–78.**

This paper describes the process involved in starting up the first four Parent–Child Home Program replications outside the model program, in 1970–1971, highlighting problems encountered and solutions found. "The overall lesson learned in this pilot experience with the service delivery of what had been a laboratory experiment was that there were few short cuts in assisting an organization to replicate the Mother-Child Home program. Every step, no matter how adapted to local needs, seemed necessary to ensure the achievement of either the scientific or practical goals of delivering this laboratory generated program to the 'real world.' "

Ginandes, J., & Roth, H. A. (1973). Replication of the Mother-Child Home Program by a foster care agency. *Child Welfare, 12*(2), **75–81.**

"An attempt at early intervention to prevent school problems in a pilot sample of undercare children by duplicating the Verbal Interaction Project's research program resulted in significant gains, analogous to those in the original research, plus positive attitudinal changes in foster mothers and professionals." The family's caseworker took on the role of the Home Visitor with the foster mothers; all fifteen invited families agreed to participate. Parent–Child Home Program children gained an average of 13 IQ points, whereas the control group's IQ fell by 0.7 point. Foster mothers reported "an increase in the pleasurable aspects of the child's learning, thus reducing the tension and the grim striving of the more ambitious foster mothers. . . . Since the characteristics of the foster child involve the feeling of 'not making a difference' as a core problem producing passivity, the 2-year-olds' new habit of initiating conversation was an important development."

Chilman, C. S. (1973). Programs for disadvantaged parents: Some major trends and related research. In B. M. Caldwell & H. N. Ricciuti (Eds.), *Review of child development research*, Vol. 3 (pp. 403–466). Chicago: University of Chicago Press.

"A review of parent education programs on which reports are available reveals that they almost uniformly failed to attract and hold more than a few parents and that measured changes in parental attitudes generally failed to occur." The Parent–Child Home Program, on the other hand, was the only one of seven such programs to obtain "enthusiasm and responsible cooperation from the mothers."

Bronfenbrenner, U. (1974). *Is early intervention effective? A report on longitudinal evaluations of preschool programs*, Vol. 2, DHEW Publication No. (OHD) 74-25. Washington, DC: U.S. Department of Health, Education and Welfare, Office of Child Development, Children's Bureau.

"It is in the social sphere that Levenstein's method is most distinctive. There are two critical aspects in which it differs from the other approaches we have examined thus far: intervention in group settings and tutoring in the home. First, Levenstein's strategy has as its target not the child but the mother-child dyad as an interactive system. Second, the principal and direct agent of intervention becomes not the teacher or the tutor, but the mother. As a result, intervention does not terminate at the end of the program, but continues as long as the patterns of joint activity and interaction between mother and child endure. . . . Moreover, since it is the product of mutual adaptation and learning, the system exhibits a distinctive hand-in-glove quality, and thereby an efficiency, that it would be hard to achieve in nonenduring relationships. Finally, since the participants remain together after intervention ceases, the momentum of the system insures some degree of continuity for the future."

Levenstein, P. (1975). A message from home: Findings from a program for nonretarded, low-income preschoolers. In M. J. Begab & S. B. Richardson (Eds.), *The mentally retarded and society: A social science perspective* (pp. 305–318). Baltimore: University Park Press.

This chapter extends earlier research to include four yearly cohorts of toddlers enrolled in the model Parent–Child Home Program, with longer follow-up. In cohorts entering the now two-year program from 1968 to 1971, children had significant IQ gains and achieved high-normal IQs by the end of the Program (pretest 90, posttest 109). "Toddlers' play using interactive language with a parent aids the developmental task of learning to learn." Parent–Child Home Program participants also showed superior coping skills in first grade, two years later, according to teachers who knew little about the Program and did not know which children had been in it: On the Child's Behavior Traits (CBT), a measure of social, emotional, and behavioral maturity, program children's mean score was 77 and controls' 66 (statistically significant, $p < .02$). At the Program's first eight sites away from the model center, "the range of IQ differences among the replications was wide, immediately suggesting that the program had varying effects on different target populations among the poor."

Hunt, J. McV. (1975). Reflections on a decade of early education. *Journal of Abnormal Child Psychology, 3*, 275–330.

"Most thoroughly tested of the programs for preventing retardation through parent education is Phyllis Levenstein's. Since the course of her investigation approaches the ideal for the development of a program of intervention more closely than any other I know of, it seems worthwhile to summarize the process in some detail. The development of this program has negotiated with promise several essential hurdles in social program development. It has moved from a promising pilot project, where a majority of such programs terminate, to a well developed program that has demonstrated repeatedly that it achieves gains in test-performance large enough to be educationally significant, and gains that persist until the children get into school. A preponderant majority of the mothers report enthusiasm for the program, and those children who gain in test-performance also acquire motivation to attend and to concentrate as well as desirable traits of social behavior. . . . a laudable example of program development."

Madden, J., Levenstein, P., & Levenstein, S. (1976). Longitudinal IQ outcomes of the Mother-Child Home Program. *Child Development, 47*, 1015–1025.

Follow-up through age eight of children from low-income families who had participated in several variations of the model Parent–Child Home Program (ninety-six children) and three groups of controls (fifty-five children), examining the relation between various program characteristics and observed outcomes. Some 95 percent of enrollees continued participation to the end of the first year, and 80 percent completed the full two years of the Program. One group of Program mothers received only selected toys and books, whereas other groups received in addition forty-six, fifty-five, or ninety-two home visits over ten to twenty-two months; follow-up was in kindergarten (Stanford-Binet IQ test) and third grade (WISC IQ test). Program children (all those who had been assigned to The Parent–Child Home Program even if they had not actually had any home sessions—intention-to-treat analyses) entered the study with comparable IQ scores to controls but had higher scores at both follow-up points (106 and 101 for the Program, 95 and 95 for controls, respectively). Results after the full two-year Program were significantly superior to those with shorter versions, but well-trained Home Visitors with a less than high school education were as successful in obtaining long-term results as graduate social workers. In fifty-two families where a younger child entered The Parent–Child Home Program a year or more after an older sibling, the mean pretest IQ scores was higher for younger siblings (95 vs. 87, $p < .001$), suggesting downward diffusion of benefits from improvements in their mothers' parenting skills. "The children who received 2 full years of the MCHP do not appear to be laboring under the cognitive disadvantage usually associated with the demographic attributes which determined their acceptance into the program."

Levenstein, P. (1976). Cognitive development through verbalized play: The Mother-Child Home Programme. In J. S. Bruner, A. Jolly, & K. Sylva (Eds.), *Play: Its role in development and evolution* (pp. 286–296). New York: Basic Books.

A summary of the method of The Parent–Child Home Program and of results in the first years of the model program (see Madden, Levenstein, & Levenstein, 1976) plus detailed data from early replication sites. Grouping the results for the first eight replications in 1971–1972, general IQ rose from 90 to 106 over one year of the Program and verbal IQ from 80 to 90 (statistically significant, $p < .001$, for both). One of the sites, run by the New Mexico Bureau of Indian Affairs among Apache and Pueblo tribes, provided raw data for eleven Program participants (pretest IQ 90, posttest 96) and ten test-only controls (86 and 86). "It is an old saying that play is the work of the young child. The truth of this statement is apparent when we think of a child's work as learning to learn. The main tool for this task of toddlers is language; toys provide the material with which they work."

Levenstein, P. (1977). The Mother-Child Home Program. In M. C. Day & R. K. Parker (Eds.), *The preschool in action* (2nd ed.) (pp. 27–49). Boston: Allyn and Bacon.

A thorough description of the theory, practice, and previously reported cognitive data of The Parent–Child Home Program (see Madden et al., 1976). In contrast to the lasting results of the two-year program, children who had only one program year made gains at the end of that year but lost them by third grade; bringing the children books and toys during the second year, without home visits, achieved little more. Apparently, a full-scale second program year serves to consolidate gains by repetition during the second year, indicating that a two-year program is substantially superior to a one-year program. A college education does not seem to be an essential qualification for Home Visitors.

Joint Dissemination Review Panel of U.S. Department of Education. (1978). *Unanimous approval of research findings, 1967–1978, Mother-Child Home Program of Verbal Interaction Project.* Freeport, NY: Verbal Interaction Project.

The unanimous 1978 approval by the Joint Dissemination Review Panel of the U.S. Department of Education and the National Institute of Education led to the inclusion of the Mother [Parent]-Child Home Program in the National Diffusion Network's annual catalogue, *Educational Programs That Work*, where it remained through the final (twenty-first) edition in 1995. The Joint Dissemination Review Panel examined and accepted evidence from the model program and its first replication sites: "The MCHP [PCHP] had credible, statistically reliable and educationally meaningful impact on mothers interactive behavior; children's significant post program *cognitive* development, normal third grade reading and arithmetic *achievement*; and third grade *socioemotional competence*." The Joint Dissemination Review Panel also approved the reliability and validity of the Maternal Interactive Behavior (MIB) instrument (see Appendix) and accepted the Program's claim to the generalizability of its results to other low-income populations.

Bradshaw-McNulty, G., & Delaney, L. (1979). *An evaluation of the Mother-Child Home Program, ESEA Title I for the Pittsfield Public School District.*

This independent report examined the performance of children who had been exposed to the Pittsfield, Massachusetts, replication of The Parent–Child Home Program as toddlers. In third grade, Program children outperformed other third graders of comparably low socioeconomic status on the total California Achievement Test (CAT) battery, with scores of 50 versus 29 (statistically significant, $p < .009$). In kindergarten, Parent–Child Home Program children's scores had clustered slightly below the 50th percentile (prereading 47th percentile, math 47th percentile, visual 47th percentile, alphabetic 43rd percentile), indicating that they were performing close to national norms. The evaluators concluded, "PCHP children seemed better able to cope with and benefit from formal schooling than children who did not participate," and commented, "the school achievement data tended to allay the fears of some observers that initial cognitive gains would 'wash-out' over time."

Levenstein, P. (1979). The parent–child network. In A. Simmons-Martin & D. K. Calvert (Eds.), *Parent-infant intervention: Communication disorders* **(pp. 245–268). New York: Grune and Stratton.**

This chapter reports the relation between parents' verbal interaction during The Parent–Child Home Program, when their child was four, measured on Parent and Child Together (PACT), and the child's social–emotional competence both at the time and on follow-up on the Child's Behavior Traits (CBT). Of the characteristics measured by the PACT—verbal interaction, nurturance, encouragement of autonomy, and parental controls—items rating verbal interaction showed the strongest associations with CBT scores. At age four, each of the CBT skills was strongly associated with at least two of the five concurrent PACT verbal interaction items. When the children's teachers were asked to rate them two years later, in first grade, each item on the task-orientation, cognitive-orientation, responsible-independence,

TABLE 11.1 CORRELATIONS OF MOTHERS' HOME VERBAL INTERACTION AT CHILD'S AGE 4 WITH CHILD COMPETENCIES IN FIRST GRADE AT AGE 6 (PEARSON'S r), $N=39$

Mothers' Verbal Interaction at Child's Age 4 (PACT)

	Responds verbally to request	Verbalizes expectation of child	Tries to talk with child	Verbalizes reasons to obey
Child Competencies in First Grade (CBT)				
Independence				
Accepts, asks for help	.38*		.38*	
Protects own rights	.33*			
Self-confident	.47*		.49*	
Task Orientation				
Completes tasks			.35*	
Enjoys mastering tasks	.48***		.54***	.36*
Cognitive Orientation				
Well organized	.39*		.41**	.35*
Verbalizes ideas	.48***		.48***	
Knows difference between fact and fancy	.61***	.34*	.61***	.52***
Creative, inventive	.40*		.52***	.44***
Emotional Stability				
Cheerful and content	.33*		.39*	.33*
Spontaneous	.42**		.47***	.34*

* $p<.05$
** $p<.01$
*** $p<.005$

and emotional-stability subscales of the CBT proved to be related to the mother's earlier verbal interaction at home (see Table 11.1). Only one PACT item, "Verbalizes approval of child," and one CBT subscale, "Social cooperation," failed to show significant associations. Thus, a supportive parent–child network seemed to have been achieved through participation in The Parent–Child Home Program.

Anastasi, A. (1979). *Fields of applied psychology* (p. 469). New York: McGraw-Hill.

"Among the various home tutoring programs launched in the 1960s and 1970s, one of the most fully developed and tested is the Mother [Parent]-Child Home Program initiated by Levenstein. . . . The program has proved to be transferable insofar as it has been successfully introduced in several areas by different agencies."

O'Hara J., Levenstein P. (1979). *Downward extension of the Mother-Child Home Program: Final report to the Rockefeller Brothers Fund.* Freeport, NY: Verbal Interaction Project.

The lower age limit for Parent–Child Home Program participation was examined by recruiting fifty mothers of children between ten and fourteen months old and randomizing them to receive the program either immediately or at the usual time, a year later. Unfortunately, both groups turned out to be unusually mobile geographically, and fewer than half of the subject families were still in the area after seven months. While these were considered too few dyads for reliable outcome evaluation, the subjective impression of staff members was that the Program's *downward extension* was welcomed warmly by mothers but that delivery was difficult both in planning and execution because home sessions were so frequently disrupted by the babies' physical needs: napping, feeding, diapering, and others. These reasons, as well as the lack of adequate outcome data, prevent The Parent–Child Home Program from advocating application of its classic model to children under the age of sixteen months, although future application of a modified version to younger children remains a possibility.

Darlington, R. B., Royce, J. M., Snipper, A. S., Murray, H. W., & Lazar, I. (1980). Preschool programs and later school competence of children from low-income families. *Science, 208*(April), 202–204.

A report of early results from the Consortium for Longitudinal Studies, which included The Parent–Child Home Program. "At follow-up in 1976, low-income children who had attended infant and preschool programs in the 1960's had significantly higher rates of meeting school requirements than did controls, as measured by lower frequency of placement in special education classes and of being retained in grade (held back)." Of 127 children of third grade age, 22.1 percent of those who had been in The Parent–Child Home Program and 43.5 percent of controls had at some point failed to meet school requirements by being placed in special education classes or being retained in grade (significant, $p = .035$).

Levenstein, P. (1981). Ethical considerations in home-based programs. In M. Bryce & J. C. Lloyd (Eds.), *Treating families in the home* (pp. 222–236). Springfield, IL: C. C. Thomas.

A discussion of ethical issues raised by social programs that visit families in their homes and a description of ten considerations to be taken into account when designing and carrying out such programs. The Parent–Child Home Program experience shows that it is possible for voluntary home-based programs to heed these ethical considerations by building in and maintaining ethical safeguards, without sacrificing program standards. (Similar material was previously presented orally as *Home-Based Programs: Nightmare or Dream of the Future*, at the Symposium on Home-Based Intervention Studies: Problems and Promised Strategies, biennial meeting of the Society for Research in Child Development, San Francisco, March 18, 1979.)

Lazar, I., & Darlington, R. (1982). Lasting effects of early education: A report from the Consortium for Longitudinal Studies. *Monographs of the Society for Research in Child Development, 47* (Serial No. 195).

This long-term follow-up study, performed in 1979 by independent researchers on the location-randomized subjects of the original model Parent–Child Home Program, tracked graduates of eleven programs in the Consortium for Longitudinal Studies through age ten, when the children should have been in fifth grade. Researchers took account of the families' baseline characteristics, using the statistical technique of multivariate regression analysis. Of 250 toddlers who had enrolled in The Parent–Child Home Program, some follow-up data were available for 186, more than twice as many subjects as in the Program's previous report (Madden et al., 1976). Before the study began, experimental children had an IQ of 84, similar to the controls' 85. Two years later, average IQ was 105 for Program participants and 96 for controls (statistically significant, $p < .001$). Program children maintained their superiority through age ten (see Table 11.2). These benefits remained significant in analyses that statistically eliminated the influence of mother's education, number of siblings, sex, ethnicity, presence/absence of the father in the house, and child's baseline IQ.

Positive effects on reading, but not math, achievement scores were also maintained through the final test point (Table 11.3).

As of third grade, fewer Parent–Child Home Program graduates than controls had been placed in special education classes (14 percent vs. 39 percent, statistically significant at $p = .005$) and somewhat fewer had been retained in grade (13 percent vs. 19 percent, $p = .53$). Again, these results held up in multivariate statistical analyses. Mothers of Program graduates were more satisfied with their children's school performance, even above and beyond their lower rates of grade retention and assignment to special education.

The authors' overall conclusion was that on the basis of their data, "Early childhood education can be advocated as one effective policy that may someday take its place within a coordinated set of public policies and private initiatives designed to address the needs of low-income families."

TABLE 11.2 MEAN IQ SCORES FOR PROGRAM AND CONTROL CHILD PARTICIPANTS IN PARENT–CHILD HOME PROGRAM

PCHP test period	Child's age in years	Mean IQ, program	Mean IQ, control	p	Program N	Control N
Entry	2	83.8	84.3	.83	176	27
Post-1 year	3	100.1	95.5	.07	134	19
Post-PCHP	4	104.8	95.6	<.001	117	33
First grade	5	107.1	103.2	.40	97	6
Second grade	6	103.4	87.3	.04	71	10
Third grade	7	102.5	99.9	.56	38	14
Fourth grade	8	100.8	96.9	.15	57	30
Fifth grade	10	101.9	93.6	<.001	51	25

Adapted from Table 14 in the monograph.

TABLE 11.3 EFFECT OF THE PARENT–CHILD HOME PROGRAM ON ACHIEVEMENT
SCORES (WIDE RANGE ACHIEVEMENT TEST, WRAT)

Test period	Math			Reading		
	Coefficient*	t	p	Coefficient	t	p
Grade 3	1.981	2.57	.012	9.423	2.83	.006
Grade 4	0.666	0.70	.488	11.688	2.71	.010
Grade 5	0.614	0.63	.533	11.420	2.52	.017

Adapted from Table 12 in the monograph.

*Coefficient for program as vs. controls, in multiple regression analyses adjusting for child's age, age-squared, sex, and pretest IQ score

Royce, J. M., Darlington, R. B., & Murray, H. W. (1983). Pooled analyses: Findings across studies. In Consortium for Longitudinal Studies, *As the twig is bent: Lasting effects of preschool programs* (pp. 411–459). Hillsdale, NJ: Erlbaum.

In this summary of their comparative evaluation of early intervention programs in the Consortium for Longitudinal Studies, independent evaluators noted that the IQ scores of model Parent–Child Home Program graduates at age ten, previously reported to be superior to those of controls (Lazar & Darlington, 1982), were also higher than those at the same age in the other five nationally known programs whose cognitive follow-up scores were available. It also reported new school data obtained when Consortium children were about age thirteen and should have been in the seventh grade, including twenty Parent–Child Home Program subjects. Model Parent–Child Home Program graduates were at this point somewhat less likely to have failed to meet school requirements by being placed in special education classes or retained in grade than twenty-six location-randomized controls (20 percent vs. 31 percent); the superiority was not statistically significant in this small group.

Levenstein, P., O'Hara, J. M., & Madden, J. (1983). The Mother-Child Home Program of the Verbal Interaction Project. In Consortium for Longitudinal Studies, *As the twig is bent: Lasting effects of preschool programs* (pp. 237–263). Hillsdale, NJ: Erlbaum.

In this chapter of the Consortium for Longitudinal Studies book, an internal team from The Parent–Child Home Program summarized Program research, saying: "It has been previously indicated that the MCHP [PCHP] can be reliably provided as a coherent, inexpensive, minimal intervention program in a wide variety of settings and across an extended period of time. . . . In short, it is a social program that is both validated and feasible for implementation on a local, state, or national level." The chapter presents previously unpublished raw follow-up data for fifty-three third graders who had received the two-year Parent–Child Home Program, twenty-six who had received the Program for one year, and 22 location-randomized controls. Parent–Child Home Program graduates had superior results on math and reading (Wide Range Achievement Tests, WRAT), grade failure, social–emotional

TABLE 11.4 GRADE 3 OUTCOMES FOR PROGRAM AND CONTROL CHILD-
PARTICIPANTS IN THE MODEL PARENT–CHILD HOME PROGRAM

Variable	Controls	PCHP 1 year	PCHP 2 years	F or	p
	(N=22)	(N=26)	(N=53)	chi²	
WRAT math	91.6	95.2	101.9	6.9	< 0.01
WRAT reading	90.2	95.8	99.9	4.7	< 0.05
Social–emotional competence	58.3*	61.7	63.3	1.3	N.S.
Special class placement	38 %	6 %	11 %	1.6	N.S.
School grade failure	30 %**	31 %	9 %	7.2	< 0.05

* N=12

** N=49

competence (Child's Behavioral Traits), and special class placement, significantly so for WRAT and grade failure (Table 11.4).

Datta, L-e. (1983). Epilogue: We never promised you a rose garden, but one may have grown anyhow. In Consortium for Longitudinal Studies, As the twig is bent: Lasting effects of preschool programs (pp. 467–479). Hillsdale, NJ: Erlbaum.

"Levenstein, O'Hara and Madden make the fewest policy claims for their program among the early interventions in this book," yet "they show most clearly that their program can be implemented and maternal behavior affected. . . . Levenstein et al., comparing long-term effects for children who had been in the program for 1 year versus 2 years, reported that reading and mathematics achievement beyond the third grade were linear functions of the amount of treatment received."

Levenstein, P. (1983). Implications of the transition period for early intervention. In R. Golinkoff (Ed.), The transition from prelinguistic to linguistic communication. Hillsdale, NJ: Erlbaum.

This chapter argued for the practical success of a program design based on language theory, concluding, "The research has already produced significant empirical evidence for the effectiveness of a theory based early intervention program [The Parent–Child Home Program], conducted during the little child's transition from paralinguistic to linguistic modes of communication and thought."

Levenstein, P., and O'Hara, J. (1983). Tracing the parent–child network. Final Report: 9/1/79–8/31/82 (Grant No. NIE G 800042). Freeport, NY: National Institute of Education, U.S. Department of Education.

This report to a granting agency presents follow-up data for thirty-seven five and a half year olds who had been in the model Parent–Child Home Program's subject-randomized 1976 cohort, a particularly well-motivated subject group (see Chapter 6).

Two years after the end of the program, Parent–Child Home Program mothers scored significantly better than did controls on seven of ten items of the MIB, an instrument developed by the Program to assess mother-child interactions during a videotaped play session (see Appendix). Overall MIB scores and longitudinal results were subsequently published (Levenstein, 1986; Madden, O'Hara, & Levenstein, 1984), but individual item scores (Table 11.5) and concurrent correlations were not. There were no differences in IQ, parental education, and other socioeconomic status indicators between children who were and were not lost to follow-up; 77 percent of attrition was reported as due to families moving out of the area rather than to their having voluntarily left the Program or declining testing.

Using statistical multiple regression analysis intended to factor out overlap among the items, behaviors examined on the MIB were shown to be related to desired outcomes. Four of the ten items rated in 1980 at age five and a half were associated with academic, socioemotional, and intellectual competencies measured concurrently, and the regression model explained a large portion (32 percent to 69 percent) of the variance in outcome scores. Several behaviors were negatively related to child's competencies: "gives label information," "gives color information," "vocalizes praise," and "mother does not reply to child's vocalization."

The authors considered that the lack of a benefit from parental labelling behaviors suggested revision of the Mother-Child Home program's curriculum: "This curriculum, which is aimed at two to four year olds, should minimize its information-giving aspects and emphasize even more the nondidactic responsiveness to children which is part of the program's current theoretical base."

TABLE 11.5 MATERNAL INTERACTIVE BEHAVIOR SCORES OF PCHP AND SUBJECT-RANDOMIZED NON-PCHP MOTHERS RECRUITED IN 1976 AND STUDIED IN 1980

MIB Item	Program Group N=19	Non-Program Group N=18	Difference
1. Gives labels	36.9	14.8	22.1**
2. Gives colors	13.5	4.7	8.8*
3. Describes actions	88.5	58.8	29.6*
4. Gives numbers, shapes	12.7	5.2	7.5*
5. Asks information	21.6	9.5	12.1*
6. Praises child	7.0	3.3	2.3
7. Aids divergence	9.4	3.8	5.5
8. Smiles at child	2.7	2.6	0.2
9. Replies to child	48.74	32.11	16.63*
10. No reply to child	12.32	17.89	5.57*
Total Positive Score[a]	241.11	134.83	106.28**
Total MIB Score[b]	228.79	116.94	111.85**

[a] Sum of Items 1–9; [b] Sum of Items 1–9, minus score for Item 10.

* $p < .05$; ** $p < .01$.

Slaughter, D. T. (1983). Early intervention and its effects on maternal and child development. *Monographs of the Society for Research in Child Development, 48*(4), Serial No. 202.

This location-randomized study in Chicago housing projects compared The Parent–Child Home Program with the Auerbach-Badger Discussion Group program and with a control group that was given weekly gifts of Program toys without home visits. Children were tested three months into the first year of the interventions (mean age, twenty-two months); seven months later at the end of the first school year; and nineteen months later (mean age forty-one months). At final testing, at the end of the second year of the intervention, Parent–Child Home Program participants had higher scores than did controls on the McCarthy IQ Test, both on its full scale (101 vs. 97, statistically significant at $p < .05$) and on its verbal subscale (again, $p < .05$). Children of discussion group mothers were comparable to those in The Parent–Child Home Program on the full-scale McCarthy, but not on the verbal subscale. Peabody Picture Vocabulary Test scores declined substantially, and similarly, in all three groups. Felton Earls said in a published commentary, "Had the same experiment been done in a more controlled setting . . . program effects on the children, especially the toy demonstration program, [The Parent–Child Home Program] might have produced greater cognitive gains."

Madden, J., O'Hara, J. M., and Levenstein, P. (1984). Home again. *Child Development, 55,* 636–647.

This study enrolled four successive cohorts of parents who either agreed to participate in randomized research (in 1973–1975, 54 percent of invited parents accepted) or volunteered for a developmental screening program (in 1976, 27 percent of eligible parents volunteered). All 112 families were individually randomized in a lottery to receive either the model Parent–Child Home Program or a control condition (yearly evaluations alone in three yearly cohorts, yearly evaluations plus toys and books without home visits in one). As compared with previous groups of Program participants who had been randomized on the basis of geographical location rather than individually (Madden et al., 1976), the *Home Again* children's baseline IQ was higher (92.5 vs. 88.2), maternal education was higher (11.1 years vs. 10.7), and the enrollment rate for eligible families was strikingly lower (48 percent vs. 85 percent). Of the subject-randomized children who began The Parent–Child Home Program, 77 percent completed the full two years; 90 percent of planned home visits were accomplished in the first year and 81 percent in the second year.

All eight groups of children, both Parent–Child Home Program and controls, performed at an average or above average cognitive level immediately postprogram and in first grade. For groups with pretest (baseline) and posttest (follow-up) IQ tests, the posttest scores—statistically adjusted to eliminate the effect of pretest IQ—were higher in Program participants than in controls immediately after home visits had ended (106 vs. 102), and performance on a Program Achievement Test of cognitive skills based on the Parent–Child Home Program curriculum was higher for experimental children. For other cognitive ratings, there were no substantial

TABLE 11.6 MATERNAL INTERACTIVE BEHAVIOR SCORES OF PARENT–CHILD HOME
PROGRAM AND SUBJECT-RANDOMIZED NON-PROGRAM MOTHERS

Cohort		1974		1975		1976	
	PCHP	Books/Toys only	PCHP	Test only	PCHP	Test only
Parental Behavior							
1. Provides label	50	25	37	19	37	18
2. Uses color name	31	17	23	13	18	20
3. Verbalizes actions	102	77	82	70	95	68
4. Verbalizes number and shape	28	12	16	5	18	6
5. Solicits information	22	14	24	16	21	12
6. Verbalizes praise	18	18	13	11	10	6
7. Encourages divergence	18	7	12	6	16	5
8. Expresses nonverbal warmth	14	14	6	7	8	5
9. Replies to child	49	45	53	46	55	35
10. Does not reply	8	15	13	14	12	18
Total MIB Score[a]	324	216	252	178	267	156

[a] Sum of Items 1–9, minus score for Item 10

differences between the groups, and neither IQs nor Wide Range Achievement Test
reading scores (program 101 vs. controls 109 for the 1973 cohort, 105 vs. 102 for
the 1976 cohort) and arithmetic scores (program 104 vs. controls 111 for the 1973
cohort, 107 vs. 105 for the 1976 cohort) were significantly different when children
were in first grade.

There were large Program effects on videotaped parent–child interactions
(MIB) immediately after the intervention (mean total MIB scores 282.6 vs. 185.8,
statistically significant, $p < .001$) (Table 11.6).

"The mean frequency of desirable behavior such as labeling and verbalizing actions was from 33 percent to 51 percent greater in PCHP groups in the three cohorts
for which data was available. . . . The results indicate that PCHP mothers are capable of producing the kind of verbal interaction intended by the program." These improvements in parents' verbal behavior as measured by the MIB persisted on
follow-up one or two years later, although to a somewhat lesser degree (mean scores
233.9 vs. 157.7, significant $p < .05$; for details see Levenstein and O'Hara, 1983).

For a detailed discussion of the methodology of this study, focussed on the contribution of self-selection to the unusually strong cognitive and academic performance of the randomized controls, see Chapter 6.

DeVito, P. J., and Karon, J. P. (1984). *Pittsfield Parent–Child Home Program, Chapter 1.
Longitudinal evaluation Pittsfield Public Schools. Final report.*

This independent evaluation of the Pittsfield, Massachusetts, Parent–Child
Home Program reported achievement results for 155 program graduates in the

1983–1984 school year. On the California Achievement Test assessing reading, language, mathematics, and total scores in second, third, fourth-fifth, and sixth-eighth grades, the Program groups surpassed the national average of 50 in twelve of sixteen results, and their lowest mean score of 48 was just under the national average. When the researchers compared Parent–Child Home Program graduates with randomly selected comparison groups of Pittsfield Title I (at that time known as Chapter I) participants, program graduates outperformed the Title I group dramatically in kindergarten, more modestly in grades one through four, and again dramatically in grades six through eight on each of the four measures. Program graduates in middle school were significantly outperformed by Pittsfield students as a whole (including all socioeconomic classes) in reading and language, but not in math or on their total scores. Attending nursery school after The Parent–Child Home Program had no impact on achievement scores.

The researchers observed that the program "selects those students for participation who appear to be most at risk at two years of age and for whom the prognosis of adequate school performance throughout their school years is doubtful. Overall, it appears that PCHP intervention for these students as two and three year olds had lasting effects since as a group throughout school they met or exceeded national achievement norms and generally outperformed the groups to which they were compared."

Ornstein, R. E. (1985). *Psychology, the study of human experience.* San Diego: Harcourt Brace Jovanovich.

"The most successful interventions to improve IQ, at least in the United States, are those that attempt to change the pattern of mother-child interaction. The most successful of these was devised by Phyllis Levenstein (1970, American Journal of Orthopsychiatry)."

Levenstein, P. (1986). Mother-child play interaction and children's educational achievement. In A. Gottfried & C. C. Brown (Eds.), *Play interactions: The contribution of play materials and parental involvement to children's development* (pp. 293–304). Lexington, MA: D.C. Heath.

This book chapter examined various characteristics of The Parent–Child Home Program model in relation to effectiveness in ten years of research data. Play and playfulness seemed crucial to strengthening the parent–child network, which in turn provided a foundation for the child's later motivation for school achievement. Previously unpublished data relate postprogram IQ with behaviors observed during home sessions: If the Home Visitor indicated that a mother "responds verbally to child's request," "tries to converse with child," and other items from the PACT, and that a child "is cheerful and content," "refrains from physical risks," "puts own needs second," and other items from the CBT, the child's postprogram IQ score was higher (significant correlations of $r=.40$, $p<.01$ and $r=.56$, $p<.01$, respectively).

A stepwise multiple regression statistical technique was then used to examine the relations between parental behavior in videotaped play sessions (MIB) and child outcomes in two stages, supplementing the concurrent analyses in a previous grant report (Levenstein & O'Hara, 1983).

Children's performance on the WRAT at the end of kindergarten was predicted by two parental behaviors two years earlier: "mother replies to child" and "mother smiles or makes other positive gesture," whereas children's socioemotional competence (CBT) was predicted by these two behaviors plus a third: "mother stimulates divergence and fantasy." There was no correlation between "gives label information" or "gives color information" and children's school age competence, and a negative correlation for "gives number and shape" and for "failure to reply to the child's vocalization."

When the MIB at age five was examined in relation to outcomes two years later, at the end of second grade, both WRAT scores and IQ were predicted by "mother replies to child" and "mother smiles or makes other positive gesture," whereas multiple socioemotional competencies were predicted by the same two items plus "mother verbalizes praise." Again, failure to reply to the child showed negative correlations.

Overall, mothers' behavior in interacting with their children was strongly predictive of their children's social–emotional and intellectual achievements. Regression models derived from the MIB at age three explained 17 percent of the variance in kindergarten reading scores, 41 percent of the variance in math scores, 43 percent of the variance in IQ scores, and 33 percent of the CBT scores, and similar regression models using the MIB at age five explained 38 percent, 31 percent, 55 percent, and 22 percent, respectively, of these scores at age seven.

The chapter concludes that these data furnish concrete evidence for suppositions underlying the creation of The Parent–Child Home Program by confirming "the existence of a triadic relationship between a mother's parenting and her child's intellectual and social–emotional growth. . . . Connecting them are countless strands of specific reciprocally reinforcing behaviors, leading not only from mother to child but from child to mother." Simple labelling and information giving have no or negative associations with later outcomes, so "the data also stand as a warning to mothers who see the latent presence of the parent–child network as a mandate to barrage their children with a flood of didactic instruction. The contradictory aspects of the multiple regression predictions indicate that the supportive parent–child network formed through parents' play interactions is a delicate one. It can be torn apart by a mother's insistence on the child's learning until it becomes a boring task and no longer play. A successful network is formed by a mother's general responsiveness whether verbal or silently nurturing. The probability seems to be that mothers who approach a young child's learning through play with spontaneous joy will have a child who continues to find joy in learning."

Levenstein, P. (1988). *Messages from home: The Mother-Child Home Program and the prevention of school disadvantage.* Columbus: Ohio State University Press.

The first edition of this book. At the time it was written, The Parent–Child Home Program was being implemented at only nineteen replication sites—there are 150 at present.

McLaren, L. (1988). **Fostering mother-child relationships.** *Child Welfare, 67*, 353–365.

This study among mainly Native Canadian Indian families (mean maternal education eighth grade, all referred by family service agencies because of child neglect) used the PACT to measure evolution in Parent–Child Home Program mothers' positive interactions with their children, using the statistical approach of a pre-post time series method. Interactions improved significantly from before the Program to after it ($p < .01$), and all the mothers reenrolled in the second year. The author commented, "For these parents, the MCHP [PCHP] experience seemed for the first time to individualize their children as separate persons with needs of their own. These mothers all benefitted from the modeling format, which offered a more concrete, accessible learning experience."

Scarr, S., & McCartney, K. (1988). **Far from home: An experimental evaluation of the Mother-Child Home Program in Bermuda.** *Child Development, 59*, 531–543.

In this study, two-thirds of a sample of 125 Bermudian families were randomized to receive The Parent–Child Home Program, and one-third constituted a control group. This chiefly middle-class population included all the willing families with two year olds in a single parish; 89 percent of eligible families were successfully contacted, and 93 percent of those contacted agreed to be randomized. Some 70 percent of mothers were high school graduates, and 31 percent had attended college; fathers (who were present in 71 percent of the homes) had even higher educational attainment (McCartney & Scarr, 1989). The toddlers started with age-normal IQs (mean, 99) and had above-average posttest IQs (program = 107; controls = 103), numerically but not significantly higher for the Parent–Child Home Program group. Two of the fifteen pre-program measures of child behavior significantly favored the controls (they did better on a toy-sorting task and were rated as less deviant), and controls were rated as having a somewhat more positive attitude at baseline, suggesting that by chance the randomization process had yielded a relatively advantaged control group. At posttesting, Parent–Child Home Program children achieved parity on *deviance* and performed significantly better than controls did on toy sorting. The only other significant difference between groups was that Program children had better communication skills, as reported by the parent. Regression analyses, including socioeconomic status, did not yield significant interaction terms, but the authors stated that the small number of controls made these analyses unreliable. The methodology and results of this study, which elicited a published commentary by Levenstein (1989), are also discussed in Chapter 6.

Levenstein P. (1989). Which homes? A response to Scarr and McCartney. *Child Development, 60*, 514–516.

In this invited commentary, Levenstein pointed out that the authors of Far from Home (Scarr & McCartney, 1988) had "shown through their research the futility and even wastefulness of using a replication of the MCHP [PCHP] to prevent educational disadvantage in children who are not in fact at risk for such disadvantage. . . . The Bermudian parents' impressive motivation to aid their preschoolers, in taking a chance on receiving either an early childhood program or only the children's periodic evaluations, can be seen not only in their very low attrition from the study over the years but especially in the high rate of their original acceptance of the study's 'lottery' condition."

Greene, B. S., & Hallinger, C. (1989). *Follow-up study of initial group of children in the Mother-Child Home Program.* White Plains, NY: Westchester Jewish Community Services.

Of the first children who participated in a Parent–Child Home Program replication site founded in 1972 in a low-income housing project in White Plains, New York, 80 percent could be traced many years later. All had graduated from high school, and many had entered college.

DeVito, P. J., and Karon, J. P. (1990). *Pittsfield Chapter 1 program. Parent–Child Home Program longitudinal evaluation.* Pittsfield Public Schools.

This study extended the long-term follow-up (Bradshaw-McNulty & Delaney, 1979; DeVito & Karon, 1984) of disadvantaged children who had received the Pittsfield, Massachusetts, Parent–Child Home Program at two and three years of age. All had started out with what the authors call a "particularly grim" educational prognosis. The achievement scores of Parent–Child Home Program completers currently in grades two through seven proved to be at or above national norms in reading, language arts, and mathematics; relatively few students (17 percent) had been retained in grade, and fewer than expected (42 percent) had required further Title I (previously, Chapter I) services. Of appropriately aged students, 42 percent had taken the College Board examinations, 67 percent had graduated from high school (30 percent had dropped out), and 72 percent of the high school graduates had gone on to higher education. To verify the continued quality of delivery of the Pittsfield Parent–Child Home Program after 20 years, researchers obtained IQ scores on the Peabody Picture Vocabulary Test for the cohorts that began the program in 1986 and 1987: pretest scores averaged 81 and posttest scores 100 (a significant improvement, $p < .01$). The authors commented, "The program has been highly successful in aiding these disadvantaged youth as they progress through school" and concluded, "The results of this study should be disseminated widely to state, local and other sources since longitudinal investigations of this scope are relatively uncommon for Chap. I, ECIA programs."

Springs, C. (1990). *Chapter 1, Mother-Child Home Program evaluation results.* Union County School Board Fact Sheet, Union, SC.

Comparison of scores on the Developmental Indicators for the Assessment of Learning-Revised (DIAL-R) before and after The Parent–Child Home Program among thirty-two five-year-old former participants in Union, South Carolina, showed that all had been considered likely to be eligible for the district's remedial services when they were two and three years old, before beginning the Program, but fewer than half actually required such services.

McCartney, K., and Howley, E. (1991). Parents as instruments of intervention in home-based preschool programs. In L. Okagaki & R. J. Sternberg (Eds.), *Directors of development: Influences on the development of children's thinking* (pp. 181–202). Hillsdale, NJ: Erlbaum.

This review, which called The Parent–Child Home Program "the prototype of home-based early childhood intervention programs," noted substantial effect sizes on cognitive outcomes (d ranging from .21 to .63). "We believe that home-based programs offer a successful model of early childhood intervention when parents become instruments of intervention through a change in their maladaptive beliefs and behaviors. . . . Certainly, we must evaluate programs to determine whether parental behavior has been changed before we draw premature negative conclusions about home-based preschool programs."

Levenstein, P. (1992). The Mother-Child Home Program of the Verbal Interaction Project, Inc. In L. R. Williams & D. P. Fromberg (Eds.), *The encyclopedia of early childhood education* (pp. 481–482). New York: Garland Press.

A synopsis of The Parent–Child Home Program's model, research data, and replication method.

Levenstein, P. (1992). The Mother-Child Home Program: Research methodology and the real world. In J. McCord & R. E. Tremblay (Eds.), *Preventing antisocial behavior* (pp. 43–66). New York: Guilford Press.

This chapter set out the goals and approach of The Parent–Child Home Program and discussed methodological pitfalls that had been encountered in three studies trying to evaluate Program outcomes. Two of these studies have been published elsewhere (Madden et al., 1984; Scarr & McCartney, 1988) and are discussed under their own entries as well as in Chapter 5 and Chapter 6 The third study, unpublished except for its mention in this book chapter, illustrated the human factor as a source of sample bias: instead of randomizing potential subjects, well-meaning Coordinators of an unnamed replication site assigned the neediest children to the active intervention group, so baseline IQ was lower for the intervention group (89) than it was for controls (98). At the end of two years, both groups met national norms with minimal difference between them. "The research problems of the MCHP [PCHP] have been described in this chapter as examples of some hazards that the best planned experimental field research may encounter in actual practice. Investigators who study social programs by using the experimental method—the research design rightly favored as an ideal by most research methodologists—should be aware, and accordingly vigilant, that this method's results may at times be threatened by unanticipated human volunteer factors which must be faced in evaluation of a social intervention in, and for, the real world."

Levenstein, P., & O'Hara, J. M. (1993). The necessary lightness of mother-child play. In K. B. MacDonald (Ed.), *Parent–child play: Descriptions and implications* (pp. 221–237). Albany: State University of New York Press.

This book chapter argued in support of The Parent–Child Home Program concept that early-childhood learning can function best in a nondidactic climate of light spontaneity and fun. Citing data published previously (Levenstein, 1986), it concluded that the more explicit teaching elements in the Program's curriculum contained in guide sheets given to parents along with the books and toys were less important than the nondidactic parental responsiveness made possible by the play elements of the intervention, and: "Lightness in mother-child play appears to be a necessary condition if children's optimal cognitive and socioemotional development is to result from the dyadic interaction."

Kamerman, S. B., & Kahn, A. J. (1995). *Starting right*. New York: Oxford University Press.

"The Mother [Parent]-Child Home Program has an impressive body of rigorous research documenting that this type of intervention with 2 and 3-year-olds 'at risk' has lasting impact on school performance, high school completion, and cognitive development. There are measurable positive child impacts as well as on mothers' verbal behavior with their children . . . This, then, is a remedial program for high-risk families, but an effective one."

Barnett, W. S. (1995). Long-term effects of early childhood programs on cognitive and school outcomes. *The Future of Children (The David and Lucile Packard Foundation)*, 5(3), 25–50.

"Only one of the quasi-experimental studies of model programs [The Parent–Child Home Program] found long-term effects on achievement. . . . In analyses of PCHP subjects and controls in third grade, the program children retained superiority on IQ tests and achievement tests. By seventh grade, they were less likely to have required placement in special education . . . or to have been left back."

After reviewing fifteen model programs and twenty-one large-scale public programs, the author concluded: "The weight of the evidence establishes that ECCE [Early Childhood Care and Education] can produce large effects on IQ during the early childhood years and sizable persistent effects on achievement, grade retention, special education, high school graduation, and socialization. . . . These effects are large enough and persistent enough to make a meaningful difference in the lives of children from low-income families: for many children, preschool programs can mean the difference between failing and passing, regular or special education, staying out of trouble or becoming involved in crime and delinquency, dropping out or graduating from high school. . . . Bringing ECCE services to all children who could benefit from them will not be cheap. . . . However, based on the evidence presented above, these costs would be offset over time by reductions in social problems that cost society far more each year."

Schultz, T., Lopez, E., & Hochberg, M. (1996). *Early childhood reform in seven communities: Front-line practice, agency management, and public policy* (ORAD 96-1320). U.S. Department of Education, Office of Educational Research and Improvement Studies of Education Reform.

"The first distinct strand of family-oriented early childhood intervention programs, in the 1960s. . . . focused on teaching mothers how to structure the home environment, and interact with their young children in more cognitively stimulating and socially appropriate ways. As was true for outcome studies of center-based programs, evaluations generally found positive short-term outcomes, but a more mixed pattern of effects over the longer term. . . . Studies of the Florida Parent Education program (Gordon, 1967), the Early Training Project (Gray and Klaus, 1968), and the Mother-Child [Parent–Child] Home Program (Levenstein, 1971) all found evidence of long-term program-favoring effects on children's school careers, as measured by promotion, special education placement, and high school graduation. . . . In reality, most child-focused programs included some form of parent involvement or education and many of the parent-focused programs provided activities for the child either in the home or in a center-based program. The idea that these foci are mutually reinforcing and that effective programs address both the child and parent is the prevalent view today."

Cordus, J., & Oudenhoven, N. v. (1997). *Early intervention: Examples of practice; Averroes programmes for children: An experience to be shared.* UNESCO Education Sector Monograph No. 8, Action Research in Family and Early Childhood.

"Klimrek (Climbing frame) . . . is the Dutch version of the American 'Mother [Parent] Child Home Program' developed in the 1960s by Phyllis Levenstein. In the Netherlands, the programme serves children aged two to four and their parents. Though the programme lasts two years, its structure and content facilitate parental participation. Evaluation research shows that the programme's methods and materials make it highly suitable for caravan-dwellers and gypsies, as well as for more traditional families."

Levenstein, P., Levenstein, S., Shiminski, J. A., & Stolzberg, J. E. (1998). Long-term impact of a verbal interaction program for at-risk toddlers: An exploratory study of high school outcomes in a replication of the Mother-Child Home Program. *Journal of Applied Developmental Psychology, 19,* 267–285.

This subject-randomized controlled trial in Pittsfield, Massachusetts, found that The Parent–Child Home Program improved high school graduation rates many years later. Among 123 young adults who had been eligible for the intervention as toddlers, those who had completed the full two years were significantly less likely than those from a small group of randomized nonprogram controls to have dropped out of high school (15.9 percent vs. 40.0 percent, $p = .03$) and more likely to have graduated (84.1 percent vs. 53.9 percent, $p = .01$). Their graduation rate matched the nationwide rate (83.7 percent) of middle-income students. When children who had completed only one year of the Program were included, the gains over controls remained statistically significant. When a statistical analysis included in the Parent–Child Home Program group all the youngsters who had ever enrolled (an intention-to-treat approach)—thus including ten youngsters who had participated in the Program for less than one year—76.9 percent of all Program subjects versus 53.9 percent of control subjects who had never been offered the program proved to have graduated from high school (approaching statistical significance, $p = .07$). The odds ratio for high school graduation (a measure of the advantage of Program participants over controls), adjusted for baseline IQ, was 2.12 for the entire group assigned to receive the intervention, 2.23 for those with baseline IQ of < 100, and 2.40 for those with baseline IQ of < 90, indicating that the greatest educational advantage from The Parent–Child Home Program was found for the lowest IQ toddlers. Initial acceptance rate for the Program had been 100 percent. Family withdrawals during the first year were attributed to a move in 52 percent of cases and to mothers' finding a job in another 24 percent. All the families who completed one year of the intervention continued through the second year unless they moved out of the area.

These data were also presented in poster form as Levenstein, P. & Walzer, S. E. (1999). Long-term impact of a verbal interaction program for at-risk toddlers. In Lamb-Parker, F., Hagen, J., Robinson. R. & Clark, C. (eds.) *Children and families in an era of rapid change: Creating a shared agenda for researchers, practitioners & policy makers*. Summary of Conference proceedings: Head Start's 4th National Research Conference, Washington, DC, July 9–12, 1998. Washington, DC: Administration on Children, Youth & Families (DHHS).

Manoil, K., & Bardzell, J. (1999). Parent–Child Home Program. In G. Manset, E. P. St. John, A. Simmons, R. Michael, J. Bardzell, D. Hodges, S. Jacob, & D. Gordon (Eds.), *Indiana's early literacy intervention grant program: Impact study for 1997–98* (pp. 151–152). Indiana Education Policy Center, Indiana University.

"Overall, the research suggests that PCHP parents develop high verbal responsiveness that continues throughout their child's school years. Such responsiveness has shown to correlate with a variety of short-term school readiness and long-term school performance outcomes including increased scores in reading, math, task orientation, self-confidence, social responsibility and IQ. There is also evidence that PCHP participants ultimately graduate from high school at higher rates than similar children who did not participate in the program. . . . The Parent–Child Home Program is a community-based intervention designed to be a tool in helping break the poverty cycle. It better enables the public educational system to prepare all children for lifelong success. By providing materials and focusing on empowering parents, PCHP increases the generalization of the skills acquired to parent–child interactions throughout a child's life. In addition, PCHP has several features that illustrate the program's emphasis on and respect for the integrity of the family unit. Sessions take place in homes at families' convenience. PCHP also respects and incorporates features of families' cultural differences. Furthermore, because there is no direct teaching involved in the sessions, the program should empower parents to experiment and adapt the interactions to meet the needs of their children."

Kendrick, D., Elkan, R., Hewitt, M., Dewey, M., Blair, M., Robinson, J., Williams, D., & Brummell, K. (2000). Does home visiting improve parenting and the quality of the home environment? A systematic review and meta analysis. *Archives of Disease in Childhood, 82,* 443–451.

This meta-analysis of thirty-four programs, including The Parent–Child Home Program, concluded, "Our review of the effectiveness of home visiting programmes suggests they are effective in increasing the quality of the home environment as measured by HOME scores [Home Observation for Measurement of the Environment], and that the majority of studies using other outcome measures also indicated significant improvements in a variety of measures of parenting. . . . Eight studies used lay workers, and the results of these studies appeared similar to those using professional visitors."

Brooks-Gunn, J., Berlin, L. J., & Fuligni, A. S. (2000). Early childhood intervention programs: What about the family? In J. P. Shonkoff & S. J. Meisels (Eds.), *Handbook of early childhood intervention* (2nd ed.) (pp. 549–588). Cambridge University Press.

In a review of effects on families of seventeen home-based interventions, The Parent–Child Home Program is included among those that lead to "more sensitive, supportive, or positive parenting behaviors."

Layzer, J. I., Goodson, B. D., Bernstein, L., Price, C., & Abt Associates Inc. (2001). *National evaluation of family support programs, final report Vol. A: The meta analysis.* Prepared by Abt Associates, Cambridge, MA, for Mary Bruce Webb, Department of Health and Human Services/Administration on Children, Youth and Families.

This meta-analysis of family services for at-risk populations in the first period of implementing welfare-to-work programs reviewed 260 family support programs with evaluable published results, including The Parent–Child Home Program. The programs overall showed small but statistically significant effects in all outcome domains studied, particularly on children's cognitive development and social–emotional development, parenting attitudes and knowledge, parenting behavior, and family functioning. The greatest impact on cognitive outcomes was reported to come, however, from programs providing early childhood education directly to children or giving parents opportunities for peer support, with weaker effects from programs using home visiting as a primary intervention.

Levenstein, P., Levenstein, S., & Oliver, D. (2002). First grade school readiness of former child participants in a South Carolina replication of the Parent–Child Home Program. *Journal of Applied Developmental Psychology, 23,* 331–353.

In this study in a semirural South Carolina setting, "exceptionally high risk toddlers were referred to The Parent–Child Home Program by welfare social workers or by teachers of older siblings, either because those siblings had demonstrated school learning problems, and/or because the parents had failed to attend planned school conferences with teachers of older siblings, and/or because home furnishings and children's appearance had evidenced physically visible deprivation." Testing in first grade showed four yearly cohorts of children who had completed The Parent–Child Home Program, 89 percent of whom were African American, to perform as well as the average for their age statewide, overcoming their predicted disadvantage. Cognitive Skills Assessment Battery scores indicating school readiness were achieved by 85 percent of all Parent–Child Home Program children (92 percent when seven with severe developmental delay were excluded) as compared with 82 percent of statewide first graders. Among free-lunch students 74 percent passed the CSAB statewide, as compared with 93 percent of free-lunch Program children without severe developmental delay (highly significant, $p < .001$). Statewide, 76 percent of African American children passed the Cognitive Skills Assessment Battery, but 93 percent of African American program children without severe developmental delay did so (statistically significant, $p < .01$). All parents invited into The Parent–Child Home Program accepted enrollment, and 96 percent of those who remained in the district completed the two-year intervention, at a cost of $2,000 per family.

Gomby, D. S. (2003). *Building school readiness through home visitation.* (Prepared for the First 5 California Children and Families Commission.)

This review of home visiting programs for the state of California found, "Some studies of programs such as Parents as Teachers, HIPPY, or the Parent–Child Home Program have demonstrated that home visited children out-perform other children in the community through the 4th, 6th, or 12th grades on measures such as school grades and achievement test scores on reading and math, suspensions, or high school graduation rates." The review commission included The Parent–Child Home Program among "the home visiting programs whose goals are most closely aligned with the school readiness focus of the California Children and Families Commission." Noting that most home visiting programs manage to deliver only about half the scheduled number of home visits, it observed, "An exception to this general pattern may be the PCHP where program administrators report a 90 percent completion rate for its twice-weekly home visits. If this is accurate, it may be because the PCHP brings toys and books into the homes of participants, and participants may be more likely to welcome visits in order to receive those tangible gifts." (Appendix A: Detailed Research Findings, pp. 25–26)

The report also describes the experience of the Eisner Pediatric and Medical Center Parent–Child Home Program in Los Angeles, serving 150 families per year since 2000, half Latino and half African American (Appendix C: National Models of Home Visiting Programs, pp. 42–46). Fewer than 5 percent of families had ended enrollment. "Families are encouraged to understand the importance of their child's early childhood education, and the importance of their own roles as their child's first teacher. Because of this program, over half the parents have returned to high school, sought employment to improve living conditions, enrolled in and completed ESL courses, and developed an interest in the future of their children. . . . Professional development for the home visitors is emphasized, and some of the home visitors are currently enrolled in college, striving to learn more about child development. Both Co-coordinators have returned to college to finish their degrees in child development and sociology."

Allen, L., Astuto, J., & Sethi, A. (2003). *The role of home visitors' characteristics and experience in the engagement and retention of Parent–Child Home Program participants: Final report.* New York: New York University, Child and Family Policy Center.

A team of independent evaluators, under the auspices of the Home Visit Forum, studied 137 parents or caregivers who had completed two years of The Parent–Child Home Program in Massachusetts, New York, or South Carolina, and the 36 Home Visitors who served those families. They aimed to identify Home Visitor characteristics associated with greater retention and engagement of families in the intervention, using qualitative focus group data and quantitative questionnaire data. Parents' overall satisfaction with the Program, an average of 4.5 out of 5, was highest if the Home Visitor was from their own racial/ethnic group and their own community. Results showed no consistent association between any outcome variables and the Home Visitors' educational level, whereas the relation between other characteristics and outcome variables varied from site to site. Home Visitors who were former program participants obtained the greatest use of community programs and the library among their clients, but they reported relatively less change in their clients' functioning and lower rates of parental participation as compared with Home Visitors who had not themselves participated in the program. Engagement quantity (defined as whether parents cancelled missed appointments ahead of time) was better for Home Visitors who had worked longer with The Parent–Child Home Program. Considerable variation was observed among communities, and the researchers concluded: "With regard to recommendations for hiring and training home visitors, the results of the current study suggest that hiring recommendations cannot be program-wide, but need to be community-specific."

Nelson, G., Westhues, A., & MacLeod, J. (2003). A meta-analysis of longitudinal research on preschool prevention programs for children. *Prevention and Treatment*, 6(Article 31).

This meta-analysis of thirty-four programs, including The Parent–Child Home Program, concluded, "Preschool prevention programs do have positive short-, medium-, and long-term impacts on several outcome domains," including cognitive impacts still evident many years later, social–emotional impacts, and parent-family wellness impacts, and observed, "Given the amount of time that has passed between the preschool period when the programs began and the follow-up to ages 9 and 18, these medium-term and long-term impacts are quite impressive."

Curtis, A., & O'Hagan, M. (2003). *Care and education in early childhood: A student's guide to theory and practice* (pp. 214–215). London: Routledge.

Klimrek, the Dutch Parent–Child Home Program, "aims at stimulating verbal interaction between parents and child and making them aware that they are the first educators of their child." It has been found to be of value "not only for traditional families from different cultural and ethnic groups, but also for travelling families."

Segall, N. (2004). *The first three years and beyond: Brain development and social policy* by Edward F. Zigler, Matia Finn-Stevenson, & Nancy W. Hall (a review). *Social Service Review*, 78, 166–168.

"Neuroscience's findings on babies and young children do not necessarily indicate that startlingly new designs are needed for policy and programming: such research primarily indicates instead the need for the enhancement and extension of programs already in existence. Indeed, Head Start, Healthy Start, Healthy Families America, Parents as Teachers, Healthy Steps, Home Instruction for Preschool Youngsters (HIPPY) [sic], the Parent–Child Home Program, the Nurse Visitor program, and the Yale Child Welfare Research program have yielded meaningful, if not dramatic, positive outcomes. The data support the premise that well-designed interventions providing supports to young children and their families can achieve important outcomes that reach far beyond early childhood. Among these outcomes are improved attitudes toward school, reduced grade retention, less need for special-education placements, reduced dropout rates, and lower pregnancy rates. Edward Zigler, Matia Finn-Stevenson, and Nancy Hall argue that the excitement generated by the media coverage of the new brain research may actually interfere with political support for successful, well-researched policies and programs."

Halpern, R. (2004). Parent support and education: Past history, future prospects. *Applied Research in Child Development*, 6, 1, 4–12.

"The parent education models of Gordon, Weikart, Levenstein, and the Deutsches . . . provided the outline and prototype for a new type of human service intervention. . . . Each of the main theoretical strands of parent support and education found a home in some of the notable program models that came to embody the field.

For instance, the parent education approach was adopted by Parents as Teachers and continued to be disseminated in Phyllis Levenstein's Mother-Child Home (now called Parent–Child Home) Program." The author noted a record of such programs having only modest effects on outcome measures, but his conclusions are balanced: "Parenting programs remain a potentially important resource for vulnerable young families. The recent public policy focus on school readiness has partially obscured the view of these programs. Yet, as with most supports, their time will come again. It is important, meanwhile, to continue to nurture the research that has helped this field develop."

Allen, L., & Sethi, A. (2004). Bridging the gap between poor and privileged. *American Educator*, Summer, 34–56.

In the professional journal of the American Federation of Teachers, two academics who have studied The Parent–Child Home Program wrote: "Phyllis Levenstein had a hunch . . . she knew that a critical step in the cycle that locks generations in poverty was dropping out of high school. The dropout rate had to be drastically reduced—but how? Levenstein knew that the path to school failure actually started before school entry. She believed that the dropout rate could be reduced by helping low-income parents see that talking with their young children is a great way to educate them.

Today, nearly 40 years later, it's clear that Levenstein's hunch was correct. Researchers know that the verbal interaction between parents and their young children—especially interaction around books and toys that inspire the children to initiate conversations—is absolutely essential to cognitive development. Researchers also know that the program that Levenstein developed, the Parent–Child Home Program (PCHP), is the most effective intervention of its kind. Dozens of studies have been conducted by Levenstein as well as by independent researchers; the results overwhelmingly indicate that PCHP is highly effective in preparing young children from low-income families for school. For example, researchers have found lasting increases in IQ scores; scores above national norms on the California Achievement Test in the second, fifth, and seventh grades; and high school graduation rates as high as those of middle-class students. Even more impressive, results like these have been found among a great variety of children (whites, blacks, non-English speakers, etc.) and in a great variety of communities (New York suburbs, inner-city Los Angeles, semirural South, etc.)."

Sweet, M. A., & Appelbaum, M. I. (2004). Is home visiting an effective strategy? A meta-analytic review of home visiting programs for families with young children. *Child Development, 75*(5), 1435–1456.

This assessment of the usefulness of home visits as a strategy for helping families across a range of outcomes covered sixty home visiting programs in a meta-analysis, including The Parent–Child Home Program, and analyzed five child and five parent outcome groups. Its primary conclusion: "Home visiting does seem to help families with young children."

Pelaez, M. B., & Novak, G. (2004). *Child and adolescent development: A behavioral systems approach.* Thousand Oaks, CA: Sage.

"The PCHP has home visitors bring a book or toy into the homes of 2- and 3-year-olds each week. The home visitor models the use of the item with the child and encourages the parents to adopt an interactive, dialogic style. . . . A recent study (Levenstein, Levenstein, and Oliver, 2002) showed that the 2 years of PCHP intervention greatly lowered the extra risk of poor school readiness that those not receiving home visits faced. . . . Thus, there is ample evidence that the mother-child dyad plays a crucial role in language skill learning."

Shiminski, J. A. (2005). *Parent–Child Home Program, Pittsfield Public Schools, Pittsfield, Massachusetts* (unpublished manuscript).

This manuscript reports two studies. The first provides further follow-up on eighty-seven high school graduates who had enrolled as disadvantaged toddlers in the Pittsfield Parent–Child Home Program between 1976 and 1980. Fifty-six were known to have been accepted into institutions of higher education (Levenstein, Levenstein, Shiminski, & Stolzberg, 1998), of whom forty-nine could be traced in the spring of 2000: Fourteen had been accepted but had not attended college (three of them entered the military), four had attended college but had not graduated, ten had graduated from a two-year college, and twenty-one had graduated from a four-year college. Thus, 89 percent of college attenders had graduated.

The second study traced in 2002 students who had been screened as toddlers for The Parent–Child Home Program between 1984 and 1987. Follow-up information was obtained on the 104 who had remained in the school system (55.9 percent of the original 186). Seventy-four had completed the full two-year Program, twenty-seven had completed one year, and twenty-three had completed less than one year. Fourteen of the screenees (13.5 percent) and seven of the students who had completed two years of the Program (9.5 percent) had dropped out of school, comparing very favorably with the estimated 31 percent dropout rate of the city of Pittsfield as a whole in 2004. Fifty-one of the seventy-three high school graduates (69.9 percent) had been accepted by college; seventeen students were still in high school.

Rafoth, M., & Knickelbein, B. (2005). *Cohort one final report: Assessment summary for the Parent Child Home Program,* an evaluation of the Armstrong Indiana County Intermediate Unit PCHP, Center for Educational and Program Evaluation at Indiana University of Pennsylvania.

This study by independent evaluators examined caretaker-child dyads who participated in a two-year Parent–Child Home Program replication in Armstrong Indiana County, Pennsylvania. The participant-families had been identified as the neediest families enrolled in the local Women, Infants and Children program. On videotapes of caretaker and child interactions recorded by the Home Visitor and scored independently by the Center for Educational and Program Evaluation, the average number of verbal interactions increased from six to 108 and from six to 119 (positive verbal and total verbal, respectively) at the midpoint evaluation, and to 203 and 208 at the final evaluation; the average number of total nonverbal interactions increased from eight to eighteen, and the number of positive nonverbal interactions from eight to seventeen. According to the final assessments by the Home Visitors, positive change occurred on all twenty items of Parent and Child Together, and positive behaviors of children increased dramatically on all twenty items of Child Behavior Traits (significant for every item, $p < .001$). On the Home Screening Questionnaire, seventeen of forty-one children (41 percent) were identified as at risk on enrollment, whereas only eight (20 percent) were found to still be at risk at Program completion. All the respondents agreed or strongly agreed with positive responses to all items in the Parent Satisfaction Survey, and all rated the overall quality of the intervention as good or excellent.

Gomby, D., Spiker, D., Golan, S., Zercher, C., Daniels, M., & Quirk, K. (2005). *Case studies of school readiness initiative promising programs and practices: A focus on early literacy.* Menlo Park: SRI International for First 5 Statewide Data Collection and Evaluation, California Children and Families Commission.

"Established in the 1960s, the Parent–Child Home Program is a home-visiting program that seeks to develop children's language and literacy skills, to strengthen the parent–child bond, and to enhance parenting skills. HABLA is an adaptation of the program for Spanish-speaking families. . . . Most families (60 percent to 70 percent) remain enrolled in the program for 2 years. Those who leave do so primarily because they move out of the area."

Gomby, D. S. (2005). Home visitation in 2005: *Outcomes for children and parents,* Invest in Kids Working Paper No. 7. Sunnyvale, CA: Committee for Economic Development, Invest in Kids Working Group.

This in-depth review of The Parent–Child Home Program, Early Head Start, Healthy Families America, Home Instruction for Parents of Preschool Youngsters, Nurse-Family Partnership, and Parents as Teachers concludes: "Home visiting programs can produce benefits for children and parents," especially for families with the greatest need, although they generally "produce benefits that are modest in magnitude." The author observes: "It is likely that results would improve if quality of home visiting services were bolstered. This would mean focusing on intensity of services that families actually receive, the skills of the home visitors, and the content of the home visiting curriculum." The analysis confirms that home visiting has the greatest benefit for families whose initial need is greatest. The author believes that interventions with mixed home-based and center-based components usually yield the greatest cognitive/academic gains; she notes that The Parent–Child Home Program has reported effects on high school graduation rates but feels that "large cognitive benefits such as these are not demonstrated reliably in high-quality randomized trials of home visiting programs."

Alexander, L. (2005). **School readiness in Buffalo, New York: Parent–Child Home Program.** www.parent-child.org/research/index.html (accessed November 28, 2006).

"At the start of the school year, staff measured the literacy skills of *all* incoming kindergarten students, all of whom were from low-income, minority families. This assessment included children who had completed The Parent–Child Home Program and those who had not participated in the program. These same students were assessed again at the end of the school year." Using the Peabody Picture Vocabulary Test to measure school readiness, "The Parent–Child Home Program graduates earned an average score of 99.9 upon entering kindergarten and an average score of 104.7 upon completing kindergarten. The Nonprogram students earned an average score of 89.4 upon entering kindergarten (10.5 points behind their PCHP counterparts) and an average score of 94.7 upon completing kindergarten (still 10 points behind their PCHP counterparts)." Parent–Child Home Program graduates exceeded the national average of 97 at both time points.

Shiminski, J. (2005). **School readiness in Pittsfield, Massachusetts.** www.parent-child.org/ research/index.html (accessed November 28, 2006).

"Kindergartners in Pittsfield, MA are all screened using the Daberon Screening for School Readiness. The Daberon score is reported as the age in months of the child developmentally and is then compared to the child's chronological age. The Pittsfield study compared the scores of those children entering kindergarten who had no Pre-K to those children who had the district's Pre-K to those children who had both the district's Pre-K and The Parent–Child Home Program (all Parent–Child Home Program participants go on to the district's Pre-K program). The children who participated in The Parent–Child Home Program perform substantially better than all other groups and better than the general population." Program graduates scored an average of 16 percent above chronological age, with only 7 percent scoring at or below chronological age. In comparison, district youngsters as a group scored 5 percent above chronological age, pre-K only graduates scored 7 percent above chronological age, and children with neither form of preschool scored 5 percent below chronological age.

Williams, P. H. (2006). *A multi-year study of program implementation and progress for Massachusetts' Parent–Child Home Program (PCHP), 2003–2006: Final Report and Recommendations* (report submitted to the Massachusetts Department of Early Education and Care).

In this study of all 604 families who enrolled in the Massachusetts Parent–Child Home Program statewide in 2003–2005 plus a forty-nine-family subset of the 2006 enrollees, 86 percent met National Center criteria as being at risk for educational disadvantage, and 70 percent had multiple risk factors. Somewhat more than half had incomes under $20,000 per year; one in three was single parent; more than one in four mothers had failed to finish high school; and two-thirds were members of an ethnic minority group. Families came from forty-six different countries. Some 38 percent of families left the program prematurely, in 39 percent of cases because of residential instability. A variety of family literacy behaviors and practices improved during the Program, especially in families with a moderate number of risk factors (two or three). Initial experience using home visits based on The Parent–Child Home Program model to help family childcare providers was reported and seemed encouraging.

Higgins, M., Krupa, K., & Williams, P. H. (2006). *Characteristics of extended family support that lead to attrition or retention among diverse families in the PCHP home visiting program.* Presented at 46th Annual Meeting of the New England Psychological Association, Southern New Hampshire University, Manchester, NH.

This study examined retention in the Massachusetts Parent–Child Home Program in relation to the support participants perceived from their extended families. All 427 families who enrolled at twenty-five sites in fall 2003 were tracked until their participation was scheduled to end in June 2005. Of 324 with complete data, 110 (34 percent) dropped out of the program prematurely. Among non-European American participants, especially Hispanics, a *greater* quantity of extended family support ("our children spend time with aunts, uncles, cousins, and relatives") on the Familia Inventory was associated with *briefer* participation in the Program. Quality of support ("we share stories about our family and other relatives with our children") was not significantly associated with outcomes. The authors hypothesized that "families with more frequent access to extended family support may perceive themselves as not needing the intervention," and concluded that programs "should inquire beforehand about the importance of the extended family" and consider trying "to educate and include all extended family members in the intervention."

Organizational Research Services. (2006). *Parent–Child Home Program/Play and Learn Group Demonstration Project: Preliminary findings report.* Seattle: Business Partnership for Early Learning.

This report presents before-and-after results for the first program year among 106 families who received a Parent–Child Home Program intervention. All but three of the participant-families had an income of $25,000 per year or less, and 64.2 percent spoke a language other than English at home. Twenty-eight percent of families were African American, 25 percent East African, 20 percent Hispanic, and 20 percent Asian. The intervention period was particularly brief because of logistic complications, and the average time between baseline and postprogram assessments was only three months. Only two families voluntarily discontinued the Program; 95.3 percent of participants received all forty-six scheduled visits. On the Parent and Child Together, parents had higher scores on all items at posttesting ($p < .01$ in all cases). The children also scored higher on every item of the posttest Child Behavior Traits ($p < .01$ on eighteen items, $p < .05$ on two items). Coordinators reported considerable success in navigating challenges related to the great cultural and linguistic diversity among their client population and among the Home Visitors, such as ensuring that customs related to hospitality did not prevent devotion of the home visit time to program activities, and the cultural unacceptability of certain books and toys.

Allen, L., Sethi, A., & Astuto, J. (2007). An evaluation of graduates of a toddlerhood home visiting program at kindergarten age. *NHSA Dialog: A Research-to-Practice Journal for the Early Intervention Field, 10*(1), 36–57.

This follow-up study by independent evaluators evaluated the effects of Nassau and Suffolk County, New York, replications of The Parent–Child Home Program on families when the children reached kindergarten, comparing sixty-eight Program graduates with forty-eight randomly selected nonprogram children from the same kindergarten classrooms. Comparison group parents were better educated (59 percent vs. 27 percent had gone to college), were less likely to be Latino (33 percent vs. 71 percent), and worked for pay more hours per week (twenty-five vs. sixteen). "Despite the challenges of limited English proficiency, low parental education, immigrant status, and poverty, children who had participated in the home visiting intervention were performing similarly to their peers on the majority of measures. . . . Teachers' reports of children's early literacy indicated no differences between the intervention and comparison groups, and there was no difference on tests of early literacy administered by research staff" including the Language and Literacy subscale of the Academic Rating Scale; Story and Print Concepts, Color Names, and Counting measures from FACES; and Shapes and Draw-A-Circle from the Kochanska Inhibitory Control battery. The Parent–Child Home Program group did perform less well on the Peabody Picture Vocabulary Test and the Test of Early Reading Ability— "in line with findings of previous researchers on children whose primary language is not English." Program children were indistinguishable from their peers on all measures of social–emotional development, including teachers' reports, parents' reports, evaluator ratings, and tests of children's inhibitory control, including the attitudes and behavior segment of the Assessment Behavior Scale and the Social Skills Rating System. The frequency of communication with teachers was equal in both groups of parents, although comparison group parents "were more likely to provide home supports for their children's learning and to participate in school-based activities."

Ewen, D. & Matthews, H. (2007, October). *Title I and early childhood programs: A look at investments in the NCLB era.* Center for Law and Social Policy Policy Paper, Child Care and Early Education Series, Paper no. 2.

This policy paper features the outcomes that have been achieved by The Parent–Child Home Program in Pittsfield, Massachusetts, summarizing previously published results and describing 2005 analyses as showing: "children who participated in the PCHP and the four-year-old Title I pre-kindergarten program experienced greater gains than children who participated in only the four-year-old program. . . . Ninety-three percent of entering kindergarteners who participated in the PCHP and the four-year-old program scored developmentally above their grade level, compared to 69 percent of entering kindergartners who attended only the four-year-old program."

Business Partnership for Early Learning (2007). *Annual Report.* www.parent-child.org/
BPEL07.pdf (accessed November 23, 2007).

Two years after the first cohort entered a new Parent–Child Home Program intervention in Seattle, Washington, 75 percent of families had completed the entire Program, with almost all dropouts due to moving from the area. Program children improved dramatically on the Child's Behavior Traits, with 95 percent better able to concentrate, 90 percent more effective at completing developmentally appropriate activities, 100 percent better able to seek help when experiencing difficulty with a task, and 89 percent better at tolerating delays at having their needs met. Parents improved in their positive parenting behavior and in the extent and quality of their interactions with their children (Parent and Child Together); for example, 85 percent engaged their child more frequently in conversation, 100 percent more clearly verbalized expectations to their child, 85 percent showed approval to their child more frequently, and 85 percent more often encouraged their child to perform activities independently.

For a Nonprofessional Audience

Over the years, The Parent–Child Home Program has been evaluated by numerous governmental agencies and foundations and has attracted the interest of many media outlets for the nonspecialist public. This list is a sampling of publications, in chronological order:

Levenstein, P. (1971). Are toys passé? *PTA Magazine, 66,* 16–18.

"A toy is defined as 'a plaything; something that is merely amusing or diverting . . . a paltry or trifling concern . . . without real or permanent value.'" For toddlers, though, "toys and books are food for the intellect." They "must be matched to the child's interests at his particular stage of development. The match can be judged good if the child finds the plaything really 'amusing'—that is, if it fascinates or challenges him. Then he will explore it joyously, building a sense of competence with each mastery of another object. . . . Parents and older brothers and sisters can nurture his intelligence by helping him discover enjoyment in words. The pleasure of playing with toys and books is enhanced by talk about them." So toys and books are "no 'paltry or trifling concern' . . . to amuse a child and keep him out of mischief. They can be of real and permanent value for intellectual growth."

U.S. Office of Education, National Center for Educational Communication (1972). *Mother-Child Home Program, Freeport, New York: Model programs, compensatory education.* Washington, DC: U.S. Government Printing Office, DHEW publication No. OE 72-84.

In 1972, the U.S. Office (now Department) of Education selected The Parent–Child Home Program as one of fifteen compensatory education programs chosen as models for the country. This booklet was created for national distribution to describe The Parent–Child Home Program in detail and to indicate the office's support of school districts and other sites in planning replications of the Program. "On the basis of data collected from tests, it can be concluded that the Mother [Parent]-Child Home Program achieved its objectives in producing statistically and educationally significant IQ results."

Lem, K. (1974, September 22). Volunteer mothers teach in homes. *New York Times*, p. 111.

"If a child from a low-income home is to have an equal chance with his middle-class schoolmates, many educators believe, the child's preschool cognitive growth must start within the family. The Mother [Parent]-Child Home program has evolved from this belief. . . . These practices, it was explained, encourage the child's use of his imagination and creativity as well as arouse his curiosity about the world around him. . . . You have to have a sense of humor in dealing with the different moods in the family. Have high expectations of the child and the mother begins to have high expectations, too."

Pitcoff, P., & Levenstein, P. (Synchro Films, Inc., Producer). (1975). *Learning in Joy* (28-minute film).

This educational and training film describes The Parent–Child Home Program's aims, approach, and curriculum, and deals with the nuts and bolts of program implementation. Segments show the recruitment of families, home visits, staff training sessions, and staff meetings, and emphasize the handling of practical, interpersonal, and ethical issues.

U.S. National Institute of Mental Health (1978). *Model parent–child program series, Report No. 1: Parent–Child Home Program, Freeport, New York*. Washington, DC: DHEW Publication No. ADM 78-659.

The U.S. National Institute of Mental Health selected the program as one of five "visible successful models of programs which enable families to play an important role in improving child mental health."

Fiske, E. B. (1979, February 20). Toys can hone preschool skills. *New York Times*, p. C1.

"The basic issue addressed by the program is the disparity in verbal and other academically relevant skills between middle-income and low-income children. 'It's not that low-income kids don't hear a lot of talking. It's the kind of talking,' explained Dr. Levenstein. . . . 'The ethics of programs such as these are crucial,' said Dr. Levenstein. 'The temptation of home-based programs is to overload the recipients with services—whether wanted or not. A worker will start giving advice on nutrition or medical help, and it's a curious fact about having people come into your home that you can't tell them to get out. A mother can become the victim of the visitor's do-goodedness. We train our workers very carefully to maintain confidentiality and to resist the temptation to get drawn into other family problems, and there is close monitoring of how they do this. We are there for one purpose only, and this involves building on the family's own strength. This is one situation where less is more.' "

Russell, A. (1979). Building concepts through verbal interaction: The key to future success in school? *Carnegie Quarterly, Carnegie Corporation of New York, 27,* 1–4.

"The story behind the Mother [Parent]-Child Home program's remarkable success is one of careful, painstaking research fraught with enough methodological problems to have defeated a less determined and visionary proponent of early intervention than Phyllis Levenstein. The M[P]CHP is basically an incentives program that builds on the emotional bond between mother and child to encourage their verbal interaction long after direct assistance has been withdrawn. Thought grows through language, and language expresses thought. The Mother [Parent]-Child Home program incorporates all these elements: conceptual capacity, curiosity, social readiness, and relationship with parents in order to preserve children's native intelligence and equip them to take advantage of school."

Gilinsky, R. M. (1981, December 6). Mothers learn to be teachers. *New York Times,* p. WC11.

"The philosophy of the Mother-Child Home Program is that the mother is the child's most important teacher, according to Carol Hallinger, the program's coordinator. . . . 'The mothers' self-concepts are usually poor, and they find it hard to believe that what they do and say to their preschool children has any effect. . . . After the first few sessions, they begin to understand that even a few minutes a day of reading to or playing with the child can make a real impact.' . . . Besides the intended objectives of the program, Mrs. Hallinger described what she called the 'fringe benefits.' 'Women who had never participated in activities outside of their homes have become active in PTA's and even become board members,' she said. . . . 'There's a great increase in their self-confidence.' . . . Families are referred for many reasons: a lack of mother-child contact or mother-child bonding, a lack of verbalization skills, or a lack of awareness of the needs of an infant or a toddler."

Silver, H., & Silver, P. (1991). *An educational war on poverty: American and British policymaking, 1960–1980* (p. 313). Cambridge University Press.

"The home visiting 'movement' was given a major impetus both by the West Riding EPA project and follow-up and by interest in American schemes, notably that pioneered by Phyllis Levenstein—a relatively structured approach to assisting mothers with child development—and a particular inspiration for a Lothian Educational home visiting Project in Scotland."

Penenberg, A. L. (1993, December 19). Untitled. *New York Times*, p. L.I. 8.

"On a recent morning in New Hyde Park, an Iranian émigré, Lida Balakhane, joined parents from Ecuador, Colombia and the West Indies to learn about being a parent. While their toddlers and preschoolers played nearby, the parents learned ways to set foundations for their children's learning. . . . The philosophy of the program . . . is to head off potential problems by laying a foundation of parent–child communication. . . . One researcher, Dr. Pasquale DeVito, evaluated children in such a program in Pittsfield, Mass., and found that 80 percent eventually graduated from high school. . . . 'We're getting a real bang for our buck,' Dr. DeVito said."

National Center for the Mother-Child Home Program (Producer). (1993). *Necessary lightness* (12-minute video).

A documentary video intended to accompany presentations of the program to community groups, policymakers, administrators, and other decision makers.

Ryan, M. (1999, August 8). They help bring stories to life. *Parade Magazine*, 8.

"This is not a literacy course. The teaching demonstrators simply try to get children to fall in love with books. Based on a model developed in Long Island, N.Y., the program has helped to produce thousands of above average readers who have excelled in school even though tests once predicted that they were likely to fail. The secret is simple, said Judy Stolzberg, who started the Pittsfield program in 1970 and now works as a consultant. 'You have to make it fun,' she explained. . . . No amount of statistics could ever capture the enthusiasm in the children as they discover the power of books. 'It brings out their creativity,' Michelle Yuknis said. 'It's amazing.' "

Hevesi, A. G. (2001). *Building foundations: Supporting parental involvement in a child's first years*. New York: City of New York Office of the Comptroller, Office of Policy Management.

This report from the comptroller of New York City summarizes the method of The Parent–Child Home Program and other programs and uses Parent–Child Home Program research findings to estimate economic benefits of early childhood intervention. On the basis of the gains in high school graduation rates and IQ in program research, he estimates that participation in the program could increase a participant's lifetime earnings potential by between $600,000 and $1,000,000, with at least $150,000 going to the government in increased tax revenues. "An investment of only $2,325 per year for a few years of a home visiting program could yield these significantly higher earnings. Failing to make that investment seems imprudent." The report calculates further savings from reduced need for special education services for Parent–Child Home Program graduates at $210,000 per child, and concludes, "Evaluations of parenting programs have shown convincingly that they make a significant difference for families, improving lifelong outcomes for both children and parents.

We must ensure that parents and society take advantage of the opportunities presented in the first few years of life. By investing in programs aimed at strengthening parents and families, the City would improve the future health of New York City's children, families and communities. This is a wise investment."

Farah, S. (2001, May 1). Helping parents and children explore books together. *The Christian Science Monitor.*

This article about the Plymouth, Massachusetts, Parent–Child Home Program explains how the program brings the joy of learning to families who face tough academic odds. "Ultimately, the visitor is merely a midwife, showing parents how a little creative conversation with their children can boost imagination and skills. . . . Home visitor Ms. McChesney explains the kids' success: 'If you learn something from the person you love most in the world, it's so much more powerful.' "

Jacobson, L. (2002, March 6). Home visiting program helps fill learning gaps. *Education Week.*

The Parent–Child Home Program is spotlighted as a successful nationally replicated home visiting program that is helping families bridge the achievement gap. "Sitting on their living room carpet with home visitor Sylvia Serrano, the girls clap for themselves when they fit the brightly colored, lower-case letters into the proper places. . . . For the full 30 minutes of Ms. Serrano's visit, the girls didn't look up from the puzzle. Ms. Winston, who had not seen the girls in a few months but was visiting them on this February day, was impressed by their attention spans. 'When I first came, they would not sit down,' Ms. Winston said. 'I feel like I'm seeing a miracle.' "

Foster, E. M., & Vazquez, A. (2002). Economic issues: Costs and benefits: Investments and returns. In C. J. Groark, K. E. Mehaffie, R. B. McCall, M. T. Greenberg, & the Universities Children's Policy Collaborative (Eds.), *From science to policy: Research on issues, programs, and policies in early care and education* (Chapter 7). (Prepared for the governor of Pennsylvania's Task Force on Early Childhood Education.)

On the basis of published research, The Parent–Child Home Program is rated as having a positive impact on nearly all the domains examined: for the child, cognitive, education, and well-being outcomes; for the caregiver, parenting development, education, and well-being. The conclusion of the authors' examination of costs and benefits in several high-quality programs is, "Early childhood best practice programs can return substantial benefits in terms of improved educational success, employment, and reduced crime."

Rauch Foundation (2003). Children and families–selected grants. www.rauchfoundation.org/66.0.html (accessed October 18, 2006).

The Rauch Foundation says of The Parent–Child Home Program: "Indications are that a child with a disadvantaged start in life who goes through the program will arrive at first grade with the same potential for success as a child from a middle class family."

A. L. Mailman Family Foundation (2003). www.mailman.org/hot/infant.htm and www
.mailman.org/recent/index.htm (accessed October 7, 2006).

"Programs like the Abecedarian Project, which provided high quality early
education beginning in infancy, and the Parent/Child Home program, which supports parents of two year olds for two years in playfully enhancing their child's
language and literacy in their home language, have shown dramatic long term effects. Despite deep poverty, low maternal education, and other profound risk factors, graduates of these programs have shown average and in many cases above
average educational achievement." In describing their 2003 grant to the Program,
the A.L. Mailman Family Foundation says, "As the child, parent, and home visitor
play or read together, the parent learns new strategies for facilitating the child's
language development. In its thirty-year history, this program has shown extraordinary results. Targeting the time of rapid language learning, they have enabled
'at-risk' children to consistently score at or above average on measures of school
readiness and of primary grade literacy and mathematical competence. The Foundation's grants are helping this play-based, culturally appropriate, family-support
program."

Radowitz, S., Friedman, D. (2004). *The state of family support on Long Island: A pioneering
assessment of where families with young children will find respect and support.* Deer
Park, NY: United Way of Long Island.

This report, after examining more than 3,000 programs, found that the most
successful ones follow the framework of *family support*, which sees needy households as partners rather than problems. "Instead of simply providing services for
families and concentrating on correcting what is supposedly wrong with them, this
new approach works with families and seeks to reinforce their strengths." The report singled out The Parent–Child Home Program as a program that could serve as
a national model for the family support principles articulated in the study: "Family
input in the delivery of services, easily accessible locations, flexible hours, respectful
attitudes, and techniques that empower and strengthen families." Announcing a
grant to support the program's "pioneering work with children of homeless families," the president of United Way of Long Island later said (United Way of Long Island's Success By 6 initiative, 2005), "We are delighted to make grants to these
stellar Long Island-based family support agencies."

Mendel, D. (2004, November). Leave no parent behind. *The American Prospect*, p. A8–10.

"How can we hope to leave no child behind if we do not first help disadvantaged
parents give their children richer and more positive support in the early years? The
question resonates further when you consider the success of programs like Phyllis Levenstein's Parent–Child Home Program. Beginning in the mid-1960s, Levenstein trained
visitors to go into the homes of new parents and help teach them positive parenting

strategies. Twice weekly for the better part of two years, these visitors went to the homes of two and three year olds, bringing gifts for the child and sitting with the parent and child while modeling positive parenting behaviors. The strategy worked, and it continues to work with more than 4,000 children each year at 139 sites nationwide."

South Carolina First Steps: Getting Children Ready for School (2004). 2004 Annual Report. www.scstatehouse.net/reports/2004FirstStepsAnnualReport.pdf (accessed July 10, 2006).

This report of the achievements of the second year of statewide implementation of the South Carolina's First Steps to School Readiness initiative, which funded Parent–Child Home Program replication sites in nine counties serving 700 children, said, "Model parent education programs such as Parents as Teachers (PAT) and Parent–Child Home (PCH) [*sic*] increase parents' ability to stimulate their child's intellectual, social and physical development. . . . Studies show that parents participating in PAT and PCH programs increase their verbal interaction with their child, resulting in an increase of the child's scores in reading, math, social and cognitive skills. Moreover, these children score higher on kindergarten readiness tests and on standardized measures in first through fourth grades."

Richman, E. (2004). Secretary of Pennsylvania's Department of Public Welfare Secretary Hon. Estelle Richman's Speech for March 18, 2004.

Announcing Pennsylvania's one-year commitment of an additional $1 million for The Parent–Child Home Program, bringing its allocation for 2004–2005 to a total of $4 million, Ms. Richman said:

"Thirty years of research demonstrates that The Parent–Child Home Program plays an important role in improving school success and high school graduation rates among at-risk children. . . . Last year, in Pennsylvania . . . we were able to see a significant increase in parent–child verbal interaction. Children enrolled in the program also scored higher on school-readiness tests and often at or above the national or state average on standardized reading and math tests. Not only has the department been able to see growth and development in the children involved in the program, the parents also significantly benefit as well. Many parents who participate experience a sense of empowerment, resulting in additional confidence in their own educational development. Many of them return to school and get their GED or find employment. When their children enter school, teachers and principals are able to recognize those parents who have participated in the program because they attend parent-teacher meetings, participate in school activities, help children with their homework, and are comfortable talking about their children's educational needs, more so than other parents in their same socio-economic situation."

Rep. Steven Cappelli commented: "Pennsylvania can't afford *not* to provide funding for this high-quality program. . . . This program will produce one of the highest returns on investment and is an essential component for our state's economic success in the twenty-first century."

The Parent–Child Home Program, Inc. (Producer). (2004). *Soaring to success through books and play* (8-minute video).

A video summarizing the background, method, and results of The Parent–Child Home Program method. Interviewees include John Silber, LaRue Allen, and Julian Gomez.

Rubin, J. (2004, September 6). Language series speaks to families: Program enlists Santa Ana parents as 'first teachers' to help their children develop skills. *Los Angeles Times*, p. B1.

This article looks at The Parent–Child Home Program's Santa Ana site, HABLA, sponsored by the University of California at Irvine, which encourages verbal interaction with young children primarily in Spanish, the first language of most participating families. Its originator, University of California at Irvine cognitive scientist Virginia Mann, said, "We know these early years are when children start to learn languages, and if Spanish is the only language you are able to teach them in, then that is what you have to do. . . . If a child has language skills in Spanish, it will translate into English."

Boston Globe. (2005, January 9). Bringing up parents (unsigned editorial). *The Boston Globe*.

The Boston Globe editorialized on Massachusetts governor Mitt Romney's parental involvement initiative, saying that the governor should focus on promoting models that have been shown to work. "Several strategies should underlie new and better statewide parenting resources. A key step is to begin early . . . to emphasize the importance of reading to even the very youngest children. This means distributing free books and encouraging illiterate parents to enroll in literacy classes. One model is the national, nonprofit Parent–Child Home Program. . . . Romney should help the state's parents, offering them voluntary opportunities that are too good to refuse."

Bailey, I. J. (2005, February 10). Setting up kids, parents for success. *The Sun News*. Also published as Miss Ruby's Kids saving children—one bedtime story at a time in the *Deseret News*, February 13, 2005.

Syndicated columnist Isaac J. Bailey visited a Parent–Child Home Program teen parent and her three-year-old daughter on Pawleys Island, South Carolina. The piece praises the program's emphasis on the home environment as an indicator of school success. "The program is designed to teach the parents and provide a bridge until the child reaches an age when formal education is available. . . . 'The object is to get the parent and the child talking, get the parent confident that they can be their child's first, best teacher,' " said Jo Fortuna, resource coordinator for the program.

Lovejoy, A., & Wright, E. (for the NGA Task Force on School Readiness). (2005). *Building the foundation for bright futures: A governor's guide to school readiness* (pp. 19–23). NGA Center for Best Practices, National Governors Association.

This guide recommends six national home visiting program models, including The Parent–Child Home Program, for consideration by states and local communities. "Intensive, family-focused initiatives such as home visiting and family literacy programs influence parent behavior and improve child outcomes, particularly when they involve high-quality, well-implemented services, are staffed by well-trained professionals, and link with other family supports."

Ryssdal, K., & Gardner, S. (2005, March 30). Marketplace morning report. National Public Radio.

The NPR morning broadcast, "Marketplace," discusses The Parent–Child Home Program's Santa Ana, California, site, HABLA, highlighting its positive impact on families for whom English is a second language.

Bardige, B. (2005). *At a loss for words: How America is failing our children and what we can do about it.* Philadelphia: Temple University Press.

This book by a developmental psychologist who works to shape early childhood policy nationwide features The Parent–Child Home Program for its "powerful impact" on disadvantaged children and its excellent research record. She pinpoints as special strengths its careful population targeting, frequent visits, choice of period for intervention, unique adaptability for immigrant groups, ludic emphasis, and potential for setting long-term changes in motion. Concluding, "In terms of outcome for the money, the PCHP is an outstanding buy," she expresses the hope that the public "will insist that all families who wish it have access to such support."

Amon, R. (2005, July 17). Giving homeless a head start. *Newsday Long Island.*

This article describes a Parent–Child Home Program site in Suffolk County that works with homeless families in temporary shelters to ensure their children enter school ready to learn. " 'It's so important for these children to get a good education to break free from the homeless cycle,' said Dennis Nowak, spokesman for the Suffolk County Department of Social Services. Bringing the home tutoring program into the shelters is a 'wonderful start.' " According to Theresa Kemp-Zielenski, the United Way's vice president for community impact, "For children in underserved and often at-risk families, the first object is to reduce hunger and improve access to health care. . . . After that, it's important to take action steps to encourage future success."

Massachusetts Department of Early Education and Care (2007). Fiscal Year 2008 Parent–Child Home Program grant application: www.eec.state.ma.us/docs/PCHP %20FY2008_Renewal_Application%20%205_18.pdf (accessed October 28, 2007).

"EEC has embraced the nationally recognized Parent Child Home Program (PCHP) model as an effective and innovative literacy and parenting program for families with young children in the Commonwealth. Since 2005, EEC has awarded grants to 25 PCHP lead agencies to serve over 800 eligible families.

PCHP is a home-based parenting, early literacy, and school readiness program designed to help strengthen verbal interaction and educational play between parents and their young children. PCHP supports and strengthens parents' skills in enhancing their children's cognitive development and school readiness. Program sites serve families challenged by poverty, low levels of education, language barriers, homelessness, and other obstacles to academic success."

Nichols, R. (2005, December 5). This preschool is for parents, too: State program sends teachers to families' homes to help them prepare toddlers for kindergarten. *The Boston Globe.*

The *Globe* looks at how The Parent–Child Home Program's Massachusetts sites help involve parents in early childhood education. "Most of the families in the program earn less than $20,000 a year, but money is only one qualifier. The home visitors, trained professionals paid by the state, visit families that struggle with limited education, homelessness, or speaking English. . . . The Department of Early Education Care, a new agency created in July, sees the program as key in a statewide effort to better prepare children for prekindergarten and kindergarten. . . . 'The value of the program in many cases is as much for the mother or parent as it is for the kid,' said James Shiminski, the program director in Pittsfield, which was the first one in Massachusetts established after the 1965 test program in New York. 'If we can get an at-risk two year old with their parent for two years, we can make an incredible difference.' "

Pennsylvania Department of Public Welfare. (2006). Preventive services—Parent–Child Home Program. www.dpw.state.pa.us/child/childwelfare/003670977.htm (accessed October 6, 2006).

"The Parent–Child Home Program (PCHP) is a proven family literacy and parenting program designed for families who have not had access to educational opportunities. Through intensive home visiting, the PCHP creates language-rich home environments for preschoolers and empowers parents to become their children's first and most important teachers.

The PCHP model is based on decades of research by the PCHP National Center on the importance of parent–child verbal interaction for early brain and language development. With a gentle touch, home visitors model verbal interaction and play; children's language and literacy skills improve; and parents experience the joy and value of reading, talking and playing with their children."

Snyder, S. (2006, March 31). Parents gain the skills to teach their toddlers. *The Philadelphia Inquirer.*

The *Inquirer* reports on a new Parent–Child Home Program site serving more than 200 Philadelphia families. "School is in session. Not just for Diamond. But for her mom, as well. The Philadelphia School District launched a new home-based program in January to educate low-income parents—whose children likely would get no preschool experience otherwise—on how best to help their toddlers learn the early essentials that will make them successful in school. . . .' If you're going to equalize the academic playing field, you've got to get the kids in early childhood programs,' Paul Vallas, the district's chief executive officer, said."

Stebbins, H. (2006). *Council connections to the earliest years.* Washington, DC.: Council of Chief State School Officers.

The Council of Chief State School Officers is a nonpartisan, nationwide, non-profit organization of public officials who head departments of elementary and secondary education in the states, the District of Columbia, the Department of Defense Education Activity, and five U.S. extra-state jurisdictions. The aim of this report was to "design an approach for connecting schools and supports for children in their first three years . . . to elaborate on the exemplary programs and practices collected in our information search and to make the lessons accessible to the stakeholders who can best put them to use." It recommended that schools and school districts implement research-based programs: "Many well-respected, research-based programs for families with infants and toddlers already exist. Schools do not need to create their own program but can leverage their existing physical and administrative infrastructure to replicate an existing program. . . . The Parent–Child Home Program is a national, research-based, home visiting model founded in 1965. The program's goal is to promote parent–child verbal interaction and early language and literacy experiences in an effort to improve school readiness. The program targets children ages 16 months–3 years in families with a variety of risk factors, including low income, low level of parental education, teen parents, and/or families facing language/cultural barriers."

Riddell, C. A. Program helps parents raise successful kids. On Family Matters. WNBC-NY television. www.wnbc.com/video/9343990/index.html (accessed November 6, 2006).

WNBC in New York shows a Parent–Child Home Program Home Visitor with an enthusiastic family, interviews a board member who was a program recipient as a child, and briefly presents the nature and goals of the program.

Fight Crime: Invest in Kids *Washington* (2007). Preventing child abuse and neglect in Washington by supporting intensive home visiting. www.fightcrime.org/reports/wacanreport .pdf (accessed May 5, 2007).

According to this report, "PCHP can serve as an important bridge between infant home visiting programs and preschool for many at-risk children. . . . Such dramatic results for at-risk children are a strong indication that the PCHP program is successful in helping at-risk children to not only catch up with children from more advantaged backgrounds, but to actually excel."

Children's Trust Fund of Washington/Washington Council for Prevention of Child Abuse and Neglect (2007). *Evidence Based Home Visiting Program Descriptions* and *Children's Trust Evidence Based Home Visiting Programs and Criteria for Inclusion.* www.wcpcan .wa.gov/ (accessed October 28, 2007).

The Children's Trust Fund of Washington endorsed The Parent–Child Home Program as one of the top three evidence-based home visiting programs, rated by its Research Advisory Group at level 2 (*good support*). "These are evidence based programs that impact parenting behaviors. There is empirical evidence that these programs reduce known risk factors and/or enhance known protective factors." The Trust observes, "Every Parent–Child Home Program site adheres to a carefully developed and well-tested model to ensure high quality services and consistent results," and: "Training in multicultural awareness and the ethics of home visiting are important components of the Parent–Child Home Program training curriculum for Site Coordinators and Home Visitors."

McCarthy, J. (2007, June 26). Program gives low-income children education boost. KING 5 television news.

This WNBC-affiliated television station in Seattle featured a home visit with an East African family and an interview with Dr. Kathryn Barnard in this news item on The Parent–Child Home Program.

Outcome Measures Created by The Parent–Child Home Program

Measure I: Parent and Child Together

The Parent and Child Together (PACT) enables a Home Visitor to evaluate parents' behavior during home sessions. Each of twenty items is rated on a scale from 1 (almost not present) to 5 (markedly present), and item scores are then tallied for a PACT score that can range from 20 to 100. When this instrument is used in The Parent–Child Home Program, an explanatory paragraph accompanies each item, with illustrative examples of parent's home session behavior toward child.

PACT Items

1. Parent tries to enforce directives.
2. Parent responds verbally to child's verbal or nonverbal request for attention.
3. Parent discourages child's overdependence.
4. Parent shows warmth toward child.
5. Parent refrains from scolding.
6. Parent clearly verbalizes to child expectations of child.
7. Parent encourages child's understanding of reasons for directives.
8. Parent verbalizes affection toward child.
9. Parent's directive gains child's attention.
10. Parent actively encourages child's independence.
11. Parent verbalizes approval of child.
12. Parent satisfies child's needs, signaled verbally or nonverbally.
13. Parent persists in enforcing directives.
14. Parent tries to converse with child.
15. Parent trains child for self-direction.

Updated versions of the PACT and CBT will be available soon.

16. Parent seems comforting to child.
17. Parent is firm with child.
18. Parent verbalizes reasons for obedience.
19. Parent seems prepared to respect child's negative reactions to directive.
20. Parent uses positive reinforcement with child. (This phrase is explained to the Home Visitor by the site's Coordinator.)

Measure II: Child's Behavior Traits (CBT)[1]

With this instrument, the child is rated either on home session behavior (by a Home Visitor) or on school behavior (by a classroom teacher) on a scale from 1 (almost not present) to 5 (markedly present) for each of twenty items. Individual item scores can then be tallied for a CBT score that can range from 20 to 100. When CBT is used in The Parent–Child Home Program, an explanatory paragraph accompanies each item in relation to both home session and classroom behavior.

CBT Items

1. Child is well organized in work or play.
2. Child seems generally cheerful and content.
3. Child refrains from physically aggressive behavior toward others.
4. Child expresses ideas in language.
5. Child initiates nondestructive, goal-directed activities.
6. Child accepts or asks for help when necessary.
7. Child is cooperative with adults.
8. Child seems to know difference between facts and make believe.
9. Child is spontaneous without being explosive.
10. Child understands and completes tasks without frequent urging.
11. Child protects own rights appropriately for his or her age group.
12. Child follows necessary rules in family or in school.
13. Child is creative, inventive.
14. Child tolerates necessary frustration (e.g., awaiting turn in a game).
15. Child enjoys mastering new tasks.
16. Child seems self-confident, not timid.
17. Child can put own needs second to those of others.
18. Child refrains from unnecessary physical risks.
19. Child seems free of sudden, unpredictable mood changes.
20. Child is attentive and concentrates on tasks.

Measure III: Maternal Interactive Behavior (MIB)

During the Home Again subject-randomized research project (Madden, O'Hara, & Levenstein, 1984), the researchers sought to evaluate the quality and the quantity of

1. Levenstein, P., Zarnost, J. G., and Feldman S. D. (1976). "Child's Behavior Traits (CBT)." In O. G. Johnson (Ed.), *Tests and measurements in child development: Handbook II, Volume I.* San Francisco: Jossey-Bass. Available from Educational Testing Service (call number TC008472) at: http://store.digitalriver.com/store/ets/DisplayProductDetailsPage/productID.39346800.

the verbal interaction techniques used by Parent–Child Home Program and control parents. To answer this question, it was necessary to find some way to compare Program with control parents in their ways of talking with their children. The researchers could not compare home session behavior because nonprogram parents, of course, had had no home sessions. They solved the dilemma by videotaping individual parents from both groups in play with their children at The Parent–Child Home Program office. The procedure, known as the Maternal Interactive Behavior scale (MIB), will be described in some detail.

The videotaping is designed to give any parents and children, whether or not they have been exposed to The Parent–Child Home Program, exactly the same opportunity to converse in a situation that is equally strange to Program and nonprogram families. The parent is invited, usually as part of the arrangements for postprogram evaluations, to be videotaped as he or she and the child play with some toys. All are offered the opportunity to view the film later; almost all accept the videotaping.

A staff member unfamiliar to the family drives the parents and children to The Parent–Child Home Program office and shows them to the video playroom. The original video playroom was actually a stripped-down office furnished mainly with a child's table and two chairs for parent and child. Two attractive toys chosen to be new to all of the dyads under study are arranged on the table, and a video camera is on a tripod in one corner. A cable connects it with a video recorder and monitor screen in the next room.

The two toys are prearranged on the table in the same way for each parent–child pair: two cars and a locomotive that can be linked by hook-eye connections to form a stylized, colorful freight train, and an unassembled form board puzzle with multicolored niches, surrounded by eight forms, of differing shapes (circle, square, oblong, triangle) and of contrasting colors, which were designed to fit into the niches.

The car driver explains: "This is the play room and toys we talked about. Here's a chair for (child) and one for you. (Child) may play with the toys after I leave you and, of course, you may help in any way you like. That video camera will take ten minutes of pictures. I'll turn it on just before I leave you and (child), and I'll turn it off when I come back. I'll be back in ten minutes." He or she answers the parent's questions, if any, by saying pleasantly, "That's up to you."

The car driver then turns on the camera and leaves, shutting the door. After ten minutes, he or she returns to shut off the camera and to escort the parent and child to the next testing station if there is one.

Some time later the videotape is viewed and scored by a trained rater who is "blind" to the treatment status of the parent and child on the videotape. He or she watches the tape four times to be able to count the exact number of times a parent shows ten kinds of interactive behaviors selected as likely to be seen during a ten-minute play session. Nine were types of interactions encouraged by the Program (Items 1–9), and one was discouraged by the program (Item 10).

MIB Items

1. Gives label information: "This is a circle."
2. Gives color information: "Blue circle."
3. Verbalizes actions: "We make the train go."

4. Gives number or shape information: "Four wheels."
5. Solicits information, not "yes" or "no": "What is this shape?"
6. Vocalizes praise: "Good!" "Uh-huh!"
7. Stimulates divergence, fantasy: "Roll the round puzzle piece."
8. Smiles or other positive gesture: hugs or pats child.
9. Replies to child's vocalization within three seconds.
10. No reply to child's vocalization within three seconds.

The rater tallies the count for each item on the MIB instrument, listing the ten interactive behavior items and space to record how often they occurred during the play session. The total count for all the MIB items, except for Item 10, becomes the total positive score. The score for Item 10 is then subtracted from that score to get a final total MIB score."

References

Adult Performance Level Project. (1975). *Adult functional competency:* A summary. Austin: University of Texas, Division of Extension.

Ainsworth, M.D.S. (1963). The development of mother–infant interaction among the Ganda. In D. M. Foss (Ed.), *Determinants of infant behavior* (Vol. 2). New York: Wiley.

Ainsworth, M.D.S. (1973). The development of infant–mother attachment. In B. M. Caldwell & H. N. Ricciuti (Eds.), *Child development and social policy*. Chicago: University of Chicago Press.

Alexander, L. (2005). School Readiness in Buffalo, New York: Parent–Child Home Program. www.parent-child.org/research/index.html (accessed November 28, 2006).

Allen, L., Astuto, J., & Sethi, A. (2003). *The role of home visitors' characteristics and experience in the engagement and retention of Parent–Child Home Program participants: Final report*. New York: Child and Family Policy Center, New York University.

Allen, L., Sethi, A., & Astuto, J. (2007). An evaluation of graduates of a toddlerhood home visiting program at kindergarten age. *NHSA Dialog: A Research-to-Practice Journal for the Early Intervention Field, 10*(1), 36–57.

Amabile, T. (1983). *The social psychology of creativity*. New York: Springer Verlag.

Anastasi, A. (1979). *Fields of applied psychology*. New York: McGraw-Hill.

Baker, A.J.L., Piotrkowski, C. S., & Brooks-Gunn, J. (1999). The Home Instruction Program for Preschool Youngsters (HIPPY). *The Future of Children. Home Visiting: Recent Program Evaluations, 9*(1), 116–133.

Barnett, W. S. (1995). Long-term effects of early childhood programs on cognitive and school outcomes. *The Future of Children (The David and Lucile Packard Foundation), 5*(3), 25–50.

Bates, E. (1976). *Language and context*. New York: Academic Press.

Baumrind, D. (1967). Child care practices anteceding three patterns of preschool behavior. *Genetic Psychology Monograph, 75*, 43–88.

Bayley, N. (1965). Comparisons of mental and motor test scores for ages 1–15 months by sex, birth order, race, geographic location and education of parents. *Child Development, 36*, 379–411.

Bee, H. L., Barnard, K. E., Eyres, S. J., Gray, C. A., Hammond, M. A., Spietz, A. L., Snyder, C., & Clark, B. (1982). Prediction of IQ and language skill from perinatal status, child performance, family characteristics, and mother–infant interaction. *Child Development, 53*(5), 1134–1156.

Bee, H. L., Van Egeren, E., Streissguth, A. P., Numan, B. A., & Leckie, M. S. (1969). Social class differences in maternal teaching strategies and speech patterns. *Developmental Psychology, 6,* 726–734.

Belsky, J. (1985). Experimenting with the family in the newborn period. *Child Development, 67,* 406–414.

Bernal, R. (2005). The effect of maternal employment and child care on children's cognitive development. Chicago: University of Chicago, Department of Economics. http://economics.uchicago.edu/download/Bernal060205.pdf (accessed March 23, 2006).

Bernstein, B. (1961). Social class and linguistic development: A theory of social learning. In A. H. Halsey, J. Floud, & C. A. Anderson (Eds.), *Education, economy and society* (pp. 288–314). New York: Free Press.

Bernstein, B. (1965). A socio-linguistic approach to social learning. In J. Gould (Ed.), *Penguin survey of the social sciences.* Baltimore: Penguin.

Berrueta-Clement, J.R.B., Schweinhart, L. J., Barnett, W. S., Epstein, A. S., & Weikart, D. P. (1984). Changed lives: Effects of the Perry Preschool Program on youth through age 19. *Monographs of the High/Scope Educational Research Foundation, 9.* Ypsilanti, MI: High/Scope Press.

Birns, B., & Golden, M. (1972). Prediction of intellectual performance at three years from infant tests and personality measures. *Merrill-Palmer Quarterly, 18,* 53–58.

Bloom, B. B. (1964). *Stability and change in human characteristics.* New York: Wiley.

Bornstein, M. H., Haynes, O. M., O'Reilly, A. W., & Painter, K. M. (1996). Solitary and collaborative pretense play in early childhood: Sources of individual variation in the development of representational competence. *Child Development, 67,* 2910–2929.

Borus, J. (1978). Issues critical to the survival of community mental health. *American Journal of Psychiatry, 135,* 1029–1035.

Bower, E. M. (1963). Primary prevention of mental and emotional disorders: A conceptual framework and actional possibilities. *American Journal of Orthopsychiatry, 33,* 832–848.

Bowlby, J. (1951). Maternal care and mental health. *World Health Organization Monograph No. 2.* Geneva, Switzerland: World Health Organization.

Bradley, R. H., & Caldwell, B. M. (1984). The relation of infants' home environments to achievement test performance in the first grade: A follow-up study. *Child Development, 55,* 803–809.

Bradley, R. H., & Caldwell, B. M. (1976). The relationship of infants' home environments to mental test performance at fifty-four months: A follow-up study. *Child Development, 47,* 1172–1174.

Bradley, R. H., Caldwell, B. M., & Rock, S. L. (1988). Home environment and school performance: A ten-year follow-up and examination of three models of environmental action *Child Development, 59*(4), 852–867.

Bradshaw-McNulty, G., & Delaney, L. (1979). *An Evaluation of the Mother–Child Home Program, ESEA, Title I, for the Pittsfield Public School District,* July. Pittsfield, MA: Pittsfield Public Schools.

Bronfenbrenner, U. (1968). Early deprivation: A cross-species analysis. In G. Newton & S. Levine (Eds.), *Early experience and behavior.* Springfield, IL: C. Thomas.

Bronfenbrenner, U. (1974). *Is early intervention effective? A report on longitudinal evaluations of preschool programs.* DHEW Publication No. (Office of Human Development) 74-25 ed. Vol. 2. U.S. Dept. of Health, Education and Welfare, Office of Child Development, Children's Bureau.

Brooks-Gunn, J. (2003). Do you believe in magic? What we can expect from early childhood intervention. *Social Policy Report: Giving Child and Youth Development Knowledge Away, 17*(1), 3–14.

Brooks-Gunn, J., & Markman, L. B. (2005). The contribution of parenting to ethnic and racial gaps in school readiness. *The Future of Children, 15*(1), 139–168.

Brown, R. (1958). *Words and things*. Glencoe, IL: Free Press.

Bruner, J. S. (1964). The course of cognitive growth. *American Psychologist, 19*, 1–15.

Bruner, J. S., Olver, R., & Greenfield, P. (1966). *Studies in cognitive growth*. New York: Wiley.

Burgess, R. L., & Conger, R. D. (1978). Family interaction in abusive, neglectful and normal families. *Child Development, 49*, 1163–1173.

Bus, A. G., & van Ijzendoorn, M. H. (1988). Mother–child interactions, attachment, and emergent literacy: A cross-sectional study. *Child Development, 59*, 1262–1272.

Bus, A. G., van Ijzendoorn, M. H., & Pellegrini, A. D. (1995). Joint book reading makes for success in learning to read: A meta-analysis on intergenerational transmission of literacy. *Review of Educational Research, 65*, 1–21.

Business Partnership for Early Learning (2007). *Annual Report*. www.parent-child.org/BPEL07.pdf (accessed November 23, 2007).

Caldwell, B. M. (1967). What is the optimal learning environment for the young child? *American Journal of Orthopsychiatry, 37*(1), 8–21.

Campbell, D. T., & Stanley, J. C. (1966). *Experimental and quasi-experimental designs for research*. Chicago: Rand McNally.

Campbell, F. A., Pungello, E. P., Miller-Johnson, S., Burchinal, M., & Ramey, C. T. (2001). The development of cognitive and academic abilities: Growth curves from an early childhood educational experiment. *Developmental Psychology, 37*, 231–242.

Campbell, F. A., Ramey, C. T., Pungello, E. P., Sparling, J., & Miller-Johnson, S. (2002). Early childhood education: Young adult outcomes from the Abecedarian Project. *Applied Developmental Science, 6*(1), 42–57.

Campbell, J. R., Donahue, P. L., Reese, C. M., & Phillips, G. W. (1996). *NAEP 1994 reading report card for the nation and the states. Findings from the National Assessment of Educational Progress and Trial State Assessment*. Washington, DC: US Department of Education, National Center for Education Statistics.

Carter, L. F. (1994). The sustaining effects study of compensatory and elementary education. *Educational Researcher, 13*, 4–13.

Cassirer, E. (1944). *An essay on man*. New Haven, CT: Yale University Press.

Cazden, C. B. (1970). The situation: A neglected source of social class differences in language use. *Journal of Social Issues, 26*, 35–60.

Cazden, C. B. (1972). *Child language and education*. New York: Holt.

Chase-Lansdale, P. L., Moffitt, R. A., Johnman, B. J., Cherlin, A. J., Coley, R. L., Pittman, L. D., Roff, J., & Votruba-Drzal, E. (2003). Mothers' transitions from welfare to work and the well-being of preschoolers and adolescents. *Science, 299*, 1548–1552.

Children's Trust Fund of Washington/Washington Council for Prevention of Child Abuse and Neglect (2007). *Evidence Based Home Visiting Program Descriptions* and *Children's Trust Evidence Based Home Visiting Programs and Criteria for Inclusion*. www.wcpcan.wa.gov/ (accessed October 28, 2007).

Clark, J. W. (2000). *A meta-analytic look at parent-focused interventions for young families in high-risk circumstances*. Doctoral dissertation in human development and family studies. University Park, PA: Penn State.

Coleman, J. S., & Campbell, E. Q. (1966). *Equality of educational opportunity*. Washington, DC: U.S. Department of Health, Education, and Welfare.

Comprehensive Adult Student Assessment System. www.casas.org (accessed November 25, 2006).

Consortium for Longitudinal Studies. (1983). *As the twig is bent: Lasting effects of preschool programs*. Hillsdale, NJ: Erlbaum.

Creasey, G., & Reese, M. (1996). Mothers' and fathers' perceptions of parenting hassles: Associations with psychological symptoms, nonparenting hassles, and child behavior problems. *Journal of Applied Developmental Psychology, 17*, 393–406.

Cross, C. T., & Independent Review Panel. (1999). *Promising results, continuing challenges.* Washington, DC: Department of Education, Planning, and Evaluation Service, Office of the Undersecretary.

Cross, K. P. (1981). *Adults as learners.* San Francisco: Jossey-Bass.

Csikszentmihalyi, M. (1990). Literacy and intrinsic motivation. *Daedalus, 119*(2), 115–140.

Darlington, R., Royce, J., Snipper, A., Murray, H., & Lazar, I. (1980). Preschool programs and later school competence of children from low-income families. *Science, 208,* 202–204.

Datta, L.-e. (1983). Epilogue: We never promised you a rose garden, but one may have grown anyhow. In Consortium for Longitudinal Studies, *As the twig is bent: Lasting effects of preschool programs* (pp. 467–479). Hillsdale, NJ: Erlbaum.

Day, M. C., & Parker, R. K. (Eds.). (1977). *The preschool in action.* Boston: Allyn and Bacon.

DeParle, J. (2004). *American dream: Three women, ten kids, and a nation's drive to end welfare.* New York: Viking/Penguin.

de Souza, N., Sardessai, V., Joshi, K., Joshi, V., & Hughes, M. (2006). The determinants of compliance with an early intervention programme for high-risk babies in India. *Child: Care, Health and Development 32*(1), 63–72.

Deutsch, M. (1965). The role of social class in language development and cognition. *American Journal of Orthopsychiatry, 35,* 78–88.

DeVito, P. J., & Karon, J. P. (1984). *Pittsfield Chapter 1 Program: Parent–Child Home Program longitudinal evaluation. Final report.* Pittsfield, MA: Pittsfield Public Schools.

DeVito, P. J., & Karon, J. P. (1990). *Pittsfield Chapter 1 Program: Parent–Child Home Program longitudinal evaluation.* Pittsfield, MA: Pittsfield Public Schools.

Duncan, G. J., & Brooks-Gunn, J. (2000). Family poverty, welfare reform, and child development. *Child Development, 71*(1), 188–196.

Education Trust. (2003). *Telling the whole truth (or not) about high school graduation, new state data analysis.* http://www2.edtrust.org/NR/rdonlyres/4DE8F2E0-4D08-4640-B3B0 -013F6DC3865D/0/tellingthetruthgradrates.pdf (accessed November 28, 2007).

Ehrenreich, B. (2001). *Nickled and dimed: On (not) getting by in America.* New York: Holt.

Elkan, R., Kendrick, D., Hewitt, M., Robinson, J., Tolley, K., Blair, M., Dewey, M., Williams, D., & Brummell, K. (2000). The effectiveness of domiciliary health visiting: A systematic review of international studies and a selective review of the British literature. *Health Technology Assessment, 4*(13), 1–139.

Fader, D. (1976). *The new hooked on books.* New York: Berkeley.

Farran, D., & Ramey, C. T. (1980). Social class differences in dyadic involvement during infancy. *Child Development, 51,* 254–257.

Feeny, N. C., Eder, R. A., & Recorla, L. (1996). Conversations with preschoolers: The feeling state content of children's narratives. *Early Education and Development, 7,* 79–97.

Findlay, D. C., & McGuire, C. (1957). Social status and abstract behavior. *Journal of Abnormal and Social Psychology, 54,* 135–137.

Fitzgerald, A. (1999). Silber pushes early childhood reading program. SouthCoast Today (*The Associated Press State & Local Wire*), January 23. http://archive.southcoasttoday.com/ daily/01-99/01-23-99/a09sr058.htm (accessed December 8, 2007).

Forster, E. M. (1909). The machine stops. *The Oxford and Cambridge Review,* November, pp. 83–122.

Frasure-Smith, N., Lesperance, F., Prince, R. H., Verrier, P., Garber, R. A., Juneau, M., Wolfson, C., & Bourassa, M. G. (1997). Randomised trial of home-based psychosocial nursing intervention for patients recovering from myocardial infarction. *Lancet, 350*(9076), 473–479.

Freeberg, N. E., & Payne, D. T. (1967). Parental influence on cognitive development in early childhood: A review. *Child Development, 38,* 66–87.

Fuller, B., Kagan, S. L., Caspary, G. L., & Gauthier, C. A. (2002). Welfare reform and child care options for low-income families. *The Future of Children: Children and Welfare Reform, 12*(1), 97–119.

Garces, E., Thomas, D., & Currie, J. (2002). Longer-term effects of Head Start. *The American Economic Review, 92*(4), 999–1012.

Gennetian, L. A., Duncan, G. J., Knox, V. W., Vargas, W. G., Clark-Kauffman, E., & London, A. S. (2002). How welfare and work policies for parents affect adolescents. New York: Manpower Demonstration Research Corporation. www.mdrc.org/Reports2002/ng _adolescent/ng_adolsyn_full.pdf (accessed March 23, 2006).

Gilinsky, R. M. (1981). Mothers learn to be "teachers." *New York Times,* December 6, p. WC-11.

Ginandes, J., & Roth, H. A. (1973). Replication of the Mother–Child Home Program by a foster care agency. *Child Welfare, 12*(2), 75–81.

Glaze, L. E., & Bonczar, T. P. (2006). Probation and parole in the United States, 2005: United States Department of Justice, Office of Justice Programs, Bureau of Justice Statistics. www.ojp.usdo.gov/bjs/abstract/ppus05.htm (accessed December 29, 2006).

Goetz, B. (2005). Adult Education and Family Literacy Act program facts: U.S. Department of Education, Office of Vocational and Adult Education. www.ed.gov/about/offices/list/ ovae/pi/AdultEd/index.html (accessed November 23, 2006).

Goldberg, M. L. (1963). Factors affecting educational attainment in depressed urban areas. In A. H. Passow (Ed.), *Education in depressed areas.* New York: Teachers College, Columbia University.

Golden, M., & Birns, B. (1968). Social class and cognitive development in infancy. *Merrill-Palmer Quarterly, 14,* 139–149.

Gomby, D. S. (2000). Promise and limitations of home visitation. *Journal of the American Medical Association, 284*(11), 1430–1431.

Gomby, D. S. (2003a). *Building school readiness through home visitation.* Sunnyvale, CA: First 5 California Children and Families Commission.

Gomby, D. S. (2003b). *Building school readiness through home visitation.* Appendix C: National models of home visiting programs. Sunnyvale, CA: First 5 California Children and Families Commission.

Gomby, D. S. (2005). Home visitation in 2005: Outcomes for children and parents (No. 7). Sunnyvale, CA: Committee for Economic Development, Invest in Kids Working Group. www.ced.org/projects/kids.php (accessed August 20, 2006).

Gomby, D. S., Culross, P. L., & Behrman, R. E. (1999). Home visiting: Recent program evaluations—analysis and recommendations. *The Future of Children, 9*(1), 4–26.

Goodson, B. D., & Hess, R. D. (1975). *Parents as teachers of young children: An evaluative review of some contemporary concepts and programs,* rev. ed. Stanford, CA: Stanford University Press.

Gordon, I. J. (1969). Stimulation via parent education. *Children, 16,* 57–59.

Gordon, I. R. (1977). Parent education and parent involvement: Retrospect and prospect. *Childhood Education, 54,* 71–79.

Gottfried, A. E., Fleming, J. S., & Gottfried, A. W. (1998). Role of cognitively stimulating home environment in children's academic intrinsic motivation: A longitudinal study. *Child Development, 69*(5), 1448–1460.

Gottfried, A. W., & Brown, C. C. (Eds.). (1986). *Play interactions: The contribution of play materials and parental involvement to children's development.* Lexington, MA: Lexington Books.

Greene, B. S., & Hallinger, C. (1989). *Follow-up study of initial group of children in the Mother–Child Home Program.* White Plains, NY: Westchester Jewish Community Services.

Greene, J. P. (2001). Civic report: High school graduation rates in the United States: The Manhattan Institute for Policy Research. www.manhattan-institute.org/html/cr_baeo.htm (accessed March 23, 2006).

Guyll, M., Spoth, R., & Redmond, C. (2003). The effects of incentives and research requirements on participation rates for a community-based preventive intervention research study. *The Journal of Primary Prevention, 24*(1), 25–41.

Hamilton, B. E., Martin, J. A., & Ventura, S. J. (2006). Births: Preliminary data for 2005. Hyattsville, MD: National Center for Health Statistics. www.cDCgov/nchs/products/pubs/pubd/hestats/prelimbirths05/prelimbirths05.htm (accessed November 22, 2006).

Hart, B., & Risley, T. R. (1992). American parenting of language-learning children: Persisting differences in family child interactions observed in natural home environments. *Developmental Psychology, 28*, 1096–1105.

Hart, B., & Risley, T. R. (1995). *Meaningful differences in the everyday experience of young American children.* Baltimore: Paul H. Brookes.

Hart, B., & Risley, T. R. (1999). *The social world of children learning to talk.* Baltimore: Paul H. Brookes.

Hartocollis, A. (2002). Dropout rate rises, but wait: 4-year graduations do, too. *New York Times*, April 25, p. 6.

Haskins, R., & Rouse, C. (2005). *Closing achievement gaps.* Washington, DC: Brookings Institution.

Heath, S. B. (1983). *Ways with words.* Cambridge, UK: Cambridge University Press.

Hebb, D. O. (1949). *The organization of behavior.* New York: Wiley.

Hebbeler, K. (1985). *An analysis of the effectiveness of Head Start and of the performance of a low-income population in MCPS.* Rockville, MD: Montgomery County Public Schools.

Herbers, J. (1986). New jobs in cities little aid to poor. *New York Times*, October 20, p. 24.

Hess, R. D., & Shipman, V. C. (1965). Early experience and the socialization of cognitive modes in children. *Child Development, 36*(4), 869–886.

Hevesi, A. G. (2001). Building foundations: Supporting parental involvement in a child's first years. New York: City of New York Office of the Comptroller, Office of Policy Management. www.comptroller.nyc.gov/bureaus/opm/Building_Foundations_Final_report.pdf (accessed December 10, 2006).

Hidi, S. (1990). Interest and its contribution as a mental resource for learning. *Review of Educational Research, 60*, 549–571.

Higgins, M., Krupa, K., & Williams, P. H. (2006). *Characteristics of extended family support that lead to attrition or retention among diverse families in the PCHP home visiting program.* Paper presented at the 46th Annual Meeting of the New England Psychological Association, Southern New Hampshire University, Manchester, October 20–21.

Home Visit Forum. (2006). About Home Visit Forum. www.gse.harvard.edu/hfrp/projects/home-visit (accessed October 7, 2006).

Hunt, J. M. (1961). *Intelligence and experience.* New York: Ronald Press.

Hunt, J. M. (1975). Reflections on a decade of early education. *Journal of Abnormal Child Psychology, 3*, 275–330.

Hunter, C. S., & Harman, D. (1979). *Adult illiteracy in the United States: A Report to the Ford Foundation.* New York: McGraw-Hill.

Irwin, O. C. (1960). Infant speech: Effect of systematic reading of stories. *Journal of Speech and Hearing Research, 3*, 187–190.

Jackson, A. P., Brooks-Gunn, J., Huang, C.-C., & Glassman, M. (2000). Single mothers in low-wage jobs: Financial strain, parenting, and preschoolers' outcomes. *Child Development, 71*(5), 1409–1423.

Jargowsky, P. A., & Sawhill, I. V. (2006). The decline of the underclass (policy brief no. 36). Washington, DC: Brookings Institution. www.brookings.edu (accessed March 15, 2006).

Jayakody, R., & Stauffer, D. (2000). Mental health problems among single mothers: Implications for work and welfare reform. *Journal of Social Issues, 56*(4), 617–634.

Jencks, C. (2005). What happened to welfare? *New York Review of Books,* December 15, pp. 76–86.

Jencks, C., & Phillips, M. (1998). *The Black–White test score gap.* Washington, DC: Brookings Institution.

Kamerman, S. B., & Kahn, A. J. (1995). *Starting right.* New York: Oxford University Press.

Kamii, C. K., & Radin, N. L. (1967). Class differences in the socialization practices of Negro mothers. *Journal of Marriage and the Family, 29,* 302–310.

Karnes, M. D., Teska, J. A., Hodgins, A. S., & Badger, E. D. (1970). Educational intervention at home by mothers of disadvantaged infants. *Child Development, 41,* 925–935.

Kendrick, D., Elkan, R., Hewitt, M., Dewey, M., Blair, M., Robinson, J., Williams, D., & Brummell, K. (2000). Does home visiting improve parenting and the quality of the home environment? A systematic review and meta analysis. *Archives of Disease in Childhood, 82,* 443–451.

Kitzman, H., Olds, D. L., Henderson, C. R., Jr., Hanks, C., Cole, R., Tatelbaum, R. C., McConnochie, K. M., Sidora, K., Luckey, D. W., Shaver, D., Engelhardt, K., James, D., & Barnard, K. E. (1997). Effect of prenatal and infancy home visitation by nurses on pregnancy outcomes, childhood injuries, and repeated childbearing: A randomized controlled trial. *Journal of the American Medical Association, 278*(8), 644–652.

Kitzman, H., Olds, D. L., Sidora, K., Henderson, C. R., Hanks, C., Cole, R., Luckey, D., Bondy, J., Cole, K., & Glazner, J. (2000). Enduring effects of nurse home visitation on maternal life course. *Journal of the American Medical Association, 283,* 1983–1989.

Kohn, M. (1977). *Social competence, symptoms and underachievement in childhood: A longitudinal perspective.* Washington, DC: Winston & Sons.

Krevans, J., & Gibbs, J. C. (1996). Parents' use of inductive discipline: Relations to children's empathy and prosocial behavior. *Child Development, 67,* 3263–3277.

Lamb, H. R., & Talbott, J. A. (1986). The homeless mentally ill. *Journal of the American Medical Association, 256,* 498–561.

Laosa, L. (1983). Families as facilitators of children's intellectual development at three years of age: A causal analysis. In L. Laosa & I. E. Sigel (Eds.), *Families as learning environments for children* (pp. 1–45). New York: Plenum Press.

Laubach, F. C., & Laubach, R. S. (1960). *Toward world literacy: The each one teach one way.* Syracuse, NY: Syracuse University Press.

Layzer, J. I., Goodson, B. D., Bernstein, L., Price, C., & Abt Associates. (2001). *National evaluation of family support programs, final report. Volume A: The meta analysis.* Cambridge, MA: Abt Associates, for Department of Health and Human Services/Administration on Children, Youth and Families.

Lazar, I., & Darlington, R. (1982). Lasting effects of early education: A report from the Consortium for Longitudinal Studies. *Monographs of Society for Research in Child Development, 7*(2–3, Serial No. 195).

Lehman, E. B., Arnold, B. E., Reeves, S. L., & Steiner, A. (1996). Maternal beliefs about children's attachment to soft objects. *American Journal of Orthopsychiatry, 66,* 427–436.

Levenstein, P. (1970). Cognitive growth in preschoolers through verbal interaction with mothers. *American Journal of Orthopsychiatry, 40,* 426–432.

Levenstein, P. (1972). But does it work in homes away from home? *Theory Into Practice, 11,* 157–162.

Levenstein, P. (1975). A message from home: Findings from a program for non-retarded, low-income preschoolers. In M. J. Begab & S. B. Richardson (Eds.), *The mentally retarded and society: A social science perspective* (pp. 305–318). Baltimore: University Park Press.

Levenstein, P. (1976). Cognitive development through verbalized play: The Mother–Child Home Programme. In J. S. Bruner, A. Jolly, & K. Sylva (Eds.), *Play: Its role in development and evolution* (pp. 286–296). New York: Basic Books.

Levenstein, P. (1977). The Mother–Child Home Program. In M. C. Day & R. K. Parker (Eds.), *The preschool in action* (2nd ed., pp. 27–49). Boston: Allyn and Bacon.

Levenstein, P. (1979a). *Home-based programs: Nightmare or dream of the future.* Paper presented at the Symposium on Home-Based Intervention Studies: Problems and Promised Strategies, biennial meeting of the Society for Research in Child Development, San Francisco, March 18, 1979.

Levenstein, P. (1979b). The parent–child network. In A. Simmons-Martin & D. K. Calvert (Eds.), *Parent–infant intervention: Communication disorders* (pp. 245–268). New York: Grune and Stratton.

Levenstein, P. (1981). Ethical considerations in home-based programs. In M. Bryce & J. C. Lloyd (Eds.), *Treating families in the home* (pp. 222–236). Springfield, IL: C.C. Thomas.

Levenstein, P. (1983). Implications of the transition period for early intervention. In R. Golinkoff (Ed.), *The transition from prelinguistic to linguistic communication* (pp. 203–218). Hillsdale, NJ: Erlbaum.

Levenstein, P. (1986). Mother–child play interaction and children's educational achievement. In A. Gottfried & C. C. Brown (Eds.), *Play interactions: The contribution of play materials and parental involvement to children's development* (pp. 293–304). Lexington, MA: DC Heath.

Levenstein, P. (1988). *Messages from home: The Mother–Child Home Program and the prevention of school disadvantage.* Columbus: Ohio State University Press.

Levenstein, P. (1989). Which homes? *A response to Scarr and McCartney. Child Development, 60*(2), 514–516.

Levenstein, P. (1992). The Mother–Child Home Program: Research methodology and the real world. In J. McCord & R. E. Tremblay (Eds.), *Preventing antisocial behavior* (pp. 43–66). New York: Guilford Press.

Levenstein, P., Kochman, A., & Roth, H. (1973). From laboratory to real world: Service delivery of the Mother–Child Home Program. *American Journal of Orthopsychiatry, 43,* 72–78.

Levenstein, P., Levenstein, S., & Oliver, D. (2002). First grade school readiness of former child participants in a South Carolina replication of the Parent–Child Home Program. *Journal of Applied Developmental Psychology, 23,* 331–353.

Levenstein, P., Levenstein, S., Shiminski, J. A., & Stolzberg, J. E. (1998). Long-term impact of a verbal interaction program for at-risk toddlers: An exploratory study of high school outcomes in a replication of the Mother–Child Home Program. *Journal of Applied Developmental Psychology, 19,* 267–285.

Levenstein, P., & O'Hara, J. M. (1993). The necessary lightness of mother–child play. In K. B. MacDonald (Ed.), *Parents and children playing* (pp. 221–237). Albany: State University of New York Press.

Levenstein, P., O'Hara, J. M., & Madden, J. (1983). The Mother–Child Home Program of the Verbal Interaction Project. In Consortium for Longitudinal Studies, *As the twig is bent: Lasting effects of preschool programs* (pp. 237–263). Hillsdale, NJ: Erlbaum.

Levenstein, P., & O'Hara, J. (1983). *Tracing the parent–child network. Final report: 9/1/79–8/31/82* (Grant no. NIE G 800042). Freeport, NY: National Institute of Education, U.S. Department of Education.

Levenstein, P., & Sunley, R. (1968). Stimulation of verbal interaction between disadvantaged mothers and children. *American Journal of Orthopsychiatry, 38,* 116–121.

Lewin, T., & Medina, J. (2003). To cut failure rate, schools shed students. *New York Times,* July 31, p. 1.

Lipschultz, D. (2006). Press Release, National Coalition for Literacy, January 30. www.national-coalition-literacy.org/ (accessed November 23, 2006).

Loeb, S., Fuller, B., Kagan, S. L., & Carrol, B. (2004). Child care in poor communities: Early learning effects of type, quality, and stability. *Child Development, 75*(1), 47–65.

Lombardi, J. (2003). Parents, early education and school readiness: Where are we now and what's next? (PowerPoint presentation). www.parent-child.org/getinvolved/resources.html (accessed October 11, 2006).

Loprest, P. J. (2001). How are families that left welfare doing? A comparison of early and recent welfare leavers (policy brief no. B-36). Washington, DC: Urban Institute. www.urban.org/url.cfm?ID=310282 (accessed March 18, 2006).

Loprest, P. J., & Wissosker, D. (2001). Employment and welfare reform in the National Survey of America's Families (No. B-36). Washington, DC: Urban Institute. www.urban.org (accessed March 19, 2006).

Madden, J., Levenstein, P., & Levenstein, S. (1976). Longitudinal IQ outcomes of the Mother–Child Home Program. *Child Development, 47,* 1015–1025.

Madden, J., O'Hara, J. M., & Levenstein, P. (1984). Home again. *Child Development, 55,* 636–647.

Maeroff, G. L. (1985). Despite Head Start, "achievement gap" persists for the poor. *New York Times,* June 11, p. C1.

Manoil, K., Bardzell, J., & Indiana Education Policy Center, I. U. (1999). *Parent–Child Home Program.* Bloomington: Indiana Department of Education.

A. L. Mailman Family Foundation. www.mailman.org/hot/infant.htm and www.mailman.org/recent/index.htm (accessed March 2, 2006).

Marcus, B., & Schütz, A. (2005). Who are the people reluctant to participate in research? Personality correlates of four different types of nonresponse as inferred from self- and observer ratings. *Journal of Personality, 73*(4), 959–984.

Massachusetts Department of Early Education and Care. (2007). Fiscal Year 2008 Parent–Child Home Program grant application. www.eec.state.ma.us/docs/PCHP%20FY2008_Renewal _Application%20%205_18.pdf (accessed October 28, 2007).

Massachusetts Department of Education. (2006). Cohort 2006 graduation rates. http://profiles.doe.mass.edu/grad_report.aspx?dist=236&sch=&orgtype=5&year=2006 (accessed July 27, 2007).

Mauer, M., & Huling, T. (1995). *Young black Americans and the criminal justice system: Five years later.* Washington, DC: The Sentencing Project.

McCall, R. B., & Green, B. L. (2004). Beyond the methodological gold standards of behavioral research: Considerations for practice and policy. *Social Policy Report, 18*(11).

McCartney, K., & Scarr, S. (1989). Far from the point: A reply to Levenstein. *Child Development, 60*(2), 517–518.

McDermott, M. M., Schmitt, B., & Wallner, E. (1997). Impact of medication nonadherence on coronary heart disease outcomes: A critical review. *Archives of Internal Medicine, 157*(17), 1921–1929.

McKinley, D. G. (1964). *Social class and family life.* New York: Free Press of Glencoe.

McLanahan, S., & Sandefur, G. (1994). *Growing up with a single parent.* Cambridge: Harvard University Press.

McLaren, L. (1988). Fostering mother–child relationships. *Child Welfare, 67,* 353–365.

Melnikow, J., Alemagno, S. A., Rottman, C., & Zyzanski, S. J. (1991). Characteristics of inner-city women giving birth with little or no prenatal care: A case-control study. *Journal of Family Practice, 32*(3), 283–288.

Meltzoff, A., & Moore, M. (1977). Imitation of facial and manual gestures by human neonates. *Science, 198*(4312), 75–78.

Moore, T. (1968). Language and intelligence: A longitudinal study of the first eight years. *Human Development, 11,* 2–24.

Morrissey, J. P., Goldman, H. H., & Klerman, L. V. (1980). *The enduring asylum: Cycles of social reform at the Worcester State Hospital.* New York: Grune and Stratton.

Moss, T. (2004). Fact sheet: Adolescent pregnancy and childbearing in the United States: Advocates for Youth. www.advocatesforyouth.org/PUBLICATIONS/factsheet/fsprechd.htm (accessed March 19, 2006).

Moynihan, D. P. (1986). *Family and nation.* New York: Harcourt Brace.

Multiple Risk Factor Intervention Trial Research Group. (1982). Multiple risk factor intervention trial: Risk factor changes and mortality results. *Journal of the American Medical Association, 248*(12), 1465–1477.

Murray, C. (1984). *Losing ground: American social policy, 1950–1980.* New York: Basic Books.

Myrdal, G. (1962). *The challenge to affluence.* New York: Pantheon.

National Center for Education Statistics. (2005). National assessment of adult literacy 2003: Key findings. http://nces.ed.gov/NAAL/index.asp?file=KeyFindings/Demographics/Overall .asp&PageId=16 (accessed November 23, 2006).

National Diffusion Network. (1979–1995). Mother–Child Home Program (MCHP) of the Verbal Interaction Project. In *Educational programs that work: Catalogue of the National Diffusion Network.* Longmont, CO: Sopris West.

National Institute for Literacy. (n.d.) Welfare and literacy facts. www.nifl.gov/nifl/facts/welfare.html (accessed March 23, 2006).

National Institute of Mental Health. (1978). *Model parent–child program series, report No. 1: Mother–Child Home Program, Freeport, New York.* (DHEW publication no. ADM 78-659). Washington, DC: Government Printing Office.

National Research Council. (1987). *Risking the future.* Washington, DC: National Academy Press.

Nell, V. (1988). *Lost in a book: The psychology of reading for pleasure.* New Haven: Yale University Press.

Nelson, G., Westhues, A., & MacLeod, J. (2003). A meta-analysis of longitudinal research on preschool prevention programs for children. *Prevention & Treatment, 6*(Article 31).

Nelson, K. (1973). Structure and strategy in learning to talk. *Monographs of Society for Research in Child Development, 38*(1–2, Serial No. 149).

New York City Department of Education. (2006). The class of 2005 four-year longitudinal report and 2004–2005 event dropout rates. http://schools.nyc.gov./daa/reports/default.asp (accessed December 30, 2006).

New York State Education Department. (2005). Approved science-based SDFSCA programs. www.emsc.nysed.gov/sss/SDFSCA/SDFSCA-Science-BasedProgramList.html (accessed November 29, 2006).

Norman-Jackson, J. (1982). Family interactions, language development, and primary reading achievement of black children in families of low income. *Child Development, 53,* 349–358.

Nucci, L., & Weber, E. K. (1995). Social interactions in the home and the development of young children's conceptions of the persona. *Child Development, 66,* 1438–1452.

O'Hara, J., & Levenstein, P. (1979). *Downward extension of the Mother–Child Home Program: Final report to the Rockefeller Brothers Fund.* Freeport, NY: Verbal Interaction Project.

Ogbu, J. U. (1990). Minority status and literacy in comparative perspective. *Daedalus, 119,* 141–168.

Olds, D. L., Eckenrode, J., Henderson, C. R., Jr., Kitzman, A. H., Powers, J., Cole, R., Sidora, K., Morris, P., Pettitt, L. M., & Luckey, D. (1997). Long-term effects of home visitation on maternal life course and child abuse and neglect: Fifteen-year follow-up of a randomized trial. *Journal of the American Medical Association, 278,* 637–643.

Olds, D. L., Henderson, C. R., Chamberlin, R., & Tatelbaum, R. (1986). Preventing child abuse and neglect: A randomized trial of nurse home visitation. *Pediatrics, 78,* 65–78.

Olds, D. L., Henderson, C. R., & Cole, R., Eckenrode, J., Kitzman, H., & Luckey, D. (1998). Long-term effects of nurse home visitation on children's criminal and antisocial behavior: 15-year follow-up of a randomized controlled trial. *Journal of the American Medical Association, 280,* 1238–1244.

Olds, D. L., Henderson, C. R., Kitzman, H. J., Eckenrode, J. J., Cole, R. E., & Tatelbaum, R. C. (1999). Prenatal and infancy home visitation by nurses: Recent findings. *Future of Children, 9*(1), 44–65.

Olds, D. L., & Kitzman, H. (1993). Review of research on home visiting for pregnant women and parents of young children. *The Future of Children: Home Visiting, 3*(3), 53–92.

Olds, D. L., Kitzman, H., Cole, R., Robinson, J., Sidora, K., Lucke, D. W., Henderson, C. R., Hanks, C., Bondy, J., & Holmberg, J. (2004). Effects of nurse home-visiting on maternal life course and child development: Age 6 follow-up results of a randomized trial. *Pediatrics, 114,* 1550–1559.

Olds, D. L., Robinson, J., O'Brien, R., Luckey, D. W., Pettitt, L. M., Henderson, C. R., Jr., Ng, R. K., Sheff, K. L., Korfmacher, J., Hiatt, S., & Talmi, A. (2002). Home visiting by paraprofessionals and by nurses: A randomized, controlled trial. *Pediatrics, 110,* 486–496.

O'Neill, J. (2006). Statement of June O'Neill, Ph.D., Wollman Distinguished Professor of Economics, Zicklin School of Business, Baruch College, New York, and Former Director of the Congressional Budget Office; Testimony Before the House Committee on Ways and Means, U.S. House of Representatives, Washington, DC. http://waysandmeans.house.gov/hearings.asp?formmode=view&id=5149 (accessed November 24, 2006).

Organizational Research Services. (2006). *Parent–Child Home Program/Play and Learn Group Demonstration Project: Preliminary findings report.* Seattle: Business Partnership for Early Learning.

Padilla-Walker, L. M., Zamboanga, B. L., Thompson, R. A., & Schmersal, L. A. (2005). Extra credit as incentive for voluntary research participation. *Teaching of Psychology, 32*(3), 150–153.

Palfrey, J., Hauser-Cram, P., Bronson, M., Warfield, M., Strin, S., & Chan, E. (2005). The Brookline Early Education Project: A 25-year follow-up study of a family-centered early health and development intervention. *Pediatrics, 116*(1), 144–152.

The Parent–Child Home Program, Inc. (2005). *Annual report for fiscal year 2005.* Port Washington, NY.

Patterson, J. T. (1981). *America's struggle against poverty, 1900–1980.* Cambridge, MA: Harvard University Press.

Pennsylvania Department of Public Welfare. (2006). Preventive services—Parent–Child Home Program. www.dpw.state.pa.us/child/childwelfare/003670977.htm (accessed October 18, 2006).

Pfannenstiel, J. C., Seitz, V., & Zigler, E. (2002). Promoting school readiness: The role of the Parents as Teachers Program. *NHSA Dialog: A Research-to-Practice Journal for the Early Intervention Field, 6*(1), 71–86.

Phillips, M., Brooks-Gunn, J., Duncan, C. J., Klebanov, P., & Crane, J. (1998). Family background, parenting practices, and the Black–White test score gap. In C. Jencks & M. Phillips (Eds.), *The Black–White test score gap.* Washington, DC: Brookings Institution.

Phillips, M., Crouse, J., & Ralph, J. (1998). Does the Black–White test score gap widen after children enter school? In C. Jencks & M. Phillips (Eds.), *The Black–White test score gap.* Washington, DC: Brookings Institution.

Piaget, J. (1952). *The origins of intelligence in children.* New York: International Universities Press.

Polansky, N. A., Borgman, R. D., & DeSaix, C. (1972). *Roots of futility.* San Francisco: Jossey-Bass.

Powell, L. N. (2004). Waking up. *New Orleans Times Picayune,* September 26, p. 6.

Rafoth, M., & Knickelbein, B. (2005). *Cohort One final report: Assessment summary for the Parent Child Home Program: An evaluation of the Armstrong Indiana County Intermediate Unit PCHP program.* Armstrong Indiana County Intermediate Unit PCHP program, Center for Educational and Program Evaluation, Indiana University of Pennsylvania.

Raikes, H., Pan, B. A., Luze, G., Tamis-LeMonda, C. S., Brooks-Gunn, J., Constantine, J., Tarullo, L. B., Raikes, H. A., & Rodriguez, E. T. (2006). Mother–child bookreading in low-income families: Correlates and outcomes during the first three years of life. *Child Development, 77*(4), 924–953.

Ramey, C. T., Campbell, F. A., & Ramey, S. L. (1999). Early intervention: Successful pathways to improving intellectual development. *Developmental Neuropsychology, 16,* 385–392.

Ramey, S. L., & Ramey, C. T. (1992). Early educational intervention with disadvantaged children: To what effect? *Applied and Preventive Psychology, 1,* 131–140.

Rapoport, D., O'Brien-Strain, M., & the SPHERE Institute. (2001). *In-home visitation programs: A review of the literature.* Santa Ana, CA: Orange County Children and Families Commission.

Rauch Foundation. (2003). Children and families—selected grants. www.rauchfoundation.org/66.0.html (accessed October 18, 2006).

Resnick, L. B. (1990). Literacy in school and out. *Daedalus, 119,* 169–185.

Reynolds, A. J., Suh-Ruu, O., & Topitzes, J. W. (2004). Paths of effects of early childhood intervention on educational attainment and delinquency: A confirmatory analysis of the Chicago Child–Parent Centers. *Child Development, 75*(5), 1299–1328.

Reynolds, A. J., Temple, J. A., Ou, S.-R., Robertson, D. L., Mersky, J. P., Topitzes, J. W., & Niles, M. D. (2007). Effects of a school-based, early childhood intervention on adult health and well-being: A 19-year follow-up of low-income families. *Archives of Pediatrics & Adolescent Medicine, 161*(8), 730–739.

Richman, E. (2004). Speech for March 18, 2004. www.dpw.state.pa.us/General/FormsPub/AdminPublications/SecretarySpeeches/003670668.htm (accessed July 10, 2006).

Rizzolatti, G., Fadiga, L., Gallese, V., & Fogassi, L. (1996). Premotor cortex and the recognition of motor actions. *Cognitive Brain Research, 3*(2), 131–141.

Rohter, L. (1985). Study finds city schools made no progress in reducing dropouts. *New York Times*, May 26, p. 30.

Rosenthal, R. (1965). The volunteer subject. *Human Relations, 18*, 389–406.

Rosenthal, R., & Rosnow, R. L. (1975). *The volunteer subject.* New York: Wiley.

Royce, J. M., Darlington, R. B., & Murray, H. W. (1983). Pooled analyses: Findings across studies. In Consortium for Longitudinal Studies, *As the twig is bent: Lasting effects of preschool programs* (pp. 411–459). Hillsdale, NJ: Erlbaum.

Russell, A. (1979). Building concepts through verbal interaction: The key to future success in school? *Carnegie Quarterly, Carnegie Corporation of New York, 27*, 1–4.

Sameroff, A. J. (1978). Caretaking or reproductive casualty? Determinants in developmental deviancy In F. D. Horowitz (Ed.), *Early developmental hazards: Predictors and precautions* (AAS Selected Symposia Service). Boulder: Westview Press.

Sameroff, A. J., & Seifer, R. (1982). Familial risks and child competence. *Child Development, 54*, 1254–1268.

Sapir, E. (1921). *Language: An Introduction to the study of speech.* New York: Harcourt Brace.

Scarborough, H. S., & Dobrich, W. (1994). On the efficacy of reading to preschoolers. *Developmental Review, 14*, 245–302.

Scarr, S., & McCartney, K. (1988). Far from home: An experimental evaluation in Bermuda. *Child Development, 59*, 531–543.

Schacter, F. F. (1979). *Everyday mother talk to toddlers.* New York: Academic Press.

Schaefer, E. S. (1969). A home tutoring program. *Children, 16*, 59–61.

Schaefer, E. S. (1970). Need for early and continuing education. In V. H. Denenberg (Ed.), *Education of the infant and young child.* New York: Academic Press.

Schemo, D. J. (2003). Graduation study suggests that some states sharply understate high school dropout rates. *New York Times*, September 17, p. 9.

Schweinhart, L. J., Barnes, H. V., & Weikart, D. P. (1993). *Significant benefits: The High/Scope Perry Preschool project study through age 27. Monograph of the High/Scope Educational Research Foundation*, 10. Ypsilanti, MI: High/Scope Press.

Schweinhart, L. J., Montie, J., Xiang, Z., Barnett, W. S., Belfield, C. R., & Nores, M. (2005). *Lifetime effects: The High/Scope Perry Preschool study through age 40. Monograph of the High/Scope Educational Research Foundation*, 14. Ypsilanti, MI: High/Scope Press.

Segall, N. (2004). Review of the first three years and beyond: Brain development and social policy, by Edward F. Zigler, Matia Finn-Stevenson, & Nancy W. Hall. *Social Service Review, 78*, 166–168.

Shiminski, J. (2005a). School readiness in Pittsfield, Massachusetts. www.parent-child.org/research/index.html (accessed November 28, 2006).

Shiminski, J. A. (2005b). *Parent–Child Home Program.* Pittsfield, MA: Pittsfield Public Schools.

Sigel, I. E. (1964). The attainment of concepts. In M. L. Hoffman & L. W. Hoffman (Eds.), *Review of child development research* (Vol. 2, pp. 209–248). New York: Russell Sage.

Sigel, I. E. (1971). Language of the disadvantaged: The distancing hypothesis. In C. S. Lavatelli (Ed.), *Language training in early childhood education.* Urbana: University of Illinois Press.

Sigel, I. E., Stinson, E. T., & Flaugher, J. (1991). Socialization of representational competence in the family: The distancing paradigm. In L. Okagaki & R. J. Sternberg (Eds.), *Directors of development: Influences on the development of children's thinking* (pp. 21–144). Hillsdale, NJ: Erlbaum.

Siller, J. (1957). Socioeconomic status and conceptual thinking. *Journal of Abnormal and Social Psychology, 55,* 365–371.

Simpson, S. H., Eurich, D. T., Majumdar, S. R., Padwal, R. S., Tsuyuki, R. T., Varney, J., & Johnson, J. A. (2006). A meta-analysis of the association between adherence to drug therapy and mortality. *BMJ, 333,* 15–19.

Singer, T., Seymour, B., O'Doherty, J., Kaube, H., Dolan, R., & Frith, C. (2004). Empathy for pain involves the affective but not sensory components of pain. *Science, 303*(5661), 1157–1162.

Skeels, H. M. (1966). Adult status of children with contrasting early life experiences. *Monographs of the Society for Research in Child Development, 31*(3, Serial No. 105).

Skeels, H. M., & Dye, H. B. (1939). A study of the effects of differential stimulation on mentally retarded children. *Proceedings: American Association on Mental Deficiency, 44,* 114–136.

Slaughter, D. T. (1983). Early intervention and its effects on maternal and child development. *Monographs of the Society for Research in Child Development, 48*(4), Serial No. 202.

Springs, C. (1990). Chapter 1, Mother–Child Home Program evaluation results, Union School Board Fact Sheet, Union, SC.

Sroufe, L. A., & Sampson, M. C. (2000). Attachment theory and systems concepts. *Human Development, 43,* 321–326.

Stebbins, H. (2006). Council connections to the earliest years. Washington, DC: Council of Chief State School Officers. www.ccsso.org/content/PDFs/COUNCILconnectionsEARLIESTyears.pdf (accessed December 1, 2006).

St. Pierre, R. G., & Layzer, J. I. (1999). Using home visits for multiple purposes: The Comprehensive Child Development Program. *The Future of Children. Home Visiting: Recent Program Evaluations, 9*(1), 134–151.

Substance Abuse and Mental Health Services Administration Office of Applied Studies. (2004). Indicators of welfare dependence: Annual report to Congress 2004. Washington, DC: U.S. Department of Health and Human Services. http://aspe.hhs.gov/HSP/indicators04/ (accessed March 10, 2006).

Substance Abuse and Mental Health Services Administration Office of Applied Studies. (2005). National Survey on Drug Use and Health, 2002–2003, summarized in the National Drug Intelligence Center's National Drug Threat Assessment 2005, Appendix B. Washington, DC: U.S. Department of Health and Human Services. www.usdoj.gov/ndic/pubs11/12620/index.htm (accessed March 15, 2006).

Sutton-Smith, B., & Rosenberg, B. G. (1970). *The sibling.* New York: Holt.

Swanson, C. B. (2004). The new math on graduation rates. *Education Week on the Web,* July 28, www.urban.org/url.cfm?ID=1000675 (accessed March 18, 2006).

Sweet, M. A., & Appelbaum, M. I. (2004). Is home visiting an effective strategy? A meta-analytic review of home visiting programs for families with young children. *Child Development, 75*(5), 1435–1456.

Szwed, J. F. (1981). The ethnography of literacy. In M. F. Whiteman (Ed.), *Variation in writing: Functional and linguistic–cultural differences* (pp. 13–23). Hillsdale, NJ: Erlbaum.

Taylor, D. (1983). *Family literacy.* Exeter, NH: Heineman.

Taylor, N., Wade, P., Blum, I., Gould, L., & Jackson, S. (1980). A study of low-literate adults: Personal, environmental and program considerations. *The Urban Review, 12,* 69–77.

Thorndike, R. L. (1977). Causation of Binet decrements. *Journal of Educational Measurements, 14*(197–202).

Toulman, S. (1978). The Mozart of psychology. *New York Review of Books, 25.*

Turkheimer, E., Haley, A., Waldron, M., D'Onofrio, B., & Gottesman, I. I. (2003). Socioeconomic status modifies heritability of IQ in young children. *Psychological Science, 14*(6), 623–628.

United Health Foundation. (2005). America's health rankings, 2005 edition: A call to action for people and their communities. www.unitedhealthfoundation.org/shr2005/components/hsgrad.html (accessed November 13, 2006).

United Way of Long Island's Success by 6 Initiative. (2005). Report on the state of family support released. www.unitedwayli.org/newsletterDetails.asp?newsletter_id=11 (accessed October 18, 2006).

U.S. Bureau of Labor Statistics, Division of Labor Force Statistics. (2005). News Release. www.bls.gov/news.release/hsgec.nr0.htm (accessed March 23, 2006).

U.S. Census Bureau. (2004). Historical poverty tables. www.census.gov/hhes/www/poverty/histpov/ (accessed March, 2006).

U.S. Conference of Mayors. (2004). A status report on hunger and homelessness in America's cities: 2004. www.usmayors.org/uscm/news/publications/ (accessed November 11, 2006).

U.S. Office of Education, National Center for Educational Communication. (1972). *Mother–Child Home Program, Freeport, New York: Model programs, compensatory education* (DHEW publication no. OE 72-84). Washington, DC: Government Printing Office.

van Heuvelen, M., Hochstenbach, J., Brouwer, W., de Greef, M., Zijlstra, G., van Jaarsveld, E., Kempen, G., van Sonderen, E., Ormel, J., & Mulder, T. (2005). Differences between participants and non-participants in an RCT on physical activity and psychological interventions for older persons. *Aging Clinical and Experimental Research, 17*(3), 236–245.

Vygotsky, L. S. (1962). *Thought and language.* Cambridge, MA: MIT Press.

Vygotsky, L. S. (1978). *Mind in society: The development of higher psychological processes.* Cambridge, MA: Harvard University Press.

Wagner, M., Spiker, D., Hernandez, F., Song, J., & Gerlach-Downie, S. (2001). Multisite Parents as Teachers evaluation experiences and outcomes for children and families (No. SRI Project P07283). Menlo Park, CA: SRI International. http://policyweb.sri.com/cehs/publications/patfinal.pdf (accessed December 10, 2007).

Wargo, M. J., Campeau, P. L., & Tallmadge, G. K. (1971). *Further examination of exemplary programs for educating disadvantaged children, final report.* Palo Alto, CA: American Institutes for Research in the Behavioral Science.

Weikart, D. P., Bond, J. T., & McNeil, J. T. (1978). The Ypsilanti Perry Preschool project: Preschool years and longitudinal results through fourth grade (vol. 3). *Monographs of the High/Scope Educational Research Foundation, 3.* Ypsilanti, MI: High/Scope Press.

Wells, G. (1985). *Language development in the pre-school years.* Cambridge, UK: Cambridge University Press.

White, R. W. (1959). Motivation reconsidered: The concept of competence. *Psychological Review, 88,* 297–333.

White, R. W. (1963). *Ego and reality in psychoanalytic theory.* New York: International Universities Press.

Whitehurst, G. J., Arnold, D. S., Epstein, J. N., Angell, A. L., Smith, M., & Fischel, J. (1994). A picture book reading intervention in day care and home for children from low-income families. *Developmental Psychology, 30,* 679–689.

Whitehurst, G. J., & Lonigan, C. J. (1998). Child development and emergent literacy. *Child Development, 69*(3), 848–872.

Whitehurst, G. J., Zevenbergen, A. A., Crone, D. A., Schultz, M. D., Velting, O. N., & Fischel, J. E. (1999). Outcomes of an emergent literacy intervention from Head Start through second grade. *Journal of Educational Psychology, 91,* 261–272.

Williams, R. B. (1998). Lower socioeconomic status and increased mortality: Early childhood roots and the potential for successful interventions. *Journal of the American Medical Association, 279*(21), 1745–1746.

Winship, S., & Jenks, C. (2004). *How did the social policy changes of the 1990s affect mate-*

rial hardship among single mothers? Evidence from the CPS Food Security Supplement (working paper no. RWP04–027). Cambridge, MA: Kennedy School of Government.

Writing Group for the Women's Health Initiative Investigators. (2002). Risks and benefits of estrogen plus progestin in healthy postmenopausal women: Principal results from the Women's Health Initiative Randomized Controlled Trial. *Journal of the American Medical Association, 288,* 321–333.

WuDunn, S. (1996). In Japan, even toddlers feel the pressure to excel; still in diapers but cramming for those competitive exams. *New York Times,* January 23, p. 3.

Zaslow, M. J., Moore, K. A., Brooks, J. L., Morris, P. A., Tout, K., Redd, Z. A., & Emig, C. A. (2002). Experimental studies of welfare reform and children. *The Future of Children: Children and Welfare Reform, 12*(1), 79–95.

Zdep, S. M., & Irvine, S. H. (1970). A reverse Hawthorne effect in educational evaluation. *Journal of School Psychology, 8,* 89–95.

Zigler, E., Haskins, R., & Lyon, G. R. (2004). Closing the achievement gap: Head Start and beyond. *Harvard Family Research Project: The Evaluation Exchange, 10*(2), 9–12.

Zigler, E., Pfannenstiel, J. C., & Seitz, V. (in press). The Parents as Teachers Program and school success: A replication and extension. *The Journal of Primary Prevention.*

Index

The Parent-Child Home Program is shortened to PCHP throughout this index